BUSINESS ENGLISH

Business English was devised and developed by Nick Brieger and Jeremy Comfort of York Associates, 116 Micklegate, York YO1 1JY, in association with JOHN GREEN TEFL TAPES.

The recordings were produced and directed by JOHN GREEN TEFL TAPES, 62B Menelik Road, London NW2 3RH, England.

© Copyright 1993 Berlitz Publishing Company, Ltd.

Hergestellt unter Aufsicht und mit Genehmigung von Berlitz Publishing, Inc.

Alle Rechte vorbehalten, insbesondere das Recht der Vervielfältigung und Verbreitung sowie der Übersetzung. Ohne schriftliche Genehmigung des Verlags ist es nicht gestattet, den Inhalt dieses Werkes oder Teile daraus auf elektronischem oder mechanischem Wege (Fotokopie, Mikrofilm, Ton- und Bildaufzeichnung, Speicherung auf Datenträger oder ein anderes Verfahren) zu reproduzieren, zu vervielfältigen oder zu verbreiten.

Berlitz International, Inc., und seine Tochtergesellschaften sind weltweit die einzigen Eigentümer des Namens Berlitz in bezug auf Sprachunterricht, Sprachlehrbücher, Sprachtonbänder und -kassetten sowie Sprachschulen. Der Gebrauch des Namens Berlitz ist anderen ausdrücklich untersagt, es sei denn, dies wurde von Berlitz durch formellen Vertrag erlaubt. Der Kauf oder Wiederverkauf dieses Titels oder irgendeiner anderen Veröffentlichung von Berlitz berechtigt weder den Käufer noch jede andere Person, den Namen Berlitz im Zusammenhang mit Sprachunterricht und in jeder anderen Verbindung zu gebrauchen.

Berlitz Markenzeichen ist durch Eintrag bei Reg. U.S. Patent Office weltweit geschützt.

Erste deutsche Ausgabe Juli 1993

ISBN 0-7511-0797-2 (Kassetten-Ausgabe)
ISBN 0-7511-0798-0 (CD-Ausgabe)

CONTENTS

UNITS

1 Introducing the company   1
2 Presenting the product   19
3 Meeting customer needs   37
4 Managing projects   57
5 Results and forecasts   75
6 Customer service   93
7 Reaching agreement   113
8 Social contact   133

RESOURCE BOOK

Key to units

1 Introducing the company   159
2 Presenting the product   168
3 Meeting customer needs   177
4 Managing projects   188
5 Results and forecasts   200
6 Customer service   211
7 Reaching agreement   223
8 Social contact   234

Structural glossary   247

Vocabulary   263

INTRODUCTION

Herzlich willkommen zu Business English von Berlitz. Dieser Sprachkurs wendet sich besonders an Geschäftsleute, die bereits über die Anfänge des Englischlernens hinaus sind und ihre Kenntnisse in Wirtschaftsenglisch verbessern möchten.

Der Sprachkurs wird Sie durch ein sorgfältig strukturiertes Programm führen, mit dessen Hilfe Sie Ihre Sprach- und Sprechfertigkeit in den verschiedensten Situationen des Tätigkeitsbereichs Wirtschaft verbessern können. Am Ende des Kurses werden Sie Englisch für Ihre eigenen geschäftlichen Zwecke sicherer und präziser einsetzen können.

Für den ganzen Sprachkurs werden Sie sowohl das Buch als auch die Aufnahme gebrauchen:

Lektionen   In Ihrem Lehrbuch finden Sie acht Lektionen mit verschiedenen Themen aus der Wirtschafts- und Geschäftswelt. Jede Lektion enthält die folgenden Abschnitte:

SAY WHAT YOU MEAN

Für diesen Abschnitt hören Sie zuerst zwei Ausschnitte auf der Aufnahme und beantworten die dazugehörenden Verständnisfragen im Lehrbuch. Darauf folgen Erläuterungen und Übungen zu Problemen der Grammatik und des Wortschatzes, die in den Texten, die Sie sich angehört haben, vorkamen. Die Sprecher auf der Aufnahme werden Sie durch das im Lehrbuch präsentierte Material leiten.

PUT IT ON PAPER

In diesem Abschnitt arbeiten Sie nur mit dem Lehrbuch und konzentrieren sich auf geschriebene Sprache; als Textgrundlage finden Sie zwei Auszüge aus Geschäftsbriefen, Werbematerialien u.a.

THE BUSINESS INTERVIEW

Auf der Aufnahme hören Sie ein authentisches Interview mit einem Gesprächspartner aus der Wirtschaft, der eigene Erfahrungen vorstellt, die mit dem Thema der Lektion zu tun haben. Im Lehrbuch finden Sie einige Verständnisfragen zu diesem Interview.

Introduction

Aufnahme

Die Aufnahme folgt dem Aufbau der einzelnen Lektionen; beim Durcharbeiten der Lektionen finden Sie klare Hinweise, wann und wie Sie mit der Aufnahme arbeiten.

Englisch ist eine Sprache, die in verschiedenen Ländern und Regionen gesprochen wird; deshalb werden Sie zahlreiche verschiedene Akzente und Aussprachen auf der Aufnahme hören. Im Lehrbuch wie auch auf der Aufnahme werden die wichtigsten Unterschiede zwischen amerikanischem und britischem Englisch besonders berücksichtigt.

Resource Book

Kein Sprachkurs zum Selbststudium ist vollständig ohne die Möglichkeit, die eigene Arbeit zu überprüfen. Alles, was Sie dazu brauchen, finden Sie bei Business Englisch im 'Resource Book' hinten in diesem Lehrbuch. Es besteht aus drei Teilen:

Key

Der Antwortenteil enthält die Texte aller wichtigen Aufnahmen, einschließlich der Dialoge, Interviews und Gespräche, mit denen Sie Ihr Hörverständnis und Ihre Sprechfertigkeit üben sollen. Wenn Sie beim Zuhören Verständnishilfen brauchen, schlagen Sie bei den Texten nach. Oder benutzen Sie die Texte nach jeder Hörübung, um unbekannte Wörter oder Redewendungen nachzuschlagen. Dieser Teil enthält auch die Antworten auf alle Übungen auf der Aufnahme und im Buch, damit Sie Ihre Arbeit zwischendurch überprüfen können. Der Antwortenteil ist nach Lektionen geordnet.

Structural glossary

Das Grammatikglossar ist eine alphabetisch geordnete Liste der wichtigsten Grammatikthemen im Buch. Für eine detailliertere Erklärung sollten Sie in einer Grammatik nachschlagen; das Grammatikglossar aber erlaubt es Ihnen, schnell die grammatischen Erklärungen nachzuschlagen, die in einer Lektion vorkommen.

Vocabulary

Dieser Teil ist ein alphabetisch geordnetes Verzeichnis der wichtigsten Vokabeln, die im Kurs vorkommen. Auf jedes Wort folgen seine deutsche Übersetzung und ein Beispielsatz im Englischen. Das Wörterverzeichnis hat als Schwerpunkt die Geschäftssprache; es soll Ihr Wörterbuch nicht ersetzen, sondern es ergänzen.

Bevor Sie anfangen, möchten wir Ihnen noch ein paar Tips geben.

Arbeiten Sie so schnell oder so langsam, wie Sie möchten. Wenn Ihnen etwas nicht ganz klar ist, unterbrechen Sie einfach und hören Sie sich z.B. die Aufnahme noch einmal an.

Introduction

Machen Sie die Aufgaben anhand des Aufgabentextes im Lehrbuch schriftlich oder gehen Sie sie erst im Buch durch, bevor Sie sie mit der Aufnahme machen.

Wenn Sie sich sicherer fühlen, dann machen Sie die Aufgaben ruhig gleich mit der Aufnahme, ohne vorher ins Buch zu sehen: Damit können Sie Ihr Hörverständnis und Ihre Sprechfertigkeit üben.

Benutzen Sie, was Sie hören! Schon wenn Sie sich die Gespräche und Interviews auf der Aufnahme einfach nur anhören, lernen Sie viele nützliche Wendungen kennen, die Sie dann in Ihren eigenen geschäftlichen Verhandlungen anwenden können.

CD-Ausgabe: Einsatzmöglichkeiten

Wir möchten Ihnen hier einige weitere Methoden vorschlagen, wie Sie Ihr Sprachstudium strukturieren können, wenn Sie die CD-Ausgabe haben.

Durch die Spuren auf der CD können Sie auf die entscheidenden Punkte in jeder Lektion zugreifen. Wenn Sie in einer Übungsstunde zum Beispiel an den Aktiv- und Passivkonstruktionen in der Itcorp-Präsentation in Lektion 1 arbeiten möchten, können Sie die Erklärung und die Begleitübung sofort durch Auswahl von Spur 5 auf CD 1 aufrufen. Wenn Sie den ganzen Itcorp-Ausschnitt zur Übung und Überprüfung noch einmal hören möchten, wählen Sie einfach Spur 2. Dank dieser Flexibilität können Sie jede Übungsstunde auf Ihre persönlichen Anforderungen zuschneiden.

Mit den CDs können Sie auch Ihre Wiederholungsarbeit besser planen. Wenn Sie Gelerntes vertiefen möchten, können Sie die relevanten oder verwandten Teile der Aufnahme ganz leicht nochmals abspielen, und wenn Sie überprüfen möchten, wie gut Sie mit dem früher Gelernten noch vertraut sind, können Sie im Handumdrehen auf vorhergehendes Material im Kurs zurückgreifen.

Diese Funktion des sofortigen Zugriffs können Sie auch zur Planung Ihrer eigenen Lern- und Wiederholungsstrategien nutzen. Nachdem Sie einen Ausschnitt angehört haben, möchten Sie ihn vielleicht nochmals hören und dabei die begleitende Niederschrift der Aufnahme im Buch lesen, um die Redewendungen und Strukturen fest in Ihrem Gedächtnis zu verankern. Oder wenn Sie Ihr Hörverständnis in bezug auf eine Vielzahl unterschiedlicher Stimmen prüfen möchten, so können Sie Ihr CD-Gerät so programmieren, daß Sie eine Auswahl der *Business Interviews* hören.

ACKNOWLEDGEMENTS

Der Verlag und die Autoren danken für die Genehmigung, die folgenden urheberrechtlich geschützten Materialien verwenden zu dürfen:

Boston Consulting Group: Auszüge aus der Informationsbroschüre;

Neil Goodenough: Auszüge aus 'Operating Environments', *Which Computer*, July 1991;

Eli Lilly & Co.: Firmenzeichen;

Papeteries de Golbey: Texte und Abbildungen aus *Golbey News*, March 1991;

Prentice-Hall, Inc.: Texte aus *Beyond Language: Intercultural Communication for English as a Second Language* von Deena Levine und Mara Adelman. Copyright © 1982;

WordPerfect U.K.: Werbematerialien.

Abbildungen und Photographien wurden freundlicherweise zur Verfügung gestellt von:

Adams Picture Library;

Barnabys Picture Library;

Format Partners Photo Library und Brenda Prince;

Pictures Colour Library Ltd.;

The Image Bank, Stockphotos Inc. und Kaz Mori, Alex Stewart, Tom Owen Edmunds, Yoshikawa Shirakawa;

Tony Stone Worldwide und John Waterman, Lester Lefkowitz, David Joel, Julian Calder.

Der Verlag und die Autoren haben sich bemüht, für die Verwendung aller urheberrechtlich geschützten Materialien die nötigen Genehmigungen einzuholen. Versehentliche Auslassungen werden sobald wie möglich nachgetragen.

UNIT 1
INTRODUCING THE COMPANY

In dieser Lektion lernen Sie, über Ihr Unternehmen zu sprechen und zu schreiben.

SAY WHAT YOU MEAN

Listening	**Hören**
A formal presentation	Eine formelle Präsentation
Talking to an agent	Ein Gespräch mit einem Vertreter
Language and communication skills	**Sprache und Kommunikation**
Presenting the organization	Sie stellen Ihr Unternehmen vor
Active and passive	Aktiv und Passiv
Structuring your presentation	Sie strukturieren Ihre Präsentation

PUT IT ON PAPER

Reading	**Lesen**
A company brochure	Ein Firmenprospekt
A recruitment advertisement	Ein Stellenangebot
Language and communication skills	**Sprache und Kommunikation**
Adjectives and adverbs	Adjektive und Adverbien
Introducing your company in writing	Sie stellen Ihre Firma schriftlich vor

THE BUSINESS INTERVIEW

Company structure	Unternehmensstrukturen

Unit 1

SAY WHAT YOU MEAN

Listening

Extract 1
A formal presentation

ITCORP, ein großes amerikanisches Unternehmen in der Computerbranche, hat vor kurzem SOFTCO übernommen, die sich auf Softwareentwicklung spezialisiert hat. Hören Sie sich auf der Aufnahme die Präsentation von Mike Kowalsky an. Er ist stellvertretender Produktionsleiter bei ITCORP. Er stellt der SOFTCO-Geschäftsführung die Unternehmensstruktur vor. Füllen Sie die Übersicht über die Organisation des Unternehmens aus.

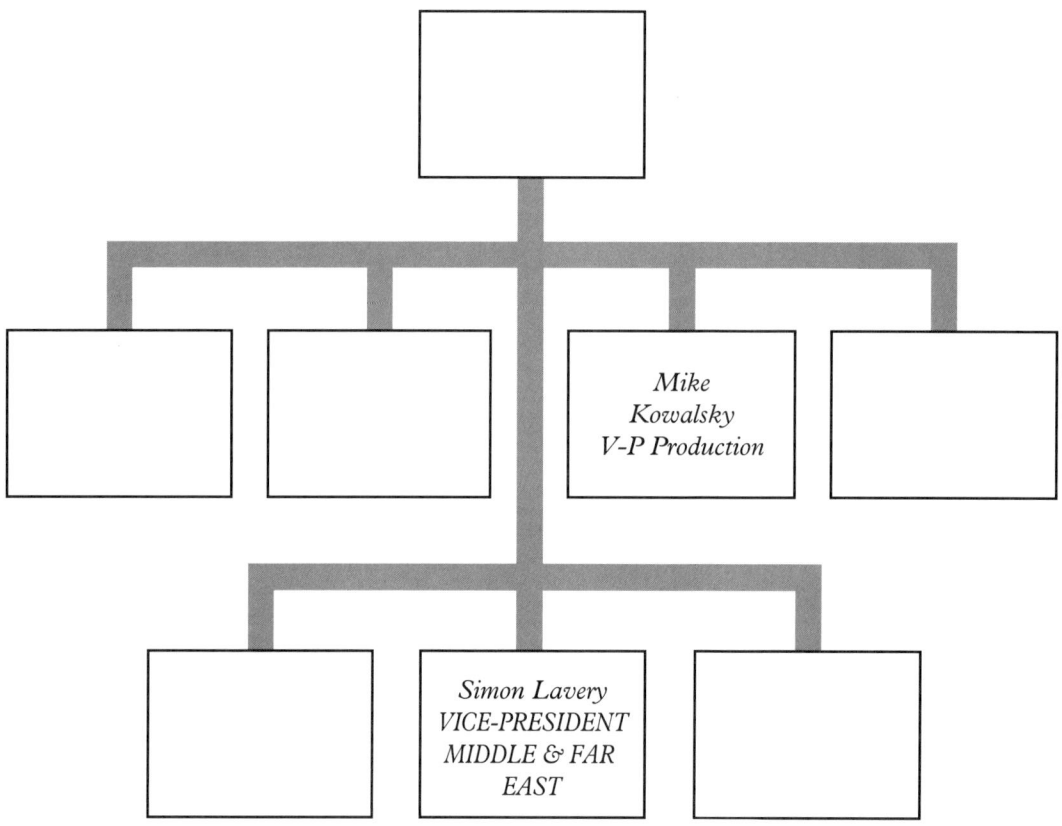

Wenn Sie fertig sind, können Sie Ihre Antworten im Lösungsteil hinten im Buch überprüfen.

Introducing the company

Extract 2
Talking to an agent

KÜBEL ist einer der führenden Küchenmöbelhersteller Europas. Paul Schneider, der Verkaufsleiter für den europäischen Markt, spricht am Messestand gerade mit einem Interessenten für eine Vertretung in Großbritannien und erklärt den Aufbau des Händler- und Vertreternetzes der Firma.

Füllen Sie beim Zuhören die Übersicht aus.

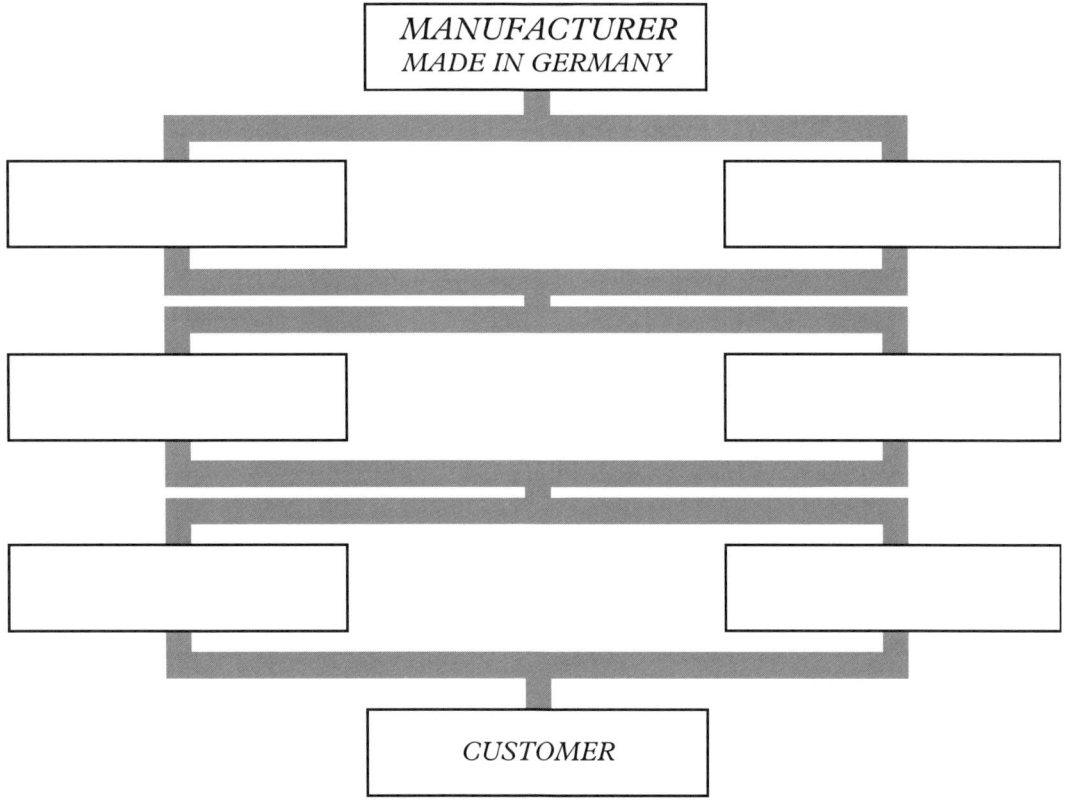

Überprüfen Sie Ihre Antworten anhand des Lösungsteils.

American/British English

Mike Kowalsky war Amerikaner. Amerikanisches und britisches Englisch unterscheiden sich u.a. darin, wie sie Unternehmen beschreiben. Im folgenden sehen Sie ein typisch britisches Organisationsschema im Vergleich mit einem amerikanischen. Achten Sie auf die unterschiedlichen Funktionsbezeichnungen.

Unit 1

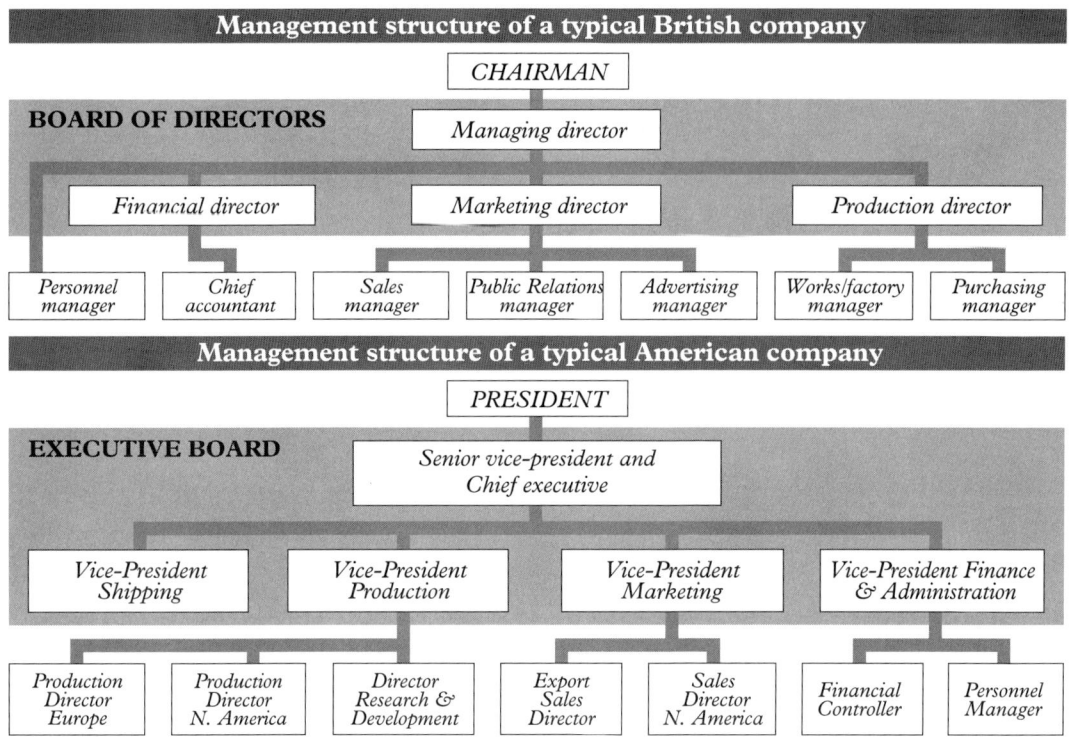

Language and communication skills

Presenting the organization

In the first extract Mike Kowalsky presented the company in terms of:

hierarchy (Hierarchie)
responsibilities and functions (Verantwortungen und Funktionen)
organization and structure (Organisation und Aufbau)

He described the hierarchy like this:

*The organization **is headed by** John De Lucca.*

*The four Vice-Presidents **report** directly **to** Mr De Lucca.*

*He **is supported by** four Vice-Presidents.*

*Each VP **is assisted by** a team of staffers.*

Here's how he described people's responsibilities and functions:

*I am the Vice-President **responsible for** production at Itcorp.*

*First, we have Paul Rosenbaum, who is **in charge of** research and development here at our headquarters.*

*And finally we have Sally Brown who **takes care of** corporate finance.*

And he described the structure of the organization as follows:

*The organization **is divided into** four key functional **departments**.*

*Our operations **are split into** three geographic areas.*

*Each **division** is like a separate **business unit**.*

*Each VP is assisted by a **team** of staffers.*

*First, North America, under Hank Martens. This consists of two **sections** - the USA and Canada.*

Division and **department** are both large sections of an organization. These can be **divided** or **split into** sections. So, a **section** is a part of a division or department; and a **team** is a group of people who work together.

Exercise 1

Diese Übung ist wie alle anderen auf der Aufnahme. Machen Sie diese Übung zuerst mit der Aufnahme. Benutzen Sie dann das Buch und schreiben Sie die Sätze in aller Ruhe auf.

Benutzen Sie die Ausdrücke in den Klammern, um die Sätze umzuformulieren. Der erste Satz zeigt Ihnen, wie es geht.

Paul is in charge of Research and Development. (responsible for)
Paul is responsible for Research and Development.

1. He is assisted by a research team.
   (supported)

2. Mike is responsible for the laboratories.
   (take care of)

3. Mike is under Paul.
   (report to)

4. The research team is divided into scientists and engineers.
   (split)

5. Susanne takes care of finance.
   (in charge)

Vervollständigen Sie die Sätze. Benutzen Sie jeweils eines der folgenden Wörter.

department   division   section   team

6. The company has four operating ....

Unit 1

7. Marketing strategy is decided in the marketing ....

8. The marketing department is divided into three ....

9. There are five of us who work together as a ....

Active and passive

Im zweiten Text unterhält sich Paul Schneider über das Vertreter- und Händlernetz der Firma Kübel.

Er benutzt das einfache Präsens im Aktiv und im Passiv.

Present simple active

*Agents **send** their orders through to us at our plant in Küberg.*

*Then our local office **processes** them and **ships** the goods to them.*

*At the same time we **invoice** the agent for the agreed amount.*

*After that the agent **delivers** the units to the customer, **collects** payment, and then **settles** our invoice.*

Present simple passive

*The order **is processed** and then the invoice **is raised**.*

*And then they **are transported** to the destination country.*

*These days they **are** usually **sent** by fax or **phoned** through to us.*

The verb phrase (Verbgruppe) consists of two parts. The first part is **am**, **is** or **are**; the second part is the past participle (Partizip Perfekt). In regular verbs (schwache Verben) the past participle ends with the letters **-ed**.

Exercise 2

Die Aufnahme wird Ihnen bei dieser Übung helfen. Sie sollen die folgenden Sätze vom Aktiv ins Passiv setzen und das Flußdiagramm ausfüllen.

Sehen Sie sich das folgende Beispiel an:

We manufacture the goods in Germany. (active)

The goods are manufactured in Germany. (passive)

Introducing the company

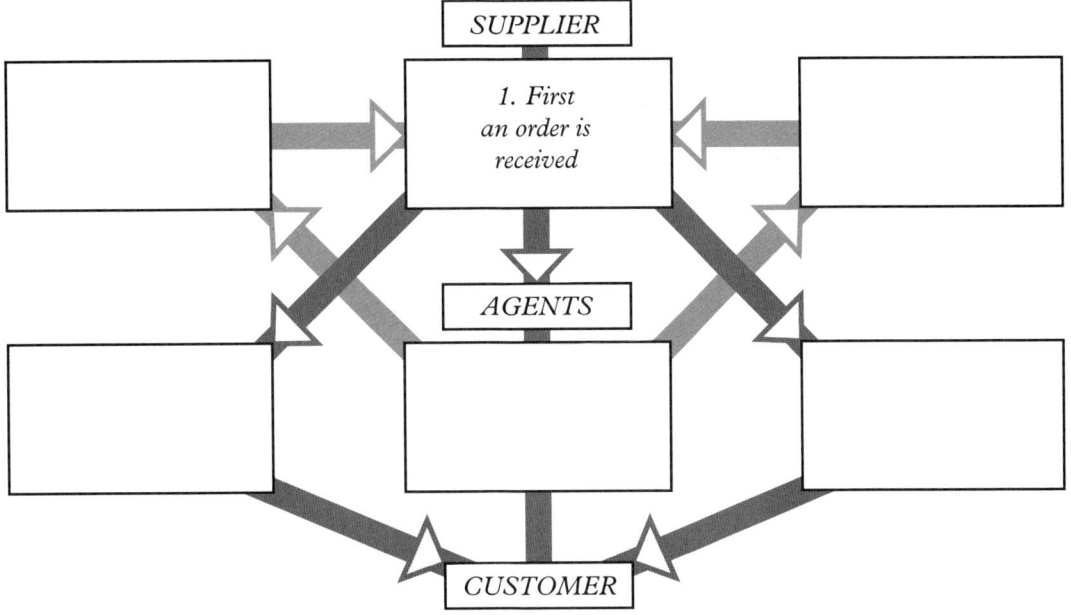

1. First we receive an order.
2. They send their orders by fax.
3. They phone an order through.
4. We ship the goods to them.
5. We sometimes transport the goods by rail.
6. We invoice the agent as soon as possible.

Structuring your presentation (1)

Wir wollen uns die erste Präsentation noch einmal ansehen, und zwar besonders die rhetorischen Mittel, die Mike Kowalsky eingesetzt hat.

Sehen wir uns das Schema an, das Mike gebraucht hat. Sie finden einige Ausdrücke, die Sie in den verschiedenen Abschnitten einer Präsentation benutzen können.

Stage 1   Greeting and welcoming your audience

Good morning/afternoon/evening, ladies and gentlemen/everyone.

I'd like to welcome you all to (company name/place).

Stage 2   Introducing yourself

My name is (name) and I am (title) responsible for production at (company name).

Unit 1

Stage 3   Introducing the subject of your talk

I'd like to give you an overview of the structure of the company/ say a few words to you today about our activities/explain to you the new organization of the company.

Stage 4   Outlining your talk

I've divided my talk into three main parts.

The subject can be looked at under three main heads.

During my presentation I'll be looking at three key areas.

First…   second…   and finally…

I'll be using some charts to highlight the key information.

To illustrate my talk I intend to use some charts.

I aim to speak for about 15 minutes.

This will take about 15 minutes.

If you have any questions, I'll be happy to answer them at the end of my talk/please feel free to interrupt.

Stage 5   The first main point

Firstly let's take a look at…

First I'd like to consider…

So that is the current structure of the organization.

So that covers the current structure of the organization.

Stage 6   The next point

Now I'd like to move on /Now let's move on /Moving on to my second point…

Exercise 3

Versuchen Sie, diese Übung zuerst nur mit der Aufnahme zu machen. Benutzen Sie dann das Buch und schreiben Sie die Sätze in aller Ruhe auf. Sie können die Übung beliebig oft wiederholen.

Sie sollen eine formelle Präsentation geben. Dafür müssen Sie die passenden Sätze formulieren. Um es Ihnen etwas leichter zu machen, finden Sie jeweils eine kurze Beschreibung dessen, was Sie sagen sollen. Sehen Sie sich die folgenden Beispiele an:

It is afternoon. You want to greet and welcome your audience. What do you say?

Introducing the company

Good afternoon, ladies and gentlemen. I'd like to welcome you all to (your company's name).

Now introduce yourself by giving your name and your position.
My name is (name) and I am the (your position).

1. Introduce the subject of your talk. Imagine you'd like to give your audience an overview of the new company structure.
2. Outline your talk. It has four main parts.
3. Explain that you will be using some charts to highlight the key information.
4. You aim to speak for about 15 minutes.

Im zweiten Teil dieser Übung finden Sie ebenfalls Hinweise auf die Sprechsituation. Außerdem sind die Schlüsselwörter angegeben, mit denen Sie passende Sätze bilden sollen.

Sehen Sie sich das folgende Beispiel an:

Explain how you want to handle questions.
(If/questions/feel free/interrupt)
If you have any questions, please feel free to interrupt.

5. Introduce your first main point.
   (First/like/consider/turnover)
6. Conclude your first point.
   (That/cover/turnover)
7. Move on to your next point.
   (Now/let/move/expenses)
8. Conclude your second point.
   (That/cover/expenses)
9. Move on to your final point.
   (Now/I/like/move/my final point)

Structuring your presentation (2)

Kehren wir noch einmal zum zweiten Text zurück. Wir wollen uns auf die rhetorischen Mittel konzentrieren, die Paul Schneider in seinem Gespräch über das Vertreter- und Händlernetz der Firma Kübel eingesetzt hat.

Pauls Gespräch folgte ebenfalls einem Schema. Sehen wir uns die verschiedenen Abschnitte und Redewendungen an.

Stage 1 Introducing the subject of your talk

This is how we operate in the UK.

Our UK operations are as follows.

Our UK operations are like this.

Stage 2 Outlining your talk

In the UK we have two kinds/types/sorts of arrangements for our customers.

Stage 3 The first main point

Let's look first of all at agents.

First of all - agents.

First - agents.

So, that's the agents.

Stage 4 The next point

OK, now moving on to the dealers.

Next there's the dealers.

Then there's the dealers.

So, that's the dealers.

Stage 5 Summarizing the main points

And those are the two arrangements.

So, we've looked at the two arrangements.

So, that covers the two arrangements.

Stage 6 Closing the talk

And if you have any questions, please get back to me.

And if anything's not clear, please contact me.

Stage 7 Inviting feedback

Is that clear?

Clear?

Is that OK?

OK?

Have you got that?

Right?

Introducing the company

Exercise 4

Sie sind auf einer Messe.

In dieser Übung geben wir Ihnen eine Gesprächssituation und Schlüsselwörter vor. Hören Sie sich die Übung zuerst mit der Aufnahme durch und schreiben Sie dann die Sätze auf.

1. First introduce the total market.
   (First/all/let/look/total market)

2. Finish that point.
   (So/total market)

3. Move on to the next point.
   (Next/German market)

4. Finish that point.
   (So/German market)

5. Summarize the two main points.
   (So/we/look/two markets/total market/German market)

6. Close the talk.
   (If/questions/get back/me)

Unit 1

PUT IT ON PAPER

Reading

Oft müssen Sie Ihr Unternehmen schriftlich vorstellen - sei es für einen Rundbrief, Werbematerialien oder für eine Stellenausschreibung. In jedem Fall müssen Sie Ihr Unternehmen überzeugend darstellen. Dazu sehen wir uns in diesem Abschnitt zwei verschiedene Textsorten an. Auf jedes Beispiel folgen einige Verständnisfragen und eine Übung zur Erweiterung des Wortschatzes.

Model 1
A company brochure

Die Boston Consulting Group ist eine der weltweit führenden Unternehmensberatungsfirmen. Im folgenden lesen Sie einen Auszug aus einem ihrer Firmenprospekte. Danach beantworten Sie bitte die Fragen.

Comprehension

Was haben Sie über BCG gelernt?

1. What is BCG's main purpose?
2. Do you think BCG has a hierarchical internal structure?
3. What type of clients does BCG work with?
4. What hierarchical level do they deal with?
5. In what three areas do they measure their success since 1980?
6. How have most of their clients responded to working with BCG?

Vocabulary development

Bilden Sie Gegensatzpaare aus diesen Adjektiven.

1. analogous   (a) similar
2. divergent   (b) tiny
3. collaborative   (c) straightforward
4. challenging   (d) different
5. outstanding   (e) inferior
6. vast   (f) conflicting

Introducing the company

THE BOSTON CONSULTING GROUP

BCG's mission is to help our clients outperform their competitors. This requires understanding the future determinants of business success. We are focused on this goal ...

BCG's team-based structure is analogous to a jazz band. Case teams forge divergent personalities into a single highly creative instrument. Senior BCG professionals set broad case objectives, while consultants fill in their parts as they think best. Consultants learn from one another, and balance each other's strengths and weaknesses. ... At BCG we are committed to respecting the potential of every individual, to creating a truly collaborative working relationship with our clients, and to maintaining the highest standards of integrity in all of our activities.

Today's most challenging business problems require both insight and the ability to turn insights into results. These capabilities allow us to work with leading firms and give us a unique reputation among CEOs worldwide ... Since 1980 we have opened offices at the rate of one per year, creating a network of 19 offices worldwide with almost 800 professionals ... This physical expansion has been accompanied by outstanding financial performance. The firm's revenues and profits have grown by over 20% per year during the last decade, and revenue per professional is at the top of the industry.

Perhaps the most important measure of our success is our client relationships. Our client base has grown, and we have forged strong relationships with leading companies in many industries. The vast majority of our clients have retained our services from one year to the next. Their loyalty is a testimony to the value that BCG can provide.

Extracts from the Boston Consulting Group's 1992/3 company brochure

N.B. CEO stands for Chief Executive Officer (Am. Eng.); Managing Director (Br. Eng.). CEO is increasingly used in an international context.

Unit 1

Model 2
A recruitment advertisement

Eli Lilly gehört zu den führenden pharmazeutischen Unternehmen der Welt. Dieser Text zeigt Ihnen, wie sich das Unternehmen in einer Stellenanzeige präsentiert. Wenn Sie den Text gelesen haben, beantworten Sie bitte die Fragen.

MEDICAL SALES

Eli Lilly and Company has been a leading manufacturer of ethical pharmaceuticals for over 100 years. Our established reputation for excellence and integrity is matched by a thorough commitment to research and innovation. These strengths were reflected in last year's global group sales of $5.7 billion.

Our field sales divisions within the UK are Lilly, Dista, and Greenfield. Due to considerable expansion in all three divisions, the success of our internal career development policy, and the continuing aim of strengthening our position in the UK market-place, the following opportunities are now available within our regional sales teams:

- We require ambitious and experienced MEDICAL REPRESENTATIVES, 22–28, educated to degree level, with up to eight years' experience in a recognized healthcare company in the GP or hospital sector.

- for positions as GRADUATE SALES TRAINEES we require confident persuasive graduates, 22–28, who are strongly motivated to enter or develop a career in field sales. Since completing your degree, you will have acquired valuable direct experience in a sales or marketing function or through an appropriate programme of management training in a top retail, industrial or commercial context.

The highly competitive remuneration package includes a non-contributory pension plan and all benefits associated with a multinational company.

Opportunities currently exist for candidates resident in the following areas:

Ethical pharmaceuticals: prescription drugs (rezeptpflichtige Medikamente)

Degree level: graduate level (Hochschulabschluß)

Comprehension

1. How long has Eli Lilly been in business?
2. What type of drugs does it produce?
3. What was its global sales figure for 1991?
4. How is the company organized in the UK?
5. What is the company's main reason for recruitment?
6. What other reasons does it give for recruiting new representatives?
7. Which sectors does Eli Lilly sell into?
8. What does it offer the successful applicant?

Introducing the company

Vocabulary development

Leiten Sie Adjektive von diesen Substantiven ab:

Nouns	Adjectives	Nouns	Adjectives
1. Excellence	(a)	5. Ambition	(e)
2. Innovation	(b)	6. Confidence	(f)
3. Success	(c)	7. Persuasion	(g)
4. Globe	(d)	8. Competition	(h)

Language and communication skills

Adjectives and adverbs

Sehen Sie sich diese Sätze aus den beiden Texten an:

Group A

highly creative instrument

truly collaborative relationship

Group B

outstanding financial performance

confident, persuasive graduates

valuable direct experience

In der Gruppe A modifiziert das Adverb *highly* das Adjektiv *creative*; in Gruppe B modifizieren beide Adjektive, *outstanding* und *financial*, das Substantiv *performance*.

Exercise 1

Ergänzen Sie die folgenden Sätze mit einem der Adjektive aus der Liste. Einige der Adjektive werden Sie als Adverbien gebrauchen müssen. Der erste Satz zeigt Ihnen, wie es geht.

real   enviable   competitive   good   technical   high

1. We work in a *highly* competitive market.
2. We need ………… qualified salesmen.
3. Our task is to achieve long-term ………… growth.
4. We have an ………… client spread.
5. It is a sophisticated ………… market.
6. We sell ………… priced products.

Unit 1

Introducing your company in writing

Sehen Sie sich diese Sätze aus den beiden Texten an:

Eli Lilly and Company has been a leading manufacturer of ethical pharmaceuticals for more than 100 years.

BCG's mission is to help their clients outperform their competitors.

These capabilities allow us to work with leading firms and give us a unique reputation among CEOs worldwide.

These strengths were reflected in last year's global group sales of $5.7 billion.

Since 1980 we have opened 19 offices worldwide.

The firm's revenues and profits have grown by over 20% per year during the last decade, and revenue per professional is at the top of the industry.

We have forged strong relationships with leading companies in many industries. Their loyalty is a testimony to the value that BCG can provide.

Unten sehen Sie einige wichtige Strukturen für die Präsentation eines Unternehmens.

---

1. Opening statement (positioning the company)

X is a	leading	manufacturer	of	pharmaceuticals
	major	producer		cosmetics
	rapidly growing	distributor		health care products

2. Supporting evidence (results, track record etc.)

Established in 19.., X has grown to ....
Last year we recorded annual sales of ....

3. Meeting needs (customers' and clients')

X is		well-placed	to	meet your needs
		in a strong position		take advantage of
		in a unique position		seize the opportunity
	can play	a significant role	in	shaping your future

4. Supporting infrastructure (organization, staff etc.)

We have	more than .... staff
	a well-qualified team
	an extensive after-sales service
	well-equipped premises
	a nationwide distribution network

Introducing the company

Exercise 2

Ordnen Sie die folgenden Aussagen so, daß sich ein gut strukturierter Text für einen Rundbrief zur Vorstellung des Unternehmens ergibt.

International Trade Fairs

- ❏ *Established in 1981, TSI has been servicing the needs of companies,*
- ❏ *... we can make sure your products or services are displayed to their full advantage.*
- ❏ *Trade Stands International (TSI) is a leading provider of exhibition stands and support services.*
- ❏ *... whether you require our simple export-pack or full, on-the-ground support.*
- ❏ *... ranging from small specialized firms entering new markets to well-established multinationals.*
- ❏ *Staffed by our 24-hour experienced teams,*
- ❏ *We are in a unique position to meet your exhibition needs,*

Unit 1

THE BUSINESS INTERVIEW

Company structure

Alan Riley, der Pressesprecher von United Biscuits Limited, spricht über den Aufbau und die Organisation des Unternehmens. Die untenstehenden Fragen, die sich auf die wichtigsten Punkte des Gesprächs beziehen, sollen Ihnen beim Zuhören helfen. Ihre Antworten können Sie dann anhand des Lösungsteils überprüfen.

McVitie's Hob-nobs, invented in Britain, are now selling well in Denmark alongside Fruit & Energy, a range produced there by Oxford Biscuits, part of the McVitie's Group.

Sophisticated technology is used to monitor the size and shape of biscuits at UB's Research and Development centre at High Wycombe, Buckinghamshire, England.

As you listen...

1. Which of these descriptions of United Biscuits matches Alan Riley's?

   (a) United Biscuits has 4 companies in the UK and 1 in the US.
   (b) United Biscuits has 4 companies in Europe and 1 in the US.
   (c) United Biscuits has 4 companies in Europe and lots of different companies in the US.

2. How does Alan Riley describe the organization of the United Biscuits companies?

3. Does Alan say his company's policy of international development is to

   (a) keep a tight control on overseas companies?
   (b) make local managers train at KP?
   (c) allow local managers to make use of their specialist knowledge and UB's central resources?

4. How does he describe the structure of the organization - is it hierarchical? How many layers of management are there?

5. How does he define the purpose of the Group centre?

UNIT 2
PRESENTING THE PRODUCT

In dieser Lektion lernen Sie, wie Sie über Ihre Produkte sprechen und schreiben.

SAY WHAT YOU MEAN

Listening	Hören
Presenting a new product idea	Wie man eine Produktidee vorstellt
Prices and delivery times	Preise und Lieferzeiten

Language and communication skills	Sprache und Kommunikation
Describing trends	Wie man Trends beschreibt
Describing change	Wie man Veränderungen beschreibt
Considering your audience	Wie man auf seine Zuhörer eingeht
Balancing your arguments	Ausgewogene Argumentation
Using visual aids	Anschauungsmaterial

PUT IT ON PAPER

Reading	Lesen
A product review and advertisement	Produktbesprechung und Werbung
Letters of enquiry and reply	Kundenanfrage und Antwortschreiben

Language and communication skills	Sprache und Kommunikation
Reinforcing your sales arguments	Wie man seine Verkaufsargumente verstärkt
Letter-writing expressions	Briefformeln
Letter-writing styles	Briefstile

THE BUSINESS INTERVIEW

Marketing and product strategy	Marketing- und Produktstrategien

Unit 2

SAY WHAT YOU MEAN

Listening

Extract 1
Presenting a new product idea

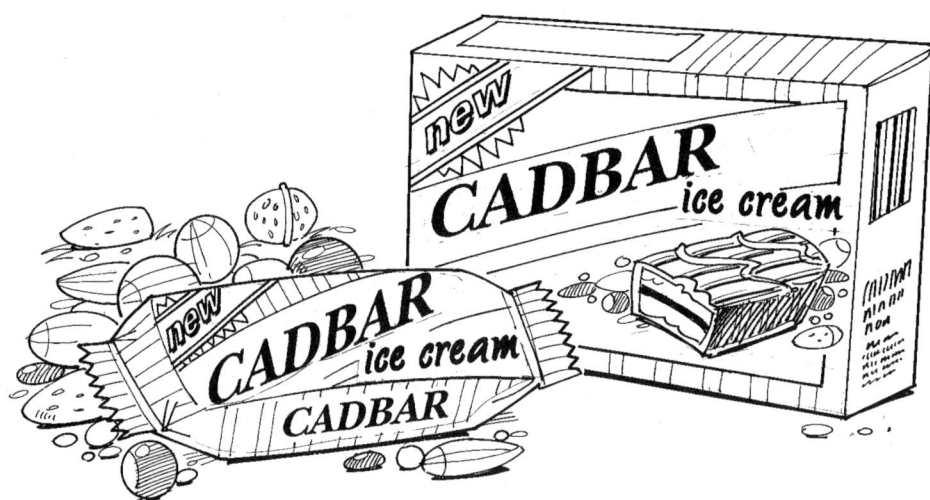

Cadtree ist einer der führenden Süßwarenhersteller der Welt. Sie hören jetzt eine Präsentation von Sarah Maxwell. Sie ist für die Entwicklung neuer Produkte verantwortlich und spricht zu den Marketingleitern des Unternehmens. Sie möchte, daß das Unternehmen auch im Speiseeissektor aktiv wird. Ihre Abteilung hat einen neuartigen Eis-Schokoladenriegel entwickelt.

Vervollständigen Sie beim Zuhören die folgenden Tabellen.

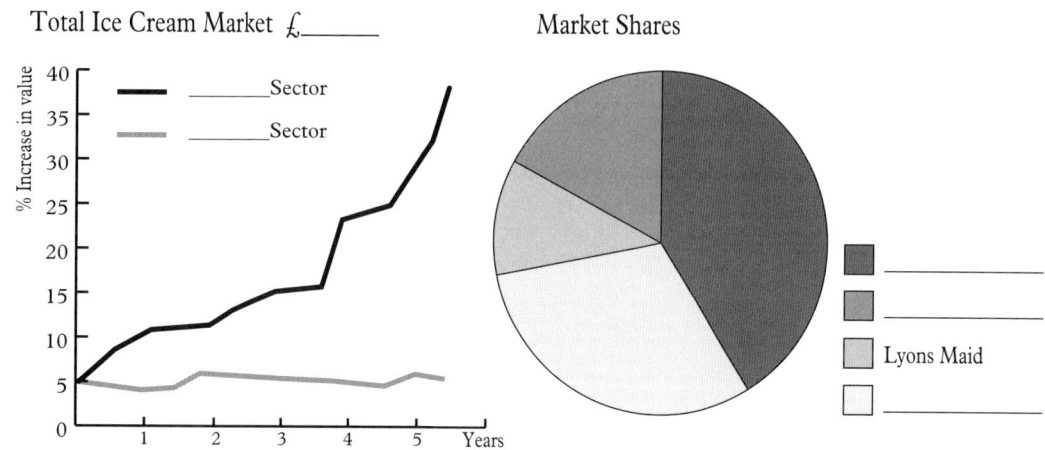

Presenting the product

Extract 2
Prices and
delivery times

Jetzt geht es auf die andere Seite des Atlantiks zu einem ganz anderen Ereignis - zur LEISUREWEAR EXPO, einer großen Messe für die Bekleidungsindustrie. Jedes Jahr stellen hier Modehäuser und Stoffhersteller ihre neuen Kollektionen vor. ZENELLI, ein italienischer Hersteller von Designerjeans aus Mailand, hat hier auch einen kleinen Stand, um die neue Kollektion zu zeigen. Francesco Pellegrini, der Verkaufsleiter, spricht mit Pete Samuelson, einem Einkäufer von Beers, einem der großen amerikanischen Warenhäuser.

Vervollständigen Sie beim Zuhören Petes Notizen über Preise.

9001	12	9	5	15	300%
9002	58	55	50	120	140%
9003	20	19	17	30	76%
9004	43	38	35	75	114%

Unit 2

American/British English

Pete Samuelson war Amerikaner. Die Unterschiede zwischen amerikanischem und britischem Englisch lassen sich in drei Kategorien einteilen:

Vocabulary

Pete said **pants**, the British would have said **trousers**. Let's look at some other words.

apartment	flat
can	tin
candy	sweets
closet	cupboard
cookie	biscuit

Spelling

Pete would have spelt it **catalog**, the British **catalogue**. Let's look at some other spellings.

color	colour
defense	defence
dialog	dialogue

Grammar

Pete said **I got that**, the British would have said **I've got that**. American English uses the past simple (Präteritum) tense more frequently as opposed to the present perfect (Perfekt), especially with **just** and **already**.

| He just arrived. | He has just arrived. |
| He already did that. | He has already done that. |

Language and communication skills

Describing trends

Sarah Maxwell used her transparencies to describe market trends (Marktentwicklungen).

You can see from this graph here, the in-hand sector has been pretty static ...

... the take-home sector has risen by about 40%.

We usually describe market trends in three ways.

1. Upward movement

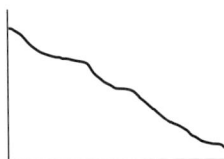

We can use verbs like **increase, rise, go up, grow, expand** in sentences like:

Sales have increased rapidly.
Profits have grown significantly.

We can also use these verbs as nouns in sentences like:

There has been a rapid increase in sales.
There has been significant growth in profits.

2. Downward movement

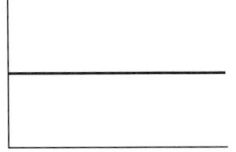

We use verbs like **decrease, fall, drop, go down, decline** or even **collapse** in sentences like:

The dollar has fallen dramatically.
Prices have collapsed completely.

Again we can also use these verbs as nouns:

There has been a dramatic fall in the value of the dollar.
There has been a complete collapse in prices.

3. No movement

Here we use words like **static**, **stable**, **constant** or even **stagnant**. We use the verb **to be** or sometimes **to remain** to make sentences like:

Share prices have remained constant.
The market was stagnant last year.

Exercise 1

Vielleicht machen Sie diese Übung lieber zuerst mit dem Buch, um genügend Zeit für die Antworten zu haben. Mit der Aufnahme üben Sie dann die Aussprache der neuen Wendungen.

Jeder der folgenden Sätze beschreibt Marktentwicklungen. Formulieren Sie die Sätze um, ohne die Bedeutung zu ändern: d.h. nehmen Sie statt des Verbs ein Substantiv und umgekehrt. Hier ist ein Beispiel:

Share prices rose dramatically last week.
There was a dramatic rise in share prices last week.

Unit 2

1. Consumer prices have fallen slightly.
2. There has been an enormous drop in demand.
3. There is a slight growth in sales.
4. Consumer confidence has collapsed.
5. The market has expanded considerably.
6. There will be a modest increase in sales.
7. Profits will decrease substantially.

Describing change

Below you will see how Francesco talked about prices.

... bringing down the price to $58 ...

... a further reduction down to $35 ...

When we talk about changes in prices, sales or any figure, we need to be careful which prepositions (Präpositionen) we use.

1. When talking about the **final figure** we use **to**:

    *We reduced the price **to** $3.*

    *We raised profits **to** 25 million.*

2. When we talk about the **difference** between the old and new figures we use a verb + **by**:

    *We **cut** our prices **by** 20 pence.*

    *We **increased** sales **by** 10%.*

    But with a noun we use **of**:

    *There was **a drop of** 2%.*

    *There was **a rise of** 10 cents per unit.*

Exercise 2

Sie erhalten Informationen über Preisänderungen oder Unternehmensgewinne. Vervollständigen Sie mit Hilfe der Aufnahme jeweils die Beschreibungen der Veränderungen mit dem richtigen präpositionalen Ausdruck.

1. Last year's turnover: £29m. This year's turnover: £27m

    Turnover has fallen ....

2. Last quarter's profits: DM 200,000. This quarter's profits: DM 250,000

    Profits have increased ....

Presenting the product

3. Last year's dividend: 25p. This year's dividend: 28p

   We have raised the dividend ....

4. This year's sales figures: 280m. Next year's sales figures: 320m

   We forecast a rise ....

5. This quarter's bank repayments: £25,000. Next quarter's bank repayments: £20,000

   We are looking forward to a reduction ....

Raise is a transitive (transitives) verb - in other words we use it when we actively do something:

My boss raised my salary.

Rise can only be used intransitively (intransitiv):

My salary rose.

Vervollständigen Sie die folgenden Sätze mit **raise** oder **rise**. Beachten Sie die unregelmäßigen Stammformen von rise (**rose, risen**).

1. They .... prices last year.
2. Inflation is forecast to .... next year.
3. The tax cuts will .... inflation.
4. My taxes .... every year of my working life.

Considering your audience

Sarah kept her talk short because she knew her audience was busy:

I know you're all on tight schedules, so I'm going to be brief today.

I'm going to take just 15 minutes.

Later we'll have time to go into more detail.

She used transparencies and handouts:

I'll be using some transparencies ... you'll find copies in the pack in front of you.

You'll find production specifications in the folder in front of you.

She guided them through her talk:

You can see from this graph here ...

As we'll see in a moment ...

... this is what I mentioned a moment ago.

Unit 2

Exercise 3

Jetzt können Sie diese Ausdrücke selbst anwenden. Stellen Sie sich vor, Sie geben eine Präsentation vor einigen ungeduldigen Kollegen! Lesen Sie sich die Sätze zuerst einmal durch und machen Sie dann die Übung mit der Aufnahme. Hier ist ein Beispiel:

You've been told they are very busy. You have just ten minutes. What do you say?

'I know you're all on tight schedules. I'm going to take just ten minutes of your time.'

1. You will have time to deal with the details later.
2. You are going to use the overhead projector and you have taken copies of the transparencies.
3. You want to indicate that you will be coming to a point in a moment.
4. You want to indicate that you are going to repeat an important point.

Balancing your arguments

Sarah also used a variety of linking expressions (Bindewörter) to balance her arguments. Let's see how she did this:

*I'm going to confine the figures to the UK market, **although** we think the product has big potential throughout Europe.*

***Nevertheless**, initially we'll almost certainly launch it in the UK ... the take-home sector has risen by 40% in value.*

***However**, most of this increase is accounted for by supermarkets' own label brands.*

She used three linking words, **although**, **nevertheless** and **however**, to draw attention to a contrast (Gegensatz) between two statements.

However and **nevertheless** start new sentences, contrasting with the previous remark.

Although comes at the beginning or in the middle of a sentence which contains a contrast of ideas.

Presenting the product

Exercise 4

Verbinden Sie jeweils diese beiden einander widersprechenden Äußerungen. Sie können die Übung mit der Aufnahme machen. Hören Sie zuerst das Beispiel:

The product was developed for the European market. It was launched in Japan.

Although *the product was developed in the European market, it was launched in Japan.*

The product was developed for the European market. **However,** *(or* **Nevertheless,**) *it was launched in Japan.*

1. The market was saturated. We launched a new product.
2. The marketing manager made a lot of mistakes. He became Managing Director.
3. The company specialized in consumer products. It bought an industrial products concern.

Using visual aids

Francesco referred to a price table:

Here we can see in the left-hand column ...

We've got prices in three columns ...

You see these last two columns ...

Sarah used charts to illustrate her message. When used well, charts and other visual aids (Anschauungsmaterial) help us to communicate more effectively.

Exercise 5

Schaubilder, Balkendiagramme, Kreisdiagramme und Tabellen können sehr nützlich sein. Welche Form würden Sie wählen, wenn Sie die folgenden Informationen präsentieren wollten?

Die 'Goldenen Regeln' auf der nächste Seite geben Ihnen einige Hinweise für den Gebrauch von Graphiken.

1. Sales in two product lines over the last five years.
2. Market share by sector over the last two years.
3. Market shares of competitors.
4. Market research results on consumer preferences.

GOLDEN RULES for using visual aids

1. Never use too many charts - **maximum** one a minute.
2. Don't put too much information on the chart.
3. Decide why you are using the chart - is it to inform, to illustrate a point?
4. Think about which type of chart to use.

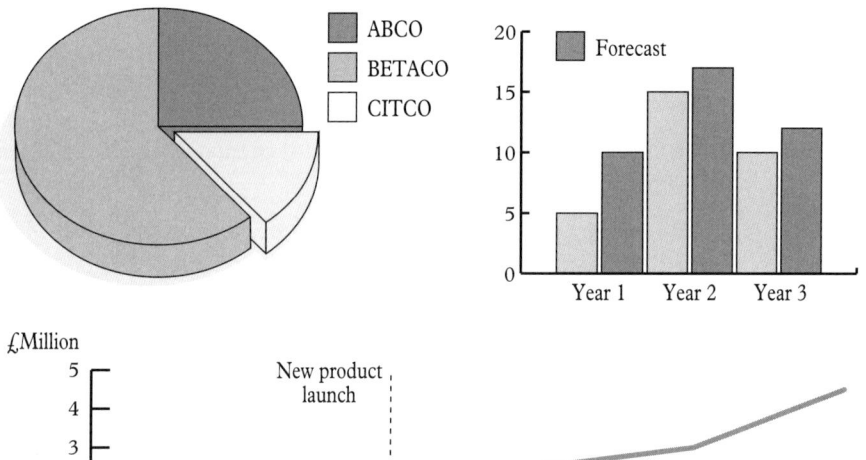

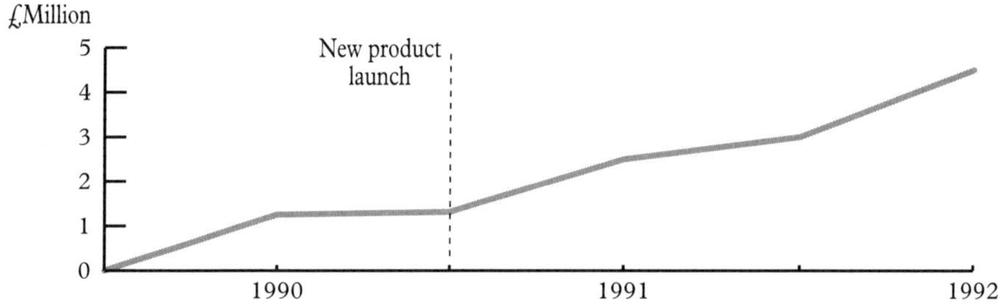

5. Don't put too much written information on the transparency.
6. Use colour, but don't overuse it!
7. Don't hide behind your charts - keep contact with your audience.

Presenting the product

PUT IT ON PAPER

Sie müssen häufig das, was Sie mit einem Kunden persönlich besprochen haben, noch durch einen Brief oder Werbematerial ergänzen. So wollen Sie vielleicht einen Antwortbrief auf eine Kundenanfrage schreiben oder in einem Rundbrief die Ausweitung Ihrer Produktpalette ankündigen. In diesem Abschnitt stellen wir Ihnen zwei verschiedene Muster solcher Mitteilungen vor, auf die dann jeweils Verständnisfragen und eine Wortschatzübung folgen.

Reading

Model 1
A product review and advertisement

WordPerfect ist ein amerikanisches Unternehmen, das sich auf Textverarbeitungsprogramme spezialisiert hat. Vor kurzem wurde ein Programm für E-Mail und Büroorganisation auf den Markt gebracht - WordPerfect Office 3.0.

Lesen Sie die kurze Produktbesprechung und die folgende Anzeige. Beantworten Sie dann die Fragen.

The major advantage of workgroup software is that group discussions (the lifeblood of business) are taking place whether or not the group can meet. Individuals can send and receive information at their convenience but each transaction is contributing to the overall discussion. And when a face to face meeting does need to take place the electronic diaries can be automatically scanned by the scheduling system and the earliest date for a meeting manageable by all parties can be identified.

There is no arguing that WordPerfect Office provides you with the full range of workgroup facilities. On top of this it is a simple task to add your other software to its menu system. And this is not just a menu system; it provides you with hot key access from any application to any other - all on a basic PC. However, its formidable power is not the only thing which earns WordPerfect Office our praise; it is also its pedigree. As a stable mate of the leading word processing package, it provides all WordPerfect users with a set of keys and commands with which they will already be familiar.

WordPerfect Office has a combined diary, memo and to do list which enables you to make three types of entry against any date. The scheduling system is well integrated with the e-mail system and the diaries. When an appointment has been scheduled all group members receive a message enabling them to accept or decline an appointment ... All in all, this is an excellent product from a proven leader.

Unit 2

'At 9.00 I had a great idea. 5 minutes later, I had the whole world convinced.'

Comprehension

1. What type of software package is WordPerfect Office?
2. What type of software is WordPerfect famous for?
3. What advantage do existing users of WordPerfect have?
4. Can you explain the headline from the advertisement?

Vocabulary development

Computerterminologie ist nie besonders 'userfriendly'. Wir wollen deshalb ein paar grundlegende Begriffe klären. Verbinden Sie die Begriffe links mit der passenden Definition auf der rechten Seite.

1. Menu system   (a) Kurzbefehl, der mit einer einzigen Taste eine andere Anwendung öffnet

2. Hot key system (b) Zugangssystem, mit dem der Benutzer aus einer Liste von Möglichkeiten auswählen kann

3. E-mail   (c) Programm, mit dem autorisierte Benutzer die Terminkalender anderer durchsehen und allgemeine Einträge machen können

4. Diaries   (d) nach Dringlichkeit geordnete Listen von Verpflichtungen mit automatischem Alarm für nahe Termine

5. Scheduler   (e) Programm, das Abschlußtermine für Projekte aufzeichnet und eine graphische Übersicht über mehrere Terminkalender für einen bestimmten Zeitraum gibt

6. To do lists   (f) Technik, mit der man Nachrichten an Einzelpersonen oder Gruppen senden kann

Model 2
Letters of enquiry and reply

Hier sehen Sie eine typische Kundenanfrage und die Antwort. Lesen Sie die beiden Briefe und beantworten Sie dann die Verständnisfragen.

The Enquiry

Equable Life Insurance
44 Broadway, Manchester M3 4PB
Tel (061) 574 2356 Fax (061) 574 2345

Our ref: 12/SB
Your ref:
Date: 7 June 1993

The Sales Manager
WordPerfect (UK)
Weybridge Business Park
Addlestone Road
Weybridge
Surrey KT15 2UU

Dear Sir/Madam

WordPerfect Office

We are interested to read the review of the above system in this month's edition of Which Computer?

We are a medium-sized insurance company with a network of agents throughout the world. At the moment we use WordPerfect as our word-processing software at headquarters. We have an increasing need to link up with our offices in the UK and agents overseas.

We would appreciate a visit from one of your technical representatives. This would give us a chance to discuss the feasibility of implementing a Workgroup package.

We look forward to hearing from you soon.

Yours faithfully

T Blackwood

T. Blackwood
Administrative Manager

WordPerfect (UK)
Weybridge Business Park
Addlestone Road
Weybridge
Surrey KT15 2UU
Tel: (0932) 850500

T. Blackwood
Administrative Manager
Equable Life Insurance
44 Broadway
Manchester M3 4PB

Your ref: 12/S
Our ref: TB/56?

11 June 1993

Dear Sir/Madam

Your enquiry of June 7 1993: WordPerfect Office

We were delighted to receive the above enquiry following the review in last month's Which Computer?

WordPerfect Office has already proved itself with a number of our customers. Staff already familiar with WordPerfect will certainly make a very swift transition to the wide range of facilities available with WordPerfect Office.

Rex Stephens, our Customer Service Manager in your area, will be phoning you in the next few days to make an appointment.

In the meantime, we are enclosing some more information about WordPerfect Office, including a case history of a customer similar to you.

Yours sincerely

Tina Brown

Tina Brown
Customer Service Assistant

encl. product documentation

The Reply

Unit 2

Comprehension

Sehen Sie sich den Brief mit der Anfrage nochmal an. Verbinden Sie jeden Absatz mit der passenden Kurzbeschreibung:

Paragraph	Purpose
1	(a) Explains the background/situation
2	(b) Makes a request
3	(c) Gives a reference for the letter
4	(d) Ends politely

Und jetzt das gleiche für den Antwortbrief:

Paragraph	Purpose
1	(a) Responds to the request
2	(b) Reinforces the sales argument
3	(c) Refers to the enquiry
4	(d) Offers more information about the enquiry

Vocabulary development

Verbinden Sie die Wörter in der rechten Spalte mit ihren Entsprechungen in der linken.

1. edition   (a) like
2. link up   (b) use
3. appreciate   (c) customer reference
4. feasibility   (d) issue
5. implement   (e) connect up
6. delighted   (f) viability
7. facility   (g) pleased
8. case history   (h) make operational

Language and communication skills

Reinforcing your sales arguments

Mit welchen sprachlichen Mitteln hat **Model 1** Sie zu überzeugen versucht?

There is no arguing that WordPerfect Office provides you with the full range ...

On top of this, it is a simple ...

This is not just a menu system ...

Its formidable power is not the only thing ..., it is also ...

All in all, this is an excellent product.

Bringing together not only ... but the most vital ...

... are not just available on your local area network ...

Alle diese Äußerungen erwecken den Eindruck, als handele es sich um ein umfassendes und multifunktionales Programm. Sehen wir uns einige der wichtigsten Ausdrücke noch einmal an:

On top of this	*All in all*
In addition	*Bringing together*
... not only ... but also	*As a whole*
... not just ...	*In total*

Exercise 1

Verwenden Sie nun diese Ausdrücke, um die folgenden Sätze zu vervollständigen:

1. This is .... a word-processing package, it is .... a time management system.

2. You can scan other colleagues' diaries. ...., you can enter proposed dates for appointments.

3. .... functions such as electronic mail and diary scheduling, the system offers the ideal networking arrangements.

4. ...., the system represents the best value for money on the market.

5. Although it has one or two minor deficiencies, ..., it meets the needs of most customers.

Letter-writing expressions

Nun zu einigen der Redewendungen aus der Anfrage und dem Antwortbrief.

We were interested to read ...

We would appreciate a visit.

Unit 2

We look forward to hearing from you.

We were delighted to receive ...

In the meantime, we are enclosing ...

Wir können diese Ausdrücke in die folgenden vier Gruppen einteilen:

Opening a letter/giving a reference

We were interested to read/see/hear about ...

Further to/With reference to ...

Thank you for your letter of ...

We were delighted to receive ...

Finishing a letter

I look forward to meeting/hearing from you.

Thanking you in advance...

Please do not hesitate to contact us if you require further information.

Requesting

We would appreciate a visit.

We would be grateful if you could ...

We would be very much obliged if you could ...

Offering information

Please find enclosed/We are enclosing ...

We wish to inform you ...

Exercise 2

Vervollständigen Sie den folgenden Brief mit den passenden Ausdrücken aus der eben besprochenen Übersicht:

Dear Mr Bradshaw

.... your letter dated 11 June 1993, we .... to read of your interest in our new accounting software.

.... the information you requested concerning prices and installation costs. .... if you could complete the attached form so that we can process your order as soon as possible.

We .... your order in the next few days. In the meantime, please .... contact us if you require further information.

Yours sincerely

Peter Matthews
Sales Coordinator

Presenting the product

American/British letter-writing style

Einige Briefformeln sind in amerikanischem und britischem Englisch unterschiedlich:

	American	British
The date	June 11, 1993 (6/11/1993)	11 June 1993 (11/6/1993)
Opening to a company	Gentlemen	Dear Sirs
Closing a letter starting **Dear Sirs/Gentlemen** or **Dear Sir/Madam**	Sincerely yours/ Very sincerely yours Truly yours/ Very truly yours	Yours faithfully
Closing a letter starting **Dear Mr/Mrs/Miss/Ms**	Sincerely yours Truly yours/ Very truly yours	Yours sincerely

N.B.

Ms .... wird in amerikanischen wie britischen Briefen immer häufiger verwendet, wenn nicht bekannt oder nicht wichtig ist, ob die angesprochene Frau verheiratet ist.

Exercise 3

Verwandeln Sie diesen britischen Brief in einen amerikanischen.

Your ref: 052/PQ
Our ref: 22/TS
Date: 2/6/93

Dear Sirs

Thank you for your letter dated 24 May 1993.

Further to your request, we enclose the documentation concerning our products.

Please do not hesitate to contact us if you require further information.

Yours faithfully

Tom Parker
Sales Director

Unit 2

THE BUSINESS INTERVIEW

Marketing and product strategy

Hören Sie jetzt Kenneth Butti, den Geschäftsführer von Electronic Book Publishing (EBP), einem Marktführer auf dem Gebiet der Veröffentlichung von Büchern auf CD. Die folgenden Fragen sollen Ihnen beim Zuhören helfen. Ihre Antworten können Sie dann im Lösungsteil des Buches überprüfen.

Kenneth Butti (seated) with
Karl Heinz Grimm, Managing Director of EPB Europe Ltd., demonstrates the Sony Electronic Book player

As you listen...

1. What three markets does Kenneth describe for his products?
2. How does he describe his market strategy? Is it

    (a) global?
    (b) local?
    (c) survival?

3. What advantage does he see in being a small company?
4. Kenneth has set about establishing a brand name globally. Has he done this by:

    (a) producing his own products?
    (b) co-producing products for well-known companies?
    (c) creating a specific name for his company?

5. Does he think electronic book publishing will take over from traditional book publishing?

UNIT 3
MEETING CUSTOMER NEEDS

In dieser Lektion lernen Sie, wie Sie Fragen nach Kundenwünschen stellen und beantworten.

SAY WHAT YOU MEAN

Listening	Hören
A marketing consultancy	Ein Beratungsgespräch
A market research assignment	Ein Marktforschungsauftrag
Language and communication skills	**Sprache und Kommunikation**
Question tags	Bestätigungsfragen
Question words	Fragewörter
Asking polite questions	Wie man höflicher fragt
Responding to questions	Wie man auf Fragen antwortet

PUT IT ON PAPER

Reading	Lesen
A customer questionnaire	Ein Kundenfragebogen
Faxes of enquiry and reply	Anfrage- und Antwortfax
Language and communication skills	**Sprache und Kommunikation**
Expressing frequency	Wie man Häufigkeiten ausdrückt
Adverbs of time	Zeitadverbien
Question types	Verschiedene Fragetypen
Formal/informal language	Formelle/informelle Sprache

THE BUSINESS INTERVIEW

Reaching the market	Erschließung des Markts

Unit 3

SAY WHAT YOU MEAN

Listening

Extract 1
A marketing consultancy

Sudouest Electronique ist eine Elektronikfirma mittlerer Größe mit Sitz in Südwestfrankreich. Ihr Besitzer und Geschäftsführer, Pierre Danton, hat beschlossen, in neue Märkte zu expandieren. Er hält den britischen Markt für sehr vielversprechend und ist deshalb in einer Besprechung mit der britischen Unternehmensberaterin Jane Stanford, um die beste Strategie für diese Expansion zu entwickeln.

Während Sie einem Ausschnitt dieser Unterredung zuhören, vervollständigen Sie bitte Janes Profil von Sudouest Electronique. Wenn Sie fertig sind, können Sie das Profil im Lösungsteil überprüfen.

COMPANY PROFILE

Name: *Sudouest Électronique*
Product: *Testing equipment for printed circuit boards*
Ownership:
Turnover:
Domestic sales:
Export sales:
Management structure:

Pierre Danton
Managing Director

Customer need:

Meeting customer needs

Extract 2
A market research assignment

Auf der anderen Seite des Atlantiks findet ebenfalls eine Besprechung statt, und zwar in Rochester (N.Y.) in der Zentrale von MEDITEC, einem Marktforschungsunternehmen für die pharmazeutische Industrie. Ein potentieller neuer Kunde, AZTEC Gesundheitspflege, möchte das Verbraucherverhalten im Bereich alternativer Medizin ermitteln. John Peters, einer der Kundenberater bei MEDITEC, bespricht die Möglichkeiten mit Claire Newman, der Leiterin der Abteilung Marketing bei AZTEC. Vervollständigen Sie beim Zuhören das Profil von AZTEC.

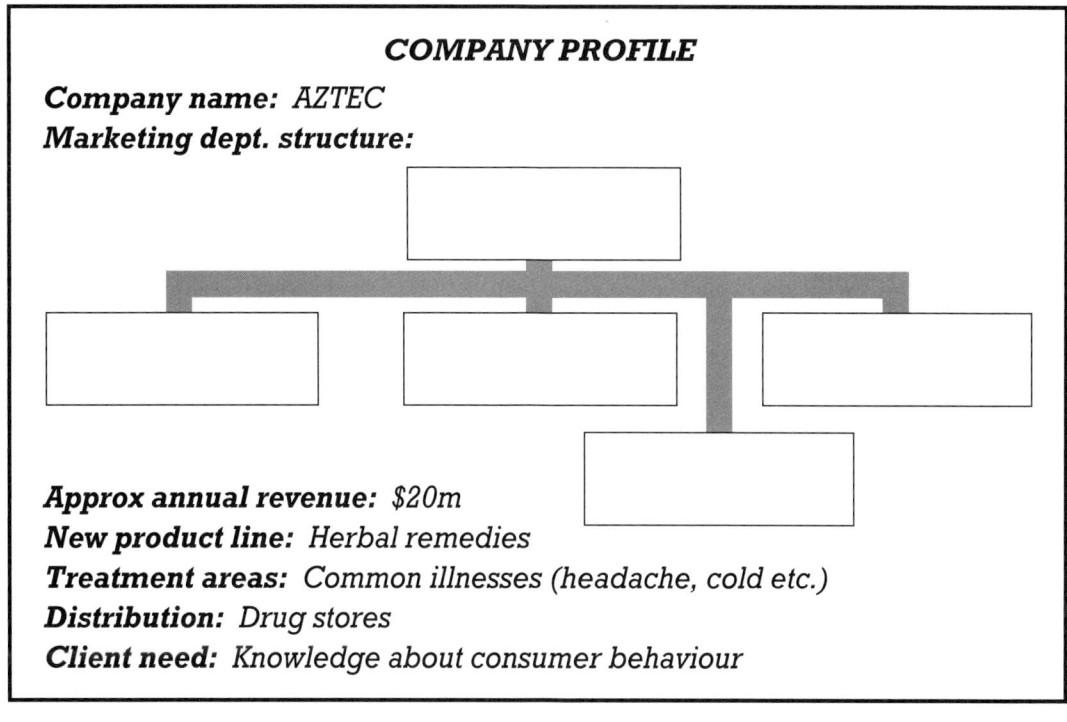

AZTEC
the natural way to **HEALTH CARE**

COMPANY PROFILE

Company name: AZTEC
Marketing dept. structure:

Approx annual revenue: $20m
New product line: Herbal remedies
Treatment areas: Common illnesses (headache, cold etc.)
Distribution: Drug stores
Client need: Knowledge about consumer behaviour

Jetzt können Sie Ihr Profil im Lösungsteil überprüfen.

Unit 3

American/British English

John Peters und Claire Newman sind Amerikaner. Sehen wir uns einige der Unterschiede zwischen amerikanischem und britischem Englisch an.

Vocabulary

John used the word **drug store**, the British would have said **chemist's**. Let's look at a few more differences:

elevator	lift
fall	autumn
first floor	ground floor
freeway	motorway

Usage

Did you notice how John repeated Claire's name frequently? This is common in America. It is often said that Americans deliberately use this technique to remember people's names. The British rarely use the name of the person they're talking to. As a result they frequently forget it!

Language and communication skills

Question tags

Sehen Sie sich zuerst noch einmal einige der Fragen an, die Jane Pierre gestellt hatte.

You and your family hold all the equity in the company?

Your turnover last year was just under 24 million francs, wasn't it?

And these sales were solely in France, I believe?

Sie haben sicherlich bemerkt, daß alle diese **Fragen** eigentlich **Aussagen** sind. Man verwendet diese Art Fragen, um sich über etwas zu vergewissern und/oder um das Gespräch in eine bestimmte Richtung zu lenken. Diese Fragen kann man auf verschiedene Weise bilden:

Meeting customer needs

1. Man läßt die Aussage unverändert und hebt einfach die Stimme gegen Ende des Satzes. Üben Sie die Intonation mit der folgenden Frage:

   You and your family own all the equity?

2. Man kann am Ende des Satzes eine kurze Frage hinzufügen, wie zum Beispiel:

   I believe?

   Is that right?

   Isn't that so?

3. Oder man kann Bestätigungsfragen verwenden. Dafür gelten die folgenden Regeln:

   (a) Subjekt und die Zeitstufe des Verbs bleiben unverändert:

   *You work**ed** for Sudouest Electronique, **did**n't you?*

   *The company **is** in bad shape, **is**n't it?*

   (b) Bejahende Sätze haben verneinende Bestätigungsfragen und umgekehrt:

   *Last year **was** a success, was**n't** it?*

   *We have**n't** exported this yet, **have** we?*

Exercise 1

Ergänzen Sie die Sätze mit passenden Bestätigungsfragen. Üben Sie dann mit Hilfe der Aufnahme die Aussprache.

1. Your family hold all the equity, ………… ?
2. You didn't export anything last year, ………… ?
3. You will appoint an agent in the UK, ………… ?
4. They haven't appointed an agent yet, ………… ?
5. Your company is based in the south west, ………… ?
6. You weren't interested in a joint venture, ………… ?

Question words

Hören Sie sich nochmal an, wie John und Claire über die Informationen sprechen, die sie benötigen:

How big are you?

Unit 3

We have to know how they behave when they get sick, what do they do, what do they think.

Es kann sehr schwierig sein, das richtige Fragewort - **how**, **what**, **which**, **when** usw. - schnell zu finden, besonders wenn man unter Streß steht. Hier ist eine kurze Übersicht über die Fragewörter:

Questions about	Question words
Place, location	Where?
People	Who?
Things	What?
Specific things/people	Which?
Reasons	Why?
Time	When?
Manner/method	How?
Duration	How long?
Distance	How far?
Age	How old?
Quantity	How much/many?
Frequency	How often?

Exercise 2

Machen Sie diese Übung zuerst mit der Aufnahme und schreiben Sie danach die Sätze in aller Ruhe auf. Das Beispiel zeigt Ihnen, wie es geht.

Ask about the number of employees.
How many do you employ?

1. Ask about the cost of the herbal remedies.
2. Ask about the place they will be sold.
3. Ask about the type of illnesses they treat.
4. Ask about the frequency of the illnesses.
5. Ask about the duration of the treatment.
6. Ask about the age of the average consumer.

Asking polite questions

Bisher haben wir gesehen, welche grammatischen Probleme sich bei Fragen ergeben. Jetzt geht es um die verschiedenen Möglichkeiten, Fragen zu stellen und zu beantworten. Hören Sie sich zuerst einige Fragen an, die Jane in ihrer Besprechung mit Pierre gestellt hat.

I'd like to start by checking some background information.

Meeting customer needs

If I understand it correctly, you and your family hold all the equity in the company?

If I might come back to one or two more questions?

I wonder if I could ask you one or two more questions?

If I could ask you a few more questions, I'd like to check over some of the figures?

Jane verwendete diese höflichen Frageformen, weil sie sehr viele Fragen stellen mußte und einige davon auch ziemlich vertrauliche Informationen berührten.

Direct questions	**Polite versions**
How old are you?	**I wonder (if I could ask you)** how old you are?
	Would you mind telling me how old you are?
	Could/Might I ask you how old you are?
	Could you tell me how old you are?
Did you make a profit?	**Could you tell me whether** you made a profit?

N.B. Das Verb der eigentlichen Frage (**you are**, **you made**) steht bei dieser Art von höflichen Fragen nicht mehr in Inversion.

Exercise 3

In dieser Übung sollen Sie ziemlich direkte Fragen in höflichere umwandeln. Sehen Sie sich zuerst ein Beispiel an:

What can you tell me about the product?
I wonder what you could tell me about the product?

Sie können diese Übung mit der Aufnahme machen. Benutzen Sie die vorgegebenen Satzanfänge.

1. Do you have plans to expand?
    Might I ask you .... ?

2. What were your profits last year?
    Could I ask you .... ?

3. What sort of problems do you have with suppliers?
    Would you mind telling me .... ?

4. How much did you export last year?
    I wonder if I could ask you .... ?

Responding to questions

Erinnern Sie sich noch, wie Pierre und Claire auf die Fragen geantwortet haben?

Yes, I can see that.

Yes, that's quite clear.

Fine.

Please go ahead.

Yes, that's right.

Correct.

We actually sold one or two test units in Italy and Spain.

Just remember I'm new to the company.

You mean in revenue terms ... gee ... I'd have to check.

No, that's not true.

Diese Antworten lassen sich in fünf Gruppen einteilen:

1. Understanding (Verständnis zeigen)

Yes, I can see that.

I see.

Yes, that's clear.

I understand what you're getting at.

2. Encouraging (Zustimmung und Entgegenkommen)

Fine.

Please go ahead.

Certainly.

Of course.

3. Confirming (Bestätigung)

Yes, that's right.

Correct.

That's perfectly correct.

4. Contradicting (Widerspruch)

No, that's not true.

We actually sold one or two units.

I'm afraid you're wrong there. We ...

That's not quite right.

5. Excusing (Wenn man eine Frage nicht beantworten kann)

Remember I'm new to the company.

I'm afraid I can't answer that.

I'm afraid I'm not in a position to answer that.

That's outside my field.

I'll have to ask one of my colleagues.

I'll have to get back to you on that.

I'm afraid I don't have the figures on me.

Exercise 4

Mit dieser Übung wiederholen Sie die Redewendungen, mit denen Sie auf Fragen antworten können. Sehen Sie sich zuerst das Beispiel an, dann machen Sie die Übung mit der Aufnahme.

Can you tell me how many people you employ?
(Make an excuse)

I'm afraid I'm new to the company.

1. If I understand you correctly, you only use distributors?
   (Confirm)
2. Would you mind me asking some personal questions?
   (Encourage)
3. You don't employ any sales staff?
   (Contradict)
4. I'd like to know about your profitability?
   (Make an excuse)
5. I need to have a deeper understanding of your market.
   (Show understanding)

Unit 3

PUT IT ON PAPER

In diesem Abschnitt konzentrieren wir uns darauf, wie man Fragen schriftlich stellt und beantwortet.

Reading

Model 1
A customer questionnaire

MEDITEC hat von AZTEC den Auftrag bekommen, das Verbraucherverhalten auf dem Gebiet alternativer Medizin, besonders bei homöopathischen Heilmitteln, zu untersuchen. Dazu werden unter anderem Passanten vor Drogerien und Apotheken befragt. Lesen Sie sich den Fragebogen durch, der als Grundlage für diese Befragung dienen soll. Beantworten Sie danach die Verständnisfragen.

CONSUMER ATTITUDE SURVEY

Alternative medicine

1. What do you understand by the term alternative medicine?
2. Are you satisfied with the health service provided by traditional medical practitioners?
3. How often are you prescribed drugs as treatment?
   - once a year
   - three times a year
   - twice a year
   - more than three times a year
4. Have you yourself ever sought professional medical advice from anybody other than your family doctor?
5. If so, which of the following have you consulted:
   - osteopath/chiropractor
   - faith healer
   - others
   - homeopath
   - herbalist
6. Were you satisfied with the treatment provided?
7. Have you ever tried any herbal remedies?
   If so, which remedies?
   If not, would you be prepared to try a herbal remedy?
8. Would you be prepared to try a herbal remedy without the prescription/advice of a medical practitioner?
9. What type of sickness do you imagine herbal remedies could cure/help?
10. How much would you be prepared to pay for the product shown below?
    $1 - $4
    $4 - $6
    $6 - $8
    $8+

Meeting customer needs

Comprehension

Was sind wohl die Gründe oder Motive für einige dieser Fragen?

1. Question 1: Is this question looking for:
   (a) a definition of alternative medicine?
   (b) an attitude towards alternative medicine?
2. Question 2: What answer does the survey hope to get?
3. Question 3: Why do you think this question is asked?
4. Question 4: If the answer is 'yes', what does this mean?
5. Question 8: Why do you think this is an important question to ask?
6. Question 10: What are they trying to establish with this question?

Vocabulary development

Sie können Ihren Wortschatz sehr effektiv und schnell erweitern, indem Sie Wortfelder um einen Wortstamm herum lernen.

Füllen Sie diese Tabelle aus. Schlagen Sie in einem Wörterbuch nach. Das erste Beispiel zeigt Ihnen, wie es geht.

Verb	Noun	Adjective
to satisfy	satisfaction	satisfactory
to prescribe	....	....
to advise	....	....
to consult	............*	....
to imagine	....	............*
to treat	....	....
to prepare	....	....
to cure	....	....

Note: *In these cases, there is more than one form!

Model 2
Faxes of enquiry and reply

Kommunikation per Fax wird immer gebräuchlicher. Ein Fax ist in der Regel weniger formell als ein Brief, aber doch ohne die Kurzformen, die beim Telex üblich sind. Nach ihrer Besprechung mit Pierre Danton von Sudouest Electronique stellt Jane Stanford fest, daß sie noch weitere Informationen benötigt, bevor sie ihren Bericht schreiben kann. Die folgenden Texte geben ein Beispiel für den Austausch per Fax.

STANFORD & PARTNERS
Marketing • Support • Services

Fax Message

From: Jane Stanford
To: Pierre Danton
Fax no: (010 33) 794 4648
Subject: Entering UK Market
Pages: 1 (including this one)

Fax no: (19 44) 203 64572
Company: Sudouest Electronique

Date: 13 March 1993

Dear Monsieur Danton,

On arrival back in the UK, I have realized there are one or two questions I still need to ask.

1. Do your current prices include transport costs?
2. Do your products conform to BS 9002?
3. What were your margins on the test units exported to Spain and Italy?

I promise you there won't be any more questions! I've already started work on the report. Thank you for looking after me so well while I was in France. I hope we will have the chance to do the same for you in the near future.

One last thing - I left a white blouse in the wardrobe in my hotel room. I'd be very grateful if you could ask them to send it on. Many thanks.

Best regards

Jane Stanford

JANE STANFORD

SUDOUEST ELECTRONIQUE
TÉLÉFAX

FAO: Jane Stanford, Stanford & Partners   Date: 14/3/93
From: Pierre Danton
Subject: Your fax of 13/3/93

Dear Jane,

Please find below the answers to your questions:

1. No, all our prices are ex-stock and do not include delivery charges. However, I do not foresee any problem quoting c.i.f. prices for UK customers.
2. I have no idea. All our equipment conforms with European quality standards. What is this BS 9002?
3. Difficult to say. We usually work on 45% margins based on manufacturing cost. I assume we achieved these margins on the few pieces of equipment we exported.

I'm sorry I can't be more helpful. It was nice to have you visit us in Albi. I have no immediate plans to visit the UK yet but will certainly go there sometime this year.

My secretary has asked the hotel to forward your blouse.
I look forward to receiving your report.

Best regards

Pierre Danton

Pierre Danton

Unit 3

Comprehension

1. Do you think c.i.f. means:

   (a) delivery cost included?
   (b) delivery cost not included?

2. Do you think BS stands for:

   (a) Business Services?
   (b) British Safety?
   (c) British Standard?

3. What does Jane mean by margins on test units?

   (a) margin of quality
   (b) margin of error
   (c) margin of profitability

4. By whom does Jane want the blouse sent on?

Vocabulary development

Im Englischen verbindet man häufig Verben mit Präpositionen oder Adverbien und bildet so Partikelverben. Sie haben sehr unterschiedliche Bedeutungen. In den beiden Fax-Briefen, die Sie gerade gelesen haben, wird das Verb **to look** in zwei ganz verschiedenen Ausdrücken verwendet.

*Thank you for **looking after** me so well.*
*I **look forward to** receiving your report.*

Es gibt noch viele andere Kombinationen. Finden Sie jeweils die passende Bedeutung.

To look + ...	**Meaning**
1. to look after	(a) We must **study** this **in greater depth**.
2. to look forward to	(b) I've been **searching for** it.
3. to look at	(c) You just need to **scan** the book.
4. to look into	(d) Why don't you **find** it **in** the directory.
5. to look for	(e) **Take care of** the children.
6. to look up	(f) Don't **stare at** me.
7. to look through	(g) I **can't wait to** see you again.

N.B.

We look forward to **something**.
We look forward to **doing something**.

For example: I look forward to your **birthday**.
             I look forward to **seeing** you.

Language and communication skills

Expressing frequency

Der Fragebogen in **Model 1** fragte danach, wie oft ein Rezept verschrieben wird.

How often are you prescribed drugs?

Once a year.

Twice a year.

Three times a year.

More than three times a year.

Fragen nach der Häufigkeit kann man auf zwei Arten beantworten:

A Definite frequency

Once		annual (adj) annually (adv)
Twice		half-yearly/six-monthly (adj)
Three times	a year =	every four months (adv)
Four times		quarterly (adj)
Six times		bi-monthly (adj)
Twelve times		monthly (adj)

B Indefinite frequency

(Adverbs of frequency)	(Approximate % frequency)
Never	0
Hardly ever/scarcely ever	5
Rarely /infrequently/seldom	10
Occasionally	35
Sometimes	50
Often/frequently	75
Usually/normally/generally	85
Nearly always/almost always	95
Always	100

Exercise 1

Finden Sie einen anderen passenden Ausdruck. Ersetzen Sie die Wörter in Klammern durch einen Ausdruck aus Liste A.

1. We hold a meeting (once a year).
2. (Every three months), we organize a social event.
3. I produce the company newsletter (once a month).
4. We are now planning our (six-monthly) conference.
5. (Three times a year), we have a strategy meeting.

Wählen Sie für die nächsten vier Sätze Ausdrücke aus Liste B.

6. I (hardly ever) leave the office before eight.
7. I'm (nearly always) the first to leave.
8. (Generally), we have lunch in the canteen.
9. I (rarely) eat out.

Adverbs of time: still/already/yet

Erinnern Sie sich noch, wie diese drei Adverbien in den Briefen verwendet wurden?

*I **still** need to ask one or two more questions.*

*I've **already** started work on my report.*

*I've no immediate plans to visit the UK **yet**.*

Adverb	Position in sentence	Example
Already	Either at the end of the sentence: or before the verb:	We've received your report already. We've already received your report.
Yet	Usually at the end of the sentence:	We haven't received the report yet.
Still	Usually before the verb:	We're still waiting for the report.

Adverb	Uses	Example
Already	Used in positive sentences to mean **by now**:	He's already visited the UK three times.
Yet	Used in negative sentences to mean **by now**:	He hasn't visited the UK yet.
Still	Used in positive and negative sentences to mean **up to now**:	He still hasn't started work on the report. We are still waiting for it to arrive.

Meeting customer needs

Exercise 2

Vervollständigen Sie die Sätze mit **already**, **still** oder **yet**. Dazu müssen Sie natürlich wissen, in welcher Situation Sie sich befinden: Die normalen Schalterstunden der Bank sind von 9.30 bis 15.30. Bei Ihrer Ankunft sind die Türen der Bank jedoch verschlossen.

1. It's 9.40. The bank .... hasn't opened!
2. It's 9.40. The bank hasn't opened .... !
3. It's 9.40. The bank's .... closed!
4. It's 15.25. The bank's .... closed!
5. It's 15.25. It should .... be open.
6. It's 15.25. It shouldn't have closed .... !

Question types

Einige der Fragen vom Fragebogen:

What do you understand by the term alternative medicine?

What type of sickness do you imagine herbal remedies could cure?

Are you satisfied with the health service?

Have you ever sought professional medical advice?

Wir können die Fragen folgendermaßen einteilen:

Open
(keine bestimmte Form der Antwort vorgegeben)

What do you think of ... ?
Could you tell me something about ... ?
I'd be interested to know about ... ?

Closed
(läßt nur bestimmte Formen der Antwort zu - im allgemeinen Ja oder Nein)

Do you think this is a good idea?
Could you tell me if you would buy this product?

Leading
(lenkt die Antwort in eine bestimmte Richtung - meistens natürlich zu der Antwort hin, die der Fragesteller hören möchte)

This is an excellent product, isn't it?
Surely you don't believe in alternative medicine?

Encouraging
(geht auf die vorige Antwort ein)

So, if I understand you, you're saying ...
Could I just check I'm with you? You are saying ... ?

Unit 3

Exercise 3 Ordnen Sie diese Fragen einer der vier Kategorien zu.

1. I'm interested to know what you feel about alternative medicine?
2. If I understand you correctly, you are saying you are in favour of it?
3. Don't you think traditional medicine does a good job?
4. Have you ever bought a herbal remedy?
5. Could you tell me something about your medical history?
6. You've had a healthy life, haven't you?

Formal/informal language Pierres Fax (Pierre ist der Kunde) war etwas weniger formell als das von Jane (die eine Dienstleistung anbietet). Erinnern Sie sich noch an einige Ausdrücke?

Thank you for looking after me so well ...

I hope we'll have the chance to do the same ...

I'd be grateful if you could ask them to ...

Difficult to say.

I've no idea.

Es ist typisch für den weniger formellen Stil im mündlichen und schriftlichen Sprachgebrauch, daß man sich kürzer faßt. Die Äußerung ist kürzer und direkter.

Formal	**Informal**
I am afraid that is difficult to say.	Difficult to say.
I am sorry, I have no idea.	No idea!
I would be grateful if you could ...	Could you ... ?
It was a pleasure to have you with us.	It was nice to see you.

Exercise 4 Kürzen Sie diese Sätze und machen Sie sie weniger formell. Versuchen Sie auch, für die Wörter in Klammern weniger formelle Alternativen zu finden.

1. I'm afraid I will be unable to (attend) the meeting.
2. (I would be grateful if) you could (forward) the package.
3. I hope we will have the (opportunity) to (reciprocate) your kindness.
4. (Please accept our apologies) (for the lateness of the delivery).

Meeting customer needs

THE BUSINESS INTERVIEW

Reaching the market

Caroline Wiggins, Marketingleiterin bei Plastico Limited, einem Hersteller von Kunststoff- und Plastikprodukten, spricht über die unterschiedlichen Verkaufstechniken, die für verschiedene Märkte erforderlich sind. Die untenstehenden Fragen, die sich auf die wichtigsten Punkte des Gesprächs beziehen, sollen Ihnen beim Zuhören helfen. Ihre Antworten können Sie dann anhand des Lösungsteils überprüfen.

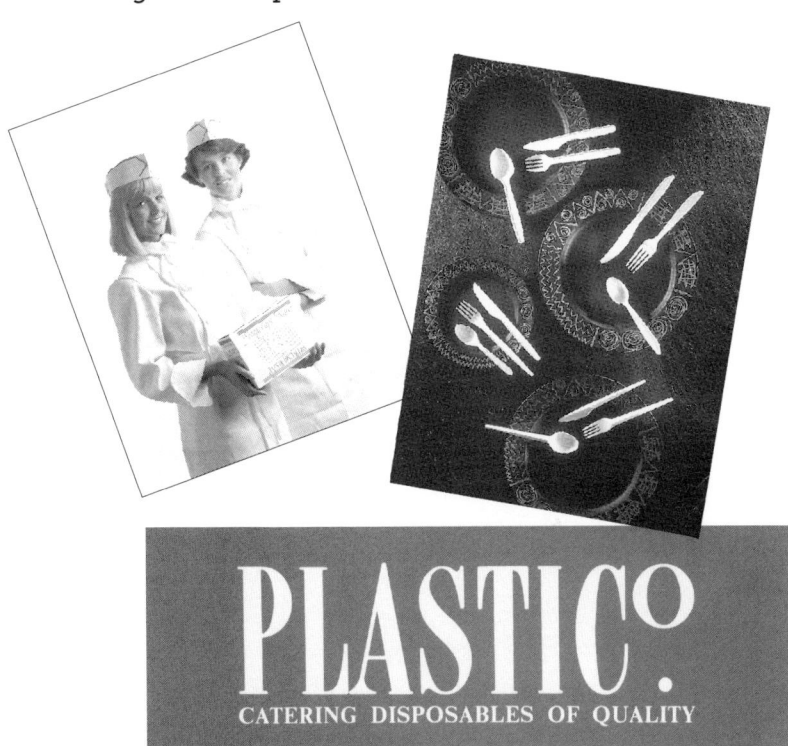

A small selection from Plastico's wide range of quality catering disposables.

PLASTICO.
CATERING DISPOSABLES OF QUALITY

As you listen...

1. What type of company is Plastico and what sort of thing does it produce?

2. Do they sell mainly through agents, or through distributors? Where do they export to?

3. What are the main differences Caroline has noticed between the markets of northern Europe, southern Europe and the Middle East?

4. What qualities does Caroline suggest a successful salesperson should have?

5. What example does she give of the results of being 'tenacious'?

UNIT 4
MANAGING PROJECTS

In dieser Lektion lernen Sie, sich an Projektbesprechungen zu beteiligen oder sie zu leiten.

SAY WHAT YOU MEAN

Listening	Hören
Discussing project timing	Der Zeitplan eines Projekts
A new quality initiative	Qualitätsoffensive
Language and communication skills	**Sprache und Kommunikation**
Prepositions of time	Zeitpräpositionen
Future: 'will' and 'going to'	Futur mit 'will' und 'going to'
Chairing meetings	Wie man Besprechungen leitet

PUT IT ON PAPER

Reading	Lesen
A project update	Ein Projektzwischenbericht
Minutes of a meeting	Protokoll einer Besprechung
Language and communication skills	**Sprache und Kommunikation**
Continuous tenses	Verlaufsform
Verbs of reporting	Verben des Berichtens
Writing for different audiences	Texte für unterschiedliche Adressaten
Writing minutes	Wie man Protokolle verfaßt

THE BUSINESS INTERVIEW

Talking about project management	Über die Leitung von Projekten

Unit 4

SAY WHAT YOU MEAN

Listening

Extract 1
Discussing
project timing

Um ein Projekt erfolgreich zu leiten, muß man vor allem genaue Zielvorgaben machen, einen realistischen Zeitplan erarbeiten und den Fortschritt ständig überwachen. Bei einem internationalen Projekt sind diese Aufgaben natürlich noch schwieriger. Da ist es unerläßlich, ein guter Kommunikator zu sein, vor allem in Projektbesprechungen.

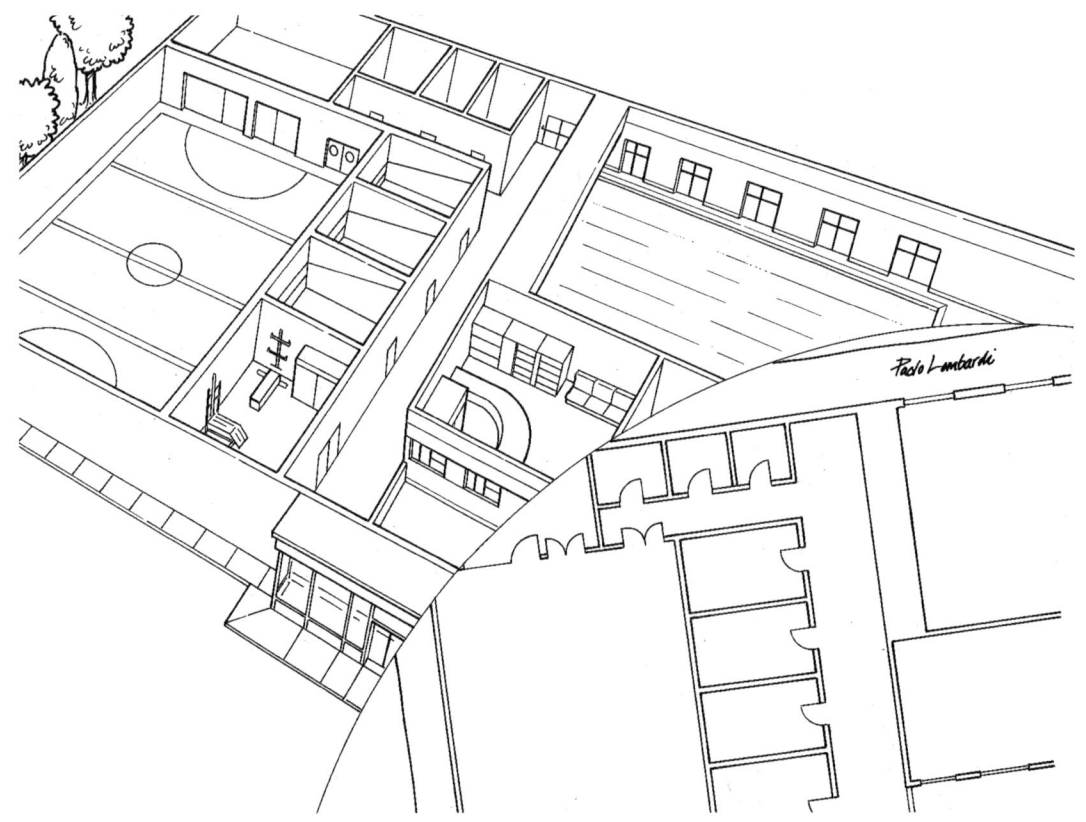

Eine britische Baugesellschaft, BRITBUILD Ltd., hat den Auftrag für den Bau eines neuen Freizeitparks außerhalb von Manchester erhalten. Sie hat einen italienischen Architekten, Paolo Lombardi, damit beauftragt, einen Entwurf vorzulegen. Wir werden bei einer Besprechung über den Zeitplan dabei sein. Chris Hughes, der Projektleiter von BRITBUILD, leitet die Besprechung. Paolo und Suzanne King, eine leitende Projektingenieurin, sind die beiden anderen Teilnehmer.

Vervollständigen Sie beim Zuhören die Angaben im Zeitplan.

Managing projects

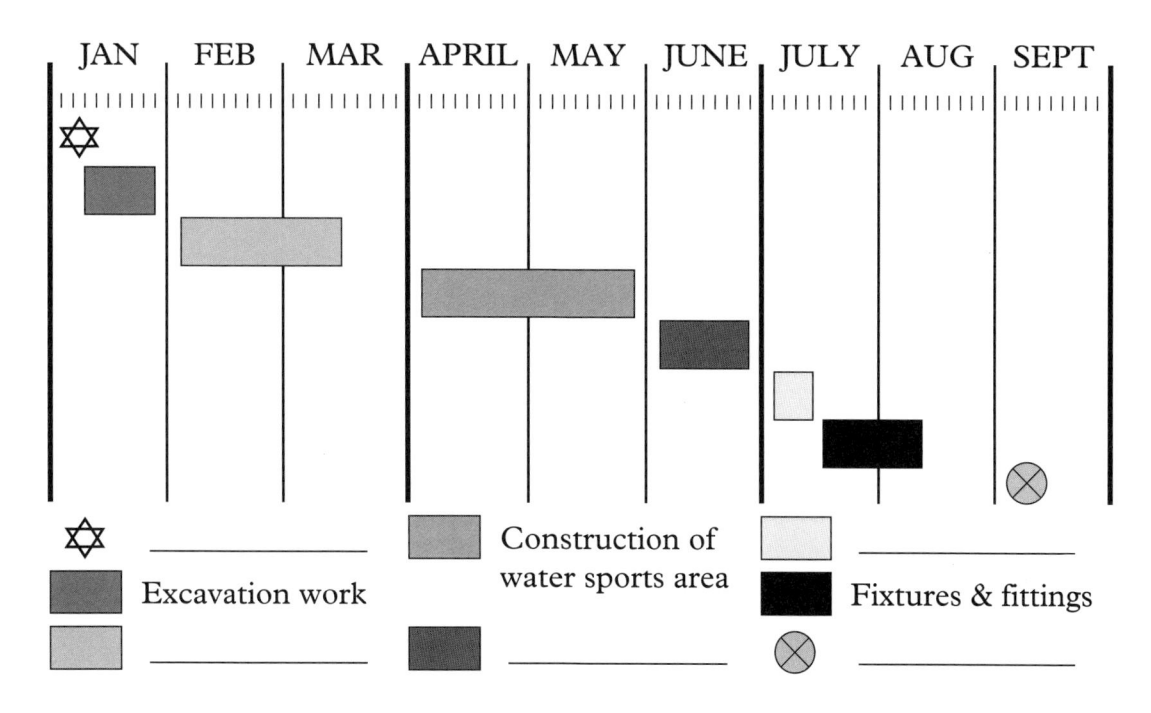

| JAN | FEB | MAR | APRIL | MAY | JUNE | JULY | AUG | SEPT |

✡ _____   Construction of   Fixtures & fittings
         Excavation work   water sports area
_____   _____   ⊗ _____

Überprüfen Sie Ihre Ergänzungen im Lösungsteil hinten im Buch.

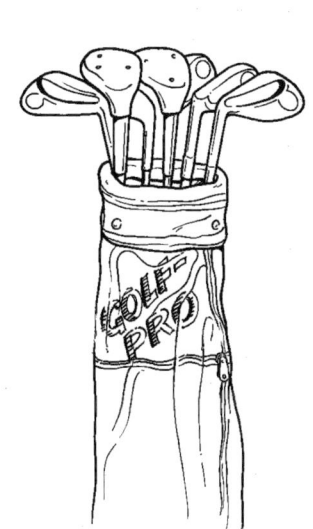

Extract 2
A new quality initiative

Eine deutsche Firma für Sportartikel, SADIMAN AG, hat einen amerikanischen Hersteller von Golfausrüstungen, GOLFPRO, gekauft. In der Herstellung gibt es dort nun einige Probleme mit der Produktqualität. Helmut Stern, der für alle GOLFPRO-Produktionsstätten verantwortlich ist, hat mit Pete Daniels, dem Produktionsleiter des Werks in Minnesota, ein Treffen vereinbart. Sie wollen in diesem Werk einen Qualitätskontrollausschuß einrichten. Pete Daniels hat Stephen Curtis, den Leiter der Qualitätskontrolle, mitgebracht. Sie diskutieren darüber, wer Mitglied im Qualitätskontrollausschuß werden soll.

Entscheiden Sie beim Zuhören, ob die folgenden Aussagen richtig oder falsch sind.

1. The quality circle will be set up in the packaging department. YES NO
2. The objective is to reduce process losses from 8% to 3%. YES NO
3. Stephen will be the team-leader. YES NO
4. Stephen will decide who is in the quality circle. YES NO
5. The purpose of the first real meeting will be to explain the objectives of the quality circle. YES NO
6. The purpose of the first real meeting will be to train them. YES NO
7. Stephen will report back on April 6. YES NO
8. Pete is sceptical about the success of the project. YES NO

Überprüfen Sie Ihre Antworten im Lösungsteil hinten im Buch.

American/British English

Pete Daniels is American, as you could hear. Let's look at some of the things he said:

The guys in the finishing plant are a pretty independent bunch.

You got to be joking!

They couldn't give a damn about quality circles.

You bet! You guys have no idea.

That's one hell of a target!

Now let's look at some differences between American and British English.

Vocabulary

gas	petrol
guy, fellow	bloke, chap
mail	post
movies	the cinema, films

Managing projects

Usage

Pete had a very direct way of speaking. While this is not necessarily typical, it is true that Americans tend to be more direct in their use of language. Let's look at how different expressions might be used either side of the Atlantic.

You got to be joking!	Are you sure that's realistic?
You guys have no idea!	I don't think you understand the problems.
That's one hell of a target!	That target's perhaps a little over-optimistic.

N.B.

As you can see the British have a tendency towards understatement. This is achieved by different means:

1. Changing statements into questions.
2. Changing positives into negatives.
3. Using words like **perhaps**, **a little**, **a bit**.

Grammar

Occasionally Americans use different prepositions from the British.

Here are two common differences:

on the weekend	**at** the weekend
different **than**	different **from**

Language and communication skills

Prepositions of time

Let's first listen to how Suzanne, Chris and Paolo talk about the project timing:

So, starting in the first week of January.

That's scheduled to take us up to the end of January.

We'd like you on site again at the beginning of February.

We aim to start by 1st April on the water sports area.

I'd want to be on site throughout this period.

61

Unit 4

We can classify the uses of time prepositions (Zeitpräpositionen) as follows:

Point of time

at	6 o'clock
	midnight
on	Saturday
	April 10
	Christmas Day
by	the end of July (indicates a deadline = at the latest)
till/until/up to	March (indicates an end point)
since	April 10, March (indicates a beginning point)

Period of time

in	July
	the autumn (Am. Eng. fall)
	the morning
	the middle of ......
at	night
	the weekend (Am. Eng. on the weekend)
during	the meeting
	the lesson
for	two days
	twelve months
throughout	August
	the project

Exercise 1

Vervollständigen Sie diese Sätze mit der richtigen Präposition. Wenn Sie möchten, können Sie diese Übung auch mit der Aufnahme machen. Wenn Sie Ihre Sätze aufschreiben, können Sie sie danach im Lösungsteil überprüfen.

1. The project is due to start .... the beginning of June.

2. We have to finish .... August 15th, no later.

3. The first phase will take us up .... the end of June.

4. We're going to work on the second phase .... July.

5. We should finish that phase .... the middle of the month.

6. We may need to work .... weekends.

7. He's been with us .... the project.

8. What's sure is that we must finish the project .... the autumn.

Future: 'will' and 'going to'

Sehen Sie sich nun die Zeitformen in der zweiten Besprechung genauer an. Wie haben die Teilnehmer über die Zukunft gesprochen?

They're going to need some guidance.

They'll work best if they're left to sort out problems themselves.

We can't have them sitting around - there won't be any production.

Who's going to decide who's in the team?

It's the only way it's going to work.

Certainly I'll do that. I'll fix it for Friday.

Sie werden bemerkt haben, daß entweder **will** oder **going to** benutzt wurde, um über die Zukunft zu sprechen.

Gewöhnen Sie sich auch an die Kurzformen, die in der gesprochenen Sprache üblich sind. Sie können sie sich auf der Aufnahme anhören.

| We will arrive late. | → | We**'ll** arrive late. |
| He will not be on time. | → | He **won't** be on time. |

Manchmal können Sie ohne Unterschied sowohl **will** als auch **going to** verwenden. Es gibt jedoch einen Unterschied in der Verwendung:

Will	1. Wenn man über etwas spricht, das gerade erst entschieden worden ist:	Could you give me those figures? I**'ll** phone them through.
	2. Wenn man hofft, glaubt oder erwartet, daß etwas stattfinden wird:	I hope they **will** sell the house.
	3. Im Hauptsatz eines einfachen Bedingungsgefüges:	Profits **won't** fall if we reduce our costs.

Unit 4

Going to	1. Wenn man über etwas schon Beschlossenes spricht:	We**'re going to** spend our holidays in Barbados.
	2. Wenn man über ein schon jetzt vorhersehbares Ereignis spricht:	The clouds are dark. It**'s going to** rain.

Exercise 2

Lesen Sie den folgenden Dialog. Verbessern Sie den Text, wo Sie es für nötig halten. Hier ist ein Beispiel:

*What film **are** you **going to** see at the cinema?*

I'll see Robin Hood ... (Better:) *I'm **going to** see Robin Hood.*

A: What **are** you **going to** do at the weekend?

B: **I'll** go away to visit friends.

A: Oh, **will** you drive?

B: No, **I'm going to** take the train.

A: How long **is** the journey **going to** take?

B: Normally it takes two hours.

A: And what **will** you do with your friends?

B: **I'll** relax, take it easy.

A: Sounds great. Before you go, could you just finish those letters for me?

B: Certainly, **I'm going to** do them now.

Sie können sich die korrigierte Version des Dialogs auf der Aufnahme anhören. Üben Sie damit auch den Gebrauch der beiden Möglichkeiten, das Futur zu bilden.

Chairing meetings (1)

Hier sehen Sie einen Ausschnitt vom Beginn der ersten Besprechung:

Anyway, we're very short of time this morning, so I suggest we get straight down to business. I've called this meeting to finalize the timing on this project. We've basically got two items on our agenda today - firstly, the construction schedule and secondly, and very important, the schedule of payments. Are there any other items, Paolo, you want to put on the agenda?

Managing projects

Dies sind ziemlich typische einleitende Worte für eine Besprechung. Wir wollen uns einige der Aufgaben der Gesprächsführung und die passenden Redewendungen genauer ansehen.

Eröffnung	Let's get started. Let's get straight down to business.
Vorstellung der Teilnehmer	I'd like to introduce a new colleague from ... Can I introduce our new sales assistant, Susan Matthews ... ?
Zweck der Besprechung	I've called this meeting to discuss the new plans ... The purpose of this meeting is to ...
Tagesordnung	Has everybody seen a copy of the agenda? There are two items of business on the agenda, firstly ... I suggest we take them in the following order ... Would anybody like to add anything to the agenda?
Von einem Punkt zum nächsten	Let's move on to the next item. I think that covers everything on that point.
Wie man Teilnehmer miteinbezieht	Would you like to add anything, Suzanne? We haven't heard from you yet, Charles.

Exercise 3

Verwenden Sie die Wörter in Klammern, um passende Sätze für die angegebenen Situationen zu bilden. Machen Sie diese Übung zuerst mit der Aufnahme; dann können Sie die Sätze aufschreiben und nochmals durchgehen. Hier ist ein Beispiel:

Start the business of the meeting.
Prompt: (short/time/start)
We're short of time, so I think we'd better get started.

1. Introduce a colleague.
   (like/introduce/new colleague/Germany)

2. Check they have seen the agenda.
   (you/seen/copy/agenda?)

3. Explain the purpose of the meeting.
   (called/meeting/discuss/new plant/location)

4. Explain the structure of the meeting.
   (three/business/agenda/firstly/the cost)

5. Move to the first point or item.
   (Right/look/first/agenda)

6. Bring someone into the discussion.
   (Philip/like/add anything?)

7. Move to the next point.
   (think/covers/point/move/item 2)

8. Keep an eye on time.
   (running/time)

Chairing meetings (2)

Now let's turn to the second meeting. This was not such an easy meeting to handle. Let's listen to a few extracts.

I think you misunderstood me ...

Come on, Pete, nobody's suggesting that.

All right, Pete. You've made your position perfectly clear.

Pete, could you drop it? I don't think your attitude's helping.

Let me just go over what we've agreed.

There are three aspects of this meeting which we want to concentrate on.

1. **Clarifying (Nachfragen und Vergewissern)**

I don't quite follow you, could you go over that again?

I'm sorry, I didn't catch that. Would you mind repeating that?

If I understand you correctly, you are saying ...

So what you are saying is ...

What exactly do you mean by ... ?

Could you be more specific/concrete?

Can you give us an example?

2. **Handling difficulties (Bewältigung von Schwierigkeiten)**

That's interesting, Pete. Could we hear from someone else?

Thank you, Pete. Your point's perfectly clear.

Could we leave it there?

I think we're getting off the point.

That's outside the scope of this meeting.

We're losing sight of the main point.

3. Summarizing and closing the meeting
   (Zusammenfassung und Abschluß der Besprechung)

So, let me summarize what has been said so far.

Can we all agree then that ... ?

Let me just go over what we've agreed.

Right, that covers everything.

Let's call it a day.

Thanks for your participation.

I declare the meeting closed. (formal, public meetings)

Exercise 4

Wir wollen einige dieser wichtigen Redewendungen wiederholen. Verwenden Sie jeweils die Wörter in Klammern. Benutzen Sie wie bei den vorhergehenden Übungen die Aufnahme, um sich an die Aussprache und das Verstehen dieser Ausdrücke zu gewöhnen. Hören Sie sich zuerst das Beispiel an:

Ask for repetition.
Prompt: (over/that/again)
Could you go over that again?

1. Ask for more precision.
   (exactly/mean/management style?)

2. Indicate irrelevance.
   (afraid/getting off/point)

3. Stop someone talking.
   (Thank/Pete/Could/move/now?)

4. Stop someone talking.
   (leave/that/now/running/short/time)

5. Summarize decisions.
   (let/summarize/we/agreed)

6. Close the meeting.
   (just/covers/call/day)

Unit 4

PUT IT ON PAPER

Reading

In diesem Abschnitt geht es vor allem darum, wie man Berichte über den Fortschritt eines Projekts schreibt. Wie Sie an den Beispielen sehen werden, könnte es sich dabei um einen Bericht für eine breitere Öffentlichkeit - wie zum Beispiel in einer Firmenzeitschrift - oder einfach um das Protokoll einer internen Projektbesprechung handeln.

Model 1
A project update

Papeteries de Golbey ist eine französische Tochtergesellschaft von Norske Skog, einem der größten Papierwarenhersteller der Welt. 1990 wurde in Nordostfrankreich mit den Bauarbeiten für die größte Papiermühle Europas begonnen. Im März 1991 erschien in der Firmenzeitschrift *Golbey News* ein Bericht über den aktuellen Stand der Arbeiten.

Lesen Sie den Auszug und beantworten Sie dann die Verständnisfragen.

The Machines are coming

Despite some of the worst weather this part of France has ever known in both December and February, the mill construction is on schedule and visibly growing by the day. This is thanks to the great efforts of the swelling number of site workers - almost 1,200. Here's an update on how the work is progressing:

January: Installation of the central boiler began, as planned. This will supply all the plant's needs for steam in the pulp and paper process. It has been designed so that it can generate heat even from tree bark.

February: Installation of the wood-store equipment began. Operating at full capacity, this will be able to handle 200,000 tons of wood and recycled paper per year. The first paper machine, soon to be installed, will process a maximum of 125,000 tons of wood a year.

March: This month administrative and technical staff will be moving into their new office block. This is being purpose-built and includes both open-plan and partitioned office space.

April: This looks like being our busiest phase so far. The paper machine will be arriving for installation over the next few months. In addition, we plan to complete site work on the water treatment plant and the paper recycling warehouse.

Managing projects

Comprehension

1. Has the weather had an impact on the project timing?
2. What is unusual about the steam boiler?
3. Why do you think they have planned for a seeming 75,000 tons over-supply of wood and recycled paper?
4. Has the new office block been completed?
5. Are they planning to assemble the paper machine on site?

Vocabulary development

Machen Sie sich nun mit Redewendungen zum Thema Projektleitung vertraut. Vielleicht brauchen Sie dazu manchmal ein Wörterbuch. Wie viele Kombinationen fallen Ihnen ein?

Base word	**Associated words**
Example: time	*Combination:* on time
1. date	
2. schedule	on, according to, as, up, to, out, of, behind, ahead
3. plan	

Überprüfen Sie Ihre Antworten im Lösungsteil.

Model 2
Minutes of a meeting

Protokolle von Besprechungen erfüllen bei der Durchführung von Projekten eine wichtige Aufgabe. Sie halten diejenigen auf dem laufenden, die an einzelnen Treffen nicht teilnehmen konnten, und erinnern an Entscheidungen, die man getroffen hat. Sehen Sie sich das Protokoll einer Besprechung an, die Sie weiter vorne in der Lektion gehört haben.

Beantworten Sie dann die Verständnisfragen.

```
MINUTES OF QUALITY ACTION GROUP MEETING

Date:      March 25, 1993
Present:   Helmut Stern, Pete Daniels, Stephen Curtis
Subject:   Quality Circle in Finishing Plant - Golfpro

We agreed to set up an experimental quality circle in the finishing plant. We
also decided the objective of this group would be to reduce process losses from
8% to 3%.

Following some discussion, it was agreed that membership of this QC (maximum:
6) would be self-selecting. We also outlined the following actions:

1.  SC to hold preliminary meeting with production workers on Friday March 27
to explain objectives and get them to select representatives.
2.  SC to attend first QC meeting (scheduled for Friday April 3) in order to
train members on methods of working.
3.  SC to report back to this action group on Monday April 6.
```

Unit 4

Comprehension

1. What are the minutes of a meeting?
2. Why are they setting up a quality circle in the finishing plant?
3. Who is going to select the quality circle members from the production workers?
4. Why is Stephen Curtis going to attend the first quality circle meeting?

Vocabulary development

Hier geht es um Wörter, die bei Besprechungen gebraucht werden. Suchen Sie rechts jeweils die beste Entsprechung für die Wörter in der linken Spalte.

1. to attend
2. to be present
3. apologies for absence
4. the agenda
5. the minutes
6. the chairman
7. actions
8. an item
9. to put on the table/to table
10. to adjourn

(a) the order of business
(b) steps to be taken
(c) the person in charge
(d) to raise an issue/point
(e) to go to a meeting
(f) the written record
(g) a point for discussion
(h) notification you cannot attend
(i) to be at a meeting
(j) to close a meeting with the plan to meet again at a later date

Language and communication skills

Continuous tenses

Look at some of the statements from *Golbey News*:

... how the work **is progressing**.

... the administrative staff **will be moving** into a new office block.

This **is being purpose-built**.

The paper machine **will be arriving** ...

We use continuous tenses (**to be** + verb + **-ing**) when we refer to an event which

1. Is happening now:

   I'm reading this exercise. (present continuous)

2. Will be happening at a definite moment in the future:

   I'll be leaving home at 07.30 tomorrow. (future continuous)

3. Was happening at a certain moment in the past:

   I was reading the newspaper when the phone rang.
   (past continuous)

N.B. In American English you will find that continuous tenses are referred to as **progressive tenses**.

Exercise 1

Vervollständigen Sie diese Sätze mit der passenden Verbform.

1. Last year I worked in Spain.
   In June .... in Seville.

2. Every day I drink 3 or 4 cups of coffee.
   At the moment .... a cup of coffee.

3. Next year we will sell 200,000 units.
   In the second half of the year, we .... 500 units a week.

4. Generally I work in Head Office.
   For the time being, I .... in our French subsidiary.

5. In 1976 I left my job in Germany.
   I .... in Germany when the terrorists kidnapped an industrialist.

6. I hope to work less hard in the future.
   I know I .... very hard next week when the negotiations start.

Verbs of reporting

We frequently use such verbs when we report meetings. Look at these examples from the minutes above.

*We **agreed to** set up an experimental quality circle.*

*We also **decided** the objective of this group would be to ...*

*We also **outlined** the following actions ...*

These verbs can be grouped as follows:

Unit 4

Describing	**Saying**		**Proposing**
to describe	to say	to notify	to suggest
to present	to tell	to inform	to recommend
to show	to announce	to report	to advise
to demonstrate	to declare	to state	to propose
	to disclose		

Thinking	**Expecting**	**Asking**
to think	to expect	to ask
to believe	to anticipate	to request
to consider	to forecast	to question
to wonder	to warn	to demand
	to threaten	

Ordering	**Agreeing**	**Disagreeing**
to order	to agree	to disagree
to command	to admit	to deny
to insist	to confirm	to refuse
to authorize	to approve	to decline
to instruct		

Exercise 2

Vervollständigen Sie diese Sätze mit einem passenden Verb aus der Übersicht. Das Beispiel zeigt Ihnen, wie es geht.

If you don't pay me, I will take you to court!
He/She threatened to take me to court.

1. He ………… saying that in court. (Disagreeing)

2. He ………… us of the danger of bankruptcy. (Proposing)

3. She ………… us how to connect the machine. (Describing)

4. He ………… me to take a holiday. (Proposing)

5. She ………… that I move my office. (Ordering)

6. He ………… the product. (Agreeing)

Managing projects

Writing for different audiences

Der Bericht in den *Golbey News* war für ein gemischtes Publikum von Mitarbeitern und Außenstehenden geschrieben.

Installation of the central boiler began, as planned. This will supply all the plant's needs for steam in the pulp and paper process. It has been designed so that it can generate heat even from tree bark.

Er enthält Informationen für Insider:

Installation of the central boiler began, as planned.

und für Außenstehende:

This will supply the plant's needs for steam in the pulp and paper process.

Solche Erklärungen (wie Zweck, Design und Kapazität) sind nur für Außenstehende interessant, die nicht direkt am Projekt mitarbeiten.

Exercise 3

Bearbeiten Sie den Bericht für *Golbey News* so, daß nur noch Informationen für Insider, d.h. die Projektmitarbeiter, enthalten sind. Ihr neuer Bericht sollte erheblich kürzer sein. Sie können Ihre Fassung dann mit dem Vorschlag im Lösungsteil vergleichen.

Writing minutes

Besprechungsprotokolle müssen selten jede einzelne Äußerung enthalten. Es ist vor allem wichtig, die getroffenen Entscheidungen festzuhalten sowie Übereinkünfte und eventuell auch Meinungsverschiedenheiten, die noch wichtig werden könnten.

Exercise 4

Hören Sie sich noch einmal den ersten Text der Lektion an. Wenn Sie möchten, können Sie den Text auch im Schlüssel lesen. Schreiben Sie ein Protokoll über den Verlauf der Besprechung und vergleichen Sie dann Ihre Fassung mit der Version im Lösungsteil.

Unit 4

THE BUSINESS INTERVIEW

Talking about project management

Dale Jennings von ORMS, einer Gruppe von Designern und Architekten, spricht über die Leitung von internationalen Projekten. Die untenstehenden Fragen, die sich auf die wichtigsten Punkte des Gesprächs beziehen, sollen Ihnen beim Zuhören helfen. Ihre Antworten können Sie dann anhand des Lösungsteils überprüfen.

ORMS' spread of work now includes residential, retail, masterplanning, interiors, graphics and corporate identity, and the firm is working in France, Germany and the Middle East.

As you listen...

1. What three examples does Dale give of ORMS' overseas projects?
2. How does he describe the task of the successful project manager?
3. According to Dale, what is the main cause of problems or 'pitfalls' in the area of project management?
4. Which of the following is his principal technique for picking up mistakes before it's too late?

    (a) having a series of stepping-stone targets?
    (b) completing the project according to a fixed programme?
    (c) having an overview of a vision of the whole project?

5. How does Dale encourage everybody to refocus their energies?
6. Who does he report to?

UNIT 5
RESULTS AND FORECASTS

In dieser Lektion lernen Sie, über Ergebnisse und Prognosen zu sprechen.

SAY WHAT YOU MEAN

Listening	Hören
Analysing past performance	Wie man Arbeitsergebnisse analysiert
Forecasting future performance	Wie man Prognosen formuliert

Language and communication skills	Sprache und Kommunikation
Present perfect and past simple	Perfekt und Präteritum
Forecasting	Prognosen
Giving opinions	Meinungen und Vermutungen
Agreeing and disagreeing	Zustimmung und Widerspruch

PUT IT ON PAPER

Reading	Lesen
A balance sheet	Eine Bilanz
A letter to shareholders	Ein Brief an die Aktionäre

Language and communication skills	Sprache und Kommunikation
Reviewing tenses	Wiederholung der Zeitformen
Giving good and bad news	Gute und schlechte Nachrichten
Individual and company letters	Korrespondenz: Einzelperson und Unternehmen

THE BUSINESS INTERVIEW

Planning for the future	Zukunftsplanung

SAY WHAT YOU MEAN

Listening

Bilanzkennzahlen und Prognosen sind für die Unternehmensleitung von zentraler Bedeutung. Deshalb ist es außerordentlich nützlich, wenn man weiß, wie man über die Bilanzkennzahlen und Planungsdaten spricht.

Extract 1
Analysing
past
performance

PEOPLEPOWER ist ein Unternehmen für Personalberatung mit Sitz in London. Das Unternehmen ist Spezialist für die Vermittlung von Computerfachleuten für kurzfristige Projekte. Der geographische Schwerpunkt seiner Tätigkeit ist Südostengland. Paul Baker und Anna Sharp leiten das Unternehmen. Beide haben langjährige Erfahrung als freiberufliche Programmierer. Sie haben sich entschlossen, PEOPLEPOWER zu gründen, um großen Firmen für ein zeitlich begrenztes Projekt hochqualifizierte und flexible Programmierer zu vermitteln, die zeitlich befristet mitarbeiten sollen.

Ihr Unternehmen ist zunächst sehr schnell gewachsen, dann aber ist die Nachfrage nach Programmierern zurückgegangen. Einige Kunden haben größere und längerfristige Projekte erst einmal zurückgestellt. Andere haben sich dazu entschlossen, Programmierer nicht mehr zeitlich befristet, sondern als ständige Mitarbeiter zu beschäftigen. Der Finanzberater für mittelständische Unternehmen bei der Eastminster Bank, Mark Cadogan, hat Paul und Anna zu einem Gespräch über die derzeitige finanzielle Situation ihres Unternehmens eingeladen.

Numerieren Sie beim Zuhören die acht Kerndaten auf der Gewinn- und Verlust-Rechnung, die sie besprechen.

PEOPLEPOWER
PROFIT & LOSS

	This year	Last year
Income		
☐ Gross turnover	445,482	425,815
☐ Cost of sales	46,183	38,514
☐ Net turnover	399,299	387,301
Direct Costs		
☐ Fees - freelancers	196,433	168,792
☐ Fees - directors	90,000	45,000
	286,433	213,792
Expenses		
☐ Salaries	32,500	24,500
☐ Rent	20,000	19,000
☐ Telecommunications	8,423	7,180
☐ Advertising and promotion	15,903	8,715
	76,826	59,395
Depreciation		
☐ Equipment	7,517	6,168
☐ Fixtures	2,319	2,041
	9,836	8,209
☐ Net profit	26,204	105,905

Wenn Sie fertig sind, überprüfen Sie Ihre Aufstellung im Lösungsteil.

Unit 5

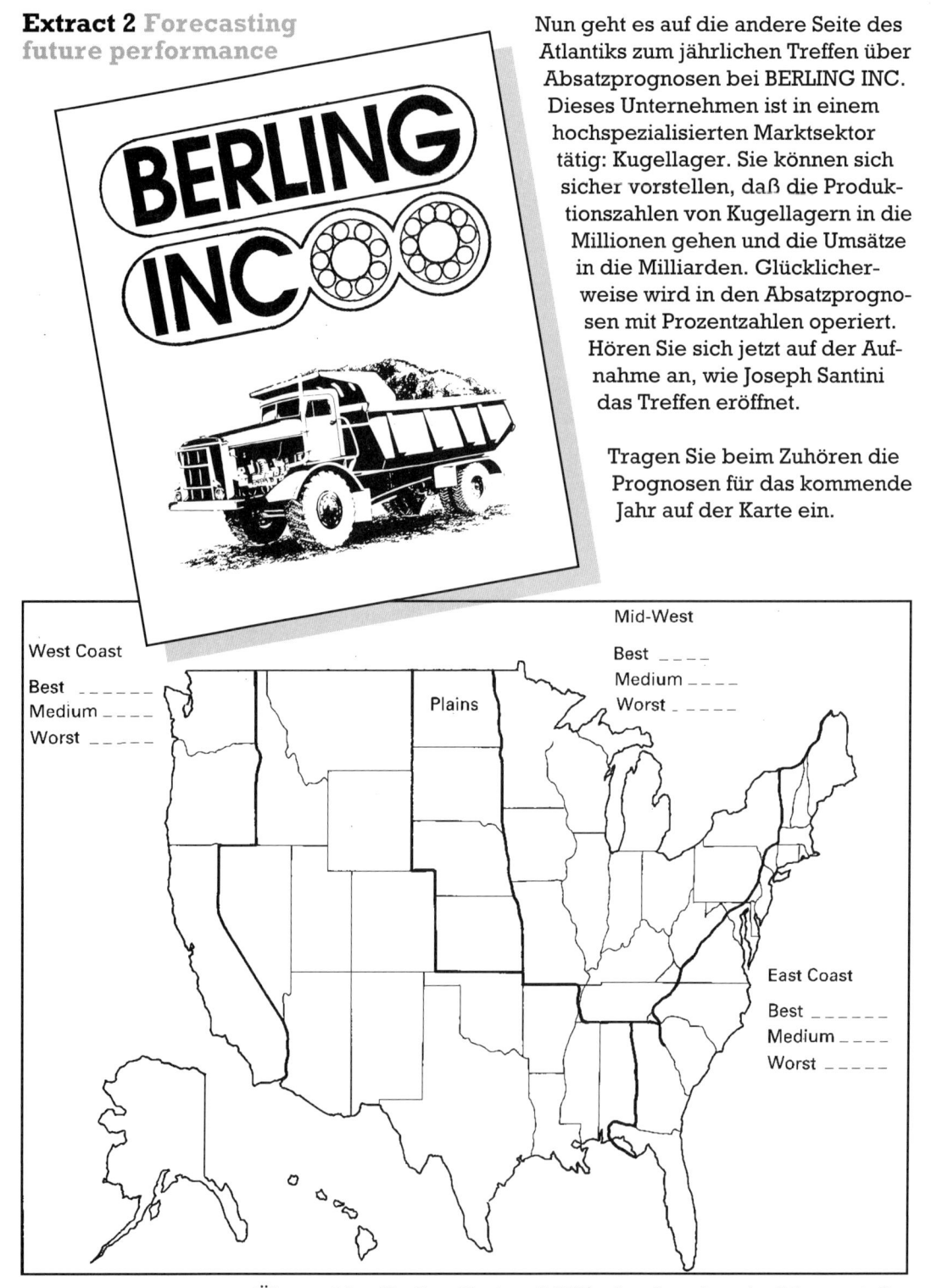

Extract 2 Forecasting future performance

Nun geht es auf die andere Seite des Atlantiks zum jährlichen Treffen über Absatzprognosen bei BERLING INC. Dieses Unternehmen ist in einem hochspezialisierten Marktsektor tätig: Kugellager. Sie können sich sicher vorstellen, daß die Produktionszahlen von Kugellagern in die Millionen gehen und die Umsätze in die Milliarden. Glücklicherweise wird in den Absatzprognosen mit Prozentzahlen operiert. Hören Sie sich jetzt auf der Aufnahme an, wie Joseph Santini das Treffen eröffnet.

Tragen Sie beim Zuhören die Prognosen für das kommende Jahr auf der Karte ein.

West Coast
Best _____
Medium _____
Worst _____

Mid-West
Best _____
Medium _____
Worst _____

Plains

East Coast
Best _____
Medium _____
Worst _____

Überprüfen Sie Ihre Karte mit Hilfe der Angaben im Lösungsteil.

Results and forecasts

American/British English

Sehen Sie sich jetzt einige der Unterschiede zwischen britischem und amerikanischem Englisch an.

Vocabulary

In American English **presently** means **at the moment**; in British English **presently** means **soon**. Let's look at a few more differences.

American	British
annual sales	turnover
bill	(bank) note
check	bill
president (company)	chairman
real estate	property
stocks	shares

Usage

Baseball is the national sport in the US. Words and expressions from the game often appear in other contexts. For example, in the meeting Joseph and his colleagues talked about **pitching** and **teams**.

Here are some other baseball expressions used in a business context. What do the words in bold mean?

*We've tried to negotiate with them, but they just refuse **to play ball**.*

*I can't tell you exactly, but a **ball park figure** would be $3.5m.*

*He knew it was urgent, so he did it **right off the bat**.*

Language and communication skills

Present perfect and past simple

Sehen Sie sich zunächst einige der Zeitformen an, die Paul, Anna und Mark in ihrem Gespräch mit der Eastminster Bank gebraucht haben.

That's why we've invited you in, just to review the situation.

I know, but it implies that something's gone wrong.

Back in the old days, we didn't need to. The clients just came to us.

When to use present perfect

Man verwendet das Perfekt - die mit **have** oder **has** gebildete Zeitform -, wenn eine Verbindung zur Gegenwart besteht:

● um eine Handlung in der unbestimmten Vergangenheit zu bezeichnen, die bis in die Gegenwart oder Zukunft hinein wirkt:

We have read the accounts. (now the reading stage is finished and we are ready to discuss them)

● um eine Handlung innerhalb einer Zeitspanne zu bezeichnen, die noch nicht abgeschlossen ist:

Our expenses have increased this year. (the year is not yet finished)

● um eine Handlung zu bezeichnen, die in der Vergangenheit begann und bis in die Gegenwart hinein dauert:

We have supplied you with programmers for the last five years. (we started to supply five years ago and we are still doing it)

When to use past simple

Man verwendet das Präteritum, wenn die Handlung ganz in der Vergangenheit stattfindet:

We read the accounts last week.

Our expenses increased last year.

We supplied you with programmers five years ago.

Exercise 1

Markieren Sie die für den Satz passende Verbform.

Hier ist ein Beispiel:

Last year our income (**increased**)/ **has increased** slightly.

Sie können für die Übung auch die Aufnahme benutzen.

1. Since last year our expenses **dropped** / **have dropped**.
2. Two months ago we **recruited** / **have recruited** a new secretary.
3. Since then we **raised** / **have raised** productivity.
4. So, you are with Smith & Partners. How long **were you** / **have you been** there?

Results and forecasts

5. Oh, I **worked / have worked** there for two years now.

Forecasting

Sehen Sie sich genauer an, wie Joseph Santini und seine Kollegen ihre Prognosen für das Kugellagergeschäft im folgenden Jahr formuliert haben. Hören Sie sich zuerst die Aufnahme an. Sie werden erkennen, daß man die folgenden fünf Abstufungen von Wahrscheinlichkeit unterscheiden kann. Anhand der Übersicht können Sie sehen, welche Redewendungen für die einzelnen Stufen verwendet werden.

Degree of likelihood	Expressions
Certain	We are definitely/certainly going to increase sales by 5%.
	Sales are bound/certain/sure to increase by at least 7%.
Probable	I'm likely to hit 6%.
	Sales should increase by 6%.
Possible	I may/might manage to repeat this year's sales.
	I could even reach 7%.
Improbable	We're unlikely to see any change.
Impossible	I definitely can't make more than 10%.
	Sales can't possibly rise by more than 10%.

Exercise 2

Benutzen Sie die Aufnahme für diese Übung. Wenn Sie wollen, schreiben Sie sich die Sätze zuerst auf. Zu den folgenden Aussagen finden Sie in der Klammer eine Angabe über ihre Wahrscheinlichkeit. Formulieren Sie diese Prognosen mit Hilfe einer passenden Phrase aus der Übersicht entsprechend um.

Hier ist ein Beispiel:

We are going to increase turnover. (certain)
We are certainly going to increase turnover.

1. Our costs will increase. (probable)

2. We will reduce our expenses. (possible)

3. Overheads will rise. (improbable)

4. We will increase our gross profit. (certain)

5. But we won't raise our percentage profit. (impossible)

Giving opinions Jetzt geht es darum, wie Sie in Besprechungen oder in Diskussionen am besten Ihre Meinung vorbringen Man kann eine Meinung überzeugt, neutral oder nur als Vermutung präsentieren. Die folgenden Redewendungen können Sie verwenden. Hören Sie sich zuerst die Aufnahme an.

Strong	I'm sure/convinced/positive … I definitely/certainly/really think … … you'll feel differently at the end of the meeting.
Neutral	As I see it, … In my opinion … I think/consider … … that has gone up quite a lot.
Weak	I tend to think … I'm inclined to think …

Exercise 3 Formulieren Sie die folgenden Aussagen mit den passenden Redewendungen aus der Liste so um, daß die Meinung überzeugt, neutral oder als Vermutung vorgebracht ist. Hören Sie sich zuerst das Beispiel auf der Aufnahme an. Sie können die Übung erweitern, indem Sie die Sätze auch noch mit allen anderen möglichen Redewendungen formulieren.

1. The short-term future isn't healthy. (neutrally)
2. The medium term looks better. (neutrally)
3. The local economy will improve. (neutrally)
4. In the long term we are in a strong position. (strongly)
5. The best policy is to maintain our prices. (weakly)

Agreeing and disagreeing In der Besprechung bei BERLING INC. waren Joseph und seine Kollegen sich in einigen Punkten einig, in anderen nicht. Hören Sie sich auf der Aufnahme einige solcher Beispiele aus der Besprechung an. Die folgende Übersicht gibt Ihnen eine Reihe von Ausdrücken, die Sie in solchen Situationen verwenden können.

Agreeing or disagreeing with a person

I totally/fully/completely agree with you.

(I'm afraid) I can't/don't agree with you.

I can't go along with you on that.

Accepting or rejecting an idea

I totally accept that.

I'm all in favour of that.

(I'm afraid) I can't/don't accept that.

I can't go along with that.

Results and forecasts

Partly agreeing or accepting

Up to a point/To a certain extent I agree/I'd agree with you, but ...

Up to a point/To a certain extent I accept/I'd accept that, but ...

Exercise 4

Üben Sie dieses kurze Gespräch mit Hilfe Ihrer Aufnahme. Antworten Sie jeweils entsprechend den Vorgaben, die Sie hören. Die folgende Skizze des Gesprächs soll Ihnen dabei helfen.

1. I think we should invest in new plant now.
   (agree)

2. ... and I really think investment should be made in the first quarter.
   (accept)

3. But first, I think we should review the investment plans.
   (partly agree; but you think we should continue the current investments)

4. Hmm. I tend to think that the forecast figures are much too optimistic.
   (reject)

5. But the demand for our products isn't growing.
   (partly accept; but it will grow in the near future)

6. I'm still not convinced that we need a major expansion policy right now.
   (disagree)

PUT IT ON PAPER

Reading

In diesem Abschnitt sehen Sie sich Bilanzen und Unternehmensgewinne genauer an. Eine Bilanz und ein Brief an die Aktionäre eines Unternehmens sind die Grundlagen für die folgenden Übungen zum Textverständnis und zum Wortschatz.

Model 1
A balance sheet

Paul Baker und Anna Sharp von Peoplepower haben auch ihre Bilanz zu dem Gespräch mit Mark Cadogan mitgebracht.

Sehen Sie sich die Bilanz an und beantworten Sie dann bitte die Verständnisfragen.

BALANCE SHEET
PEOPLEPOWER

As at 31 December

	This year	Last year
Fixed assets		
Intangible assets		23,000
Tangible assets	78,630	76,700
	78,630	99,700
Current assets		
Stock	3,110	2,030
Debtors	83,110	86,950
Property held for disposal	5,430	2,200
Cash at bank and in hand	13,600	13,880
	105,250	105,060
Current liabilities		
Creditors: amounts falling due within one year	(104,760)	(20,990)
Net current assets	490	84,070
Total assets less current liabilities	79,120	183,770
Creditors: amounts falling due after more than one year (including loans)	(27,480)	(34,640)
Provisions	(690)	
Net assets	50,950	149,130

84

Results and forecasts

Comprehension

Welche Informationen erhält man aus der Bilanz eines Unternehmens?

1. A balance sheet shows
    (a) the company's general financial position.
    (b) a snapshot of the company's financial position at a certain date.

2. Assets (Vermögenswerte) are what a company
    (a) owes.
    (b) owns.

3. Fixed assets (feste Anlagen) tie up a company's money on
    (a) a long-term basis.
    (b) a short-term basis.

4. Current assets (Umlaufvermögen) are those which
    (a) can be easily converted into cash.
    (b) can't be easily converted into cash.

5. The net assets (Reinvermögen) are calculated on the basis of
    (a) the real market value (Marktwert) of the company's assets.
    (b) the cost to buy the company's assets.

6. From the balance sheet we can interpret
    (a) the financial situation of the company.
    (b) the general health of the company.

Vocabulary development

Nun geht es um die Definitionen von Begriffen aus dem Finanzwesen. Im folgenden finden Sie die Begriffe aus der Bilanz und ihre Definitionen. Was gehört zusammen?

1. Tangible assets   (a) people to whom your company owes money
2. Loans   (b) money set aside for liabilities that cannot be accurately forecast
3. Stock (Am. Eng. inventory) (c) hardware owned by the company and used to operate its activities
4. Liabilities   (d) after all deductions have been made
5. Debtors   (e) money your company has borrowed
6. Creditors   (f) money owed by your company
7. Due   (g) people who owe money to you
8. Net   (h) value of goods ready for sale
9. Provisions   (i) owed, which must be paid

85

Unit 5

Model 2
A letter to
shareholders

Kurz nach der Verkaufsbesprechung mit Joseph Santini liefen in Wall Street Gerüchte um, BERLING stehe kurz vor der Übernahme durch ROLLERBALL. Um Befürchtungen bei den Aktionären zu zerstreuen, schrieb Marvin P. Goldwater, Vorstandsvorsitzender von BERLING, den Rundbrief, den wir auf der folgenden Seite abgedruckt haben.

Comprehension

1. What is the British English equivalent of stockholder?
2. What does the President state to highlight the long-term potential of Berling's products?
3. Is Berling accelerating or slowing down its investment program to increase productivity?
4. What is Berling's current position in its sector?

Vocabulary
development

Sie können Ihren Wortschatz sehr effektiv erweitern, indem Sie Wortfelder zu bestimmten Grundwörtern lernen. Die folgende Tabelle gibt Ihnen ein Beispiel dafür. Ermitteln Sie mit Hilfe eines Wörterbuchs die Bedeutung der übrigen Wörter und füllen Sie die Lücken aus.

Verb →	Noun →	Adjective
signify	significance	significant
....	....	impressive
....	....	continued
....	proof	....
maximize (Am. Eng.) maximise (Br. Eng.)		
....	profit	....
....	productivity	....
assure	....	....
....	leader	....

Dear Stockholder,

I am delighted to announce another year of significant growth. It is therefore your Board's unanimous view that Rollerball's offer for your stocks fails to reflect the true worth of Berling's products. The following details highlight our impressive performance over recent years and our plans for continued growth in the future.

First, we are pleased to inform you that last year Berling brands outperformed all their rivals, earning trading margins of over 15 points in the US. Regrettably, Rollerball are unable to match or even approach our margins.

Second, over the past five years, we have launched more than 20 new brands in the US market. And we feel justifiably delighted that the Berball ranges have all continued to increase market share. This is proof of the long-term potential of our products.

Third, we are presently engaged in a strategy to maximize profits. I am sure that many of you will be aware of the investments we are making to increase productivity at all our plants. These are progressing at a steady pace, although we regret that the current economic climate is forcing us to exercise caution.

And what of the future? Let me assure you that we at Berling will continue to invest in new product development; that we aim to push up our margins as well as our market share; and that we will maintain our position as market leader in the US.

For these reasons we, the Board of Berling, urge you to reject Rollerball's offer.

Sincerely yours

Marvin P. Goldwater

Marvin P. Goldwater
PRESIDENT AND CEO

Unit 5

Language and communication skills

Reviewing tenses

Sehen Sie sich nun genauer an, wie Marvin P. Goldwater in seinem Brief die verschiedenen Zeitformen benutzt.

The present continuous

Die Continuous-Form des Präsens wird verwendet, wenn ein Ereignis oder eine Tätigkeit sich gerade abspielt oder nur vorübergehend ist.

I am sure that many of you will be aware of the investments we are making to increase productivity at all our plants. These are progressing at a steady pace, although we regret that the current economic climate is forcing us to exercise caution.

The past simple

Das Präteritum wird für Ereignisse oder Tätigkeiten verwendet, die abgeschlossen sind und eindeutig in der Vergangenheit stattgefunden haben.

Last year Berling brands outperformed all their rivals.

The present perfect

Das Perfekt wird verwendet, wenn sich Ereignisse oder Tätigkeiten in einem Zeitraum abspielen, der bis in die Gegenwart reicht oder wenn der Zeitraum nicht genau angegeben ist.

Secondly, over the past five years, we have launched more than 20 new brands in the US market.

And we feel justifiably delighted that the Berball ranges have all continued to increase market share.

The future with 'will'

Diese Zeitform wird für Ereignisse oder Tätigkeiten verwendet, die in der Zukunft stattfinden.

Let me assure you that we at Berling will continue to invest in new product development.

And that we will maintain our position as market leader in the US.

Exercise 1

Vervollständigen Sie diesen Brief, indem Sie jeweils das Verb in Klammern in die richtige Zeitform setzen. Sie können Ihre Lösungen im Lösungsteil überprüfen.

Results and forecasts

Dear Shareholder,

Later this year you .... (1.have to) decide on the future of this company. And I .... (2.write) to you now to explain the options. But first I'd like to remind you of how Investalot .... (3.perform) over recent years.

In the 1980s we .... (4.turn round) a badly-managed company and .... (5.give) it a new position in the investment market. As a result Investalot .... today .... (6.become) a company attractive to investors from all over the world.

Last year .... (7.be) tough. I am well aware of that. Like many other investment companies, we .... (8.have to) fight our way through an international recession. But most experts now .... (9.agree) that we have put Investalot on course for steady and sustained growth. And right now we .... (10.begin) to see the signs of an upturn. But I promise you one thing. We, at Investalot, ... (11.continue) to look for the best opportunities for our investors.

Just over a year ago, Morton Securities .... (12.start) negotiations to get a controlling interest in Investalot. Since then we .... (13.do) much to consolidate Investalot's position. But there is much more to do. So, I hope that you .... (14.share) my vision and reject Morton's offer.

Finally, please feel free to contact your local office if you .... (15.wish) to discuss this letter in more detail.

Yours sincerely

Harvey Copper-Smythe

Harvey Copper-Smythe
CHAIRMAN

Unit 5

Giving good and bad news Marvin P. Goldwater konnte sich sehr zufrieden über die positiven Entwicklungen bei BERLING äußern; andererseits mußte er mit Bedauern auch auf einige Schwächen hinweisen. Die folgenden Redewendungen sind sehr nützlich, wenn Sie gute oder schlechte Nachrichten formulieren müssen.

Giving good news

I am delighted
I feel (very) pleased
I am glad
... to announce another year of significant growth.

We are pleased to
... inform you
... tell you
... advise you
that last year Berling brands outperformed their rivals.

Giving bad news

We regret
... are afraid
... are sorry
that the current economic climate is forcing us to exercise caution.

Regrettably,
We regret to inform you
... tell you
... advise you
that Rollerball are unable to match or even approach our margins.

Exercise 2 Bilden Sie aus den folgenden Stichwörtern ganze Sätze, die entweder gute oder schlechte Nachrichten enthalten.

1. regret/inform/job application/be/unsuccessful
2. pleased/advise/we/accept/your offer
3. regrettably/we/unable/use/services
4. delighted/welcome/you/our team
5. sorry/I/not able/attend/meeting/last week

Results and forecasts

Individual and company letters

Wenn Sie einen Geschäftsbrief auf Firmenbriefpapier schreiben, möchten Sie manchmal sicherlich unterscheiden zwischen Ideen und Vorschlägen, die Sie als Einzelperson vorbringen, und solchen, die im Namen des Unternehmens stehen. Ebenso muß man beim Adressaten unterscheiden, ob es sich um eine Einzelperson handelt oder um ein Unternehmen. Im Englischen gibt es dafür die folgenden Konventionen:

The writer	**as individual**	**as company**
	I	we
	e.g. I am pleased …	we are sorry …
	I am writing …	we are writing …
The reader	Dear Sir (man, name unknown)	Dear Sirs (Br. Eng.) Gentlemen (Am. Eng)
	Dear Madam (woman, name unknown)	
	Dear Mr Brown	
	Dear Mrs Smith (married woman)	
	Dear Ms Jones (woman, marital status unspecified)	

Exercise 3

Wie würden Sie in den folgenden Situationen einen Brief beginnen? Formulieren Sie die Anrede und den ersten Satz.

1. To a British company to which your company wants to give bad news.
2. To an American company to which your company wants to give some information.
3. To Mrs Brown to whom you, as an individual, want to give good news.
4. To a man to whom your company wants to give bad news.
5. To a woman to whom you, as an individual, want to give some information.

Unit 5

THE BUSINESS INTERVIEW

Planning for the future

Jonathan Harris, ein leitender Bilanzbuchhalter, beantwortet Fragen zur Bedeutung von Berichten zur Bilanzlage eines Unternehmens. Die untenstehenden Fragen, die sich auf die wichtigsten Punkte des Gesprächs beziehen, sollen Ihnen beim Zuhören helfen. Ihre Antworten können Sie dann anhand des Lösungsteils überprüfen.

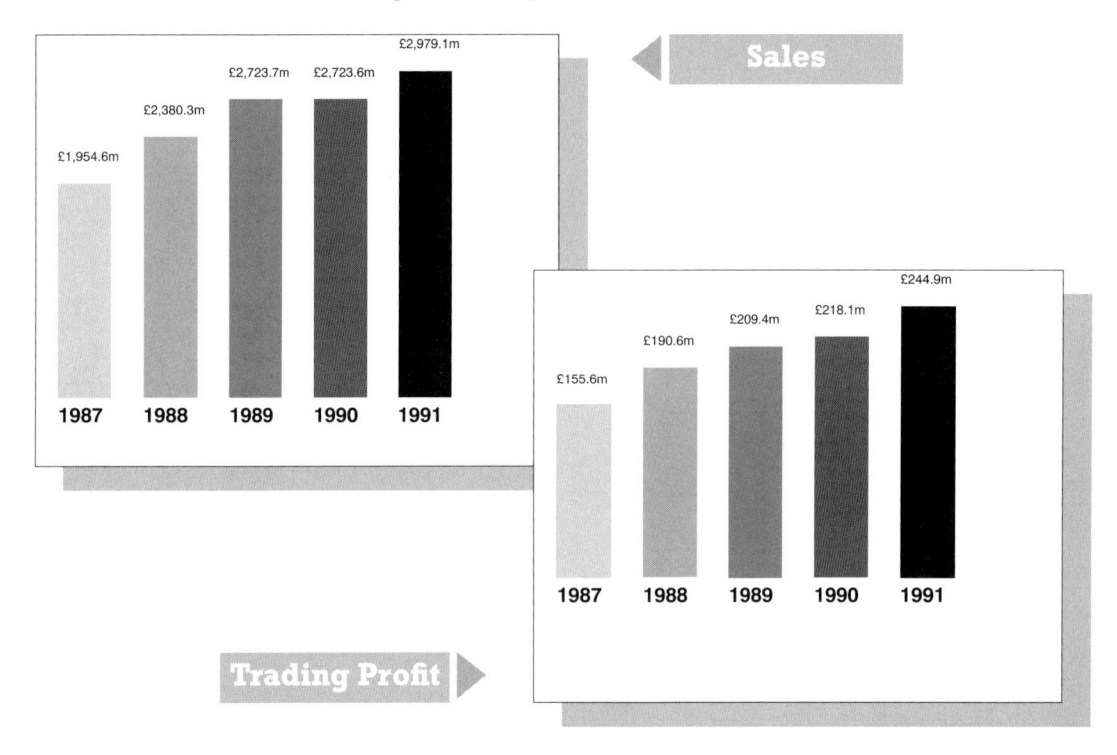

Sales

1987	1988	1989	1990	1991
£1,954.6m	£2,380.3m	£2,723.7m	£2,723.6m	£2,979.1m

Trading Profit

1987	1988	1989	1990	1991
£155.6m	£190.6m	£209.4m	£218.1m	£244.9m

Extracts from UB's five year and annual (1991) financial reports

As you listen...

1. How does Jonathan describe his current area of responsibility at United Biscuits?

2. What are the two key factors he highlights in successful financial reporting?

3. Does Jonathan say

   (a) financial reports are the same the world over?
   (b) different countries may have different emphases in their reporting?
   (c) some countries report only to their shareholders?

4. What two examples does Jonathan give of possible confusions in terminology between the UK and the United States?

UNIT 6
CUSTOMER SERVICE

In dieser Lektion sehen Sie sich verschiedene Bereiche des Kundendienstes an.

SAY WHAT YOU MEAN

Listening	Hören
Checking service conditions	Kundendienstleistungen
An insurance claim	Ein Schadensersatzanspruch

Language and communication skills	Sprache und Kommunikation
Conditional sentences	Bedingungssätze
Offering to help	Wie man Hilfe anbietet
Structuring a phone call	Wie man ein Telefongespräch gliedert
Communicating by phone	Wie man sich am Telefon verständigt

PUT IT ON PAPER

Reading	Lesen
A customer letter	Ein Brief an einen Kunden
An insurance policy	Eine Versicherungspolice

Language and communication skills	Sprache und Kommunikation
Noun + preposition/preposition + noun	Substantiv + Präposition/Präposition + Substantiv
Other conditional constructions	Weitere Bedingungsgefüge
Using different communication channels	Wie man unterschiedliche Kommunikationsmittel benutzt
Expressing obligation in writing	Wie man Verpflichtungen schriftlich formuliert

THE BUSINESS INTERVIEW

The service element	Serviceleistungen

SAY WHAT YOU MEAN

Listening

Kundendienst wird immer wichtiger für Unternehmen. In diesem Abschnitt geht es um geschäftliche Telefongespräche und die passenden Redewendungen und darum, wie man mit Verständigungsproblemen umgeht.

Extract 1
Checking service conditions

BOOTIT ist ein britisches Versandhaus, das sich auf Standardcomputerzubehör, in der Regel von bekannten Markenherstellern, spezialisiert hat. Die meisten Kunden sind entweder Privatpersonen oder kleine Unternehmen. Das Versandhaus hat regelmäßig Anzeigen in Tageszeitungen und Zeitschriften mit attraktiven Angeboten, die erheblich billiger als bei der Konkurrenz sind. Anfragen kommen in der Regel per Fax oder übers Telefon, Bestellungen werden per Fax oder Brief angenommen. Die Waren werden durch Kurierdienste an die Kunden ausgeliefert. Alle Produkte, die BOOTIT vertreibt, haben eine Garantie von zwölf oder 24 Monaten ab Kaufdatum; außerdem bietet BOOTIT auch verschiedene Serviceverträge an. Jetzt hören Sie eine telefonische Anfrage über einen Bubble-Jet-Drucker.

Füllen Sie beim Zuhören die Notizen des Anrufers über die Kundendienstleistungen aus.

Customer service

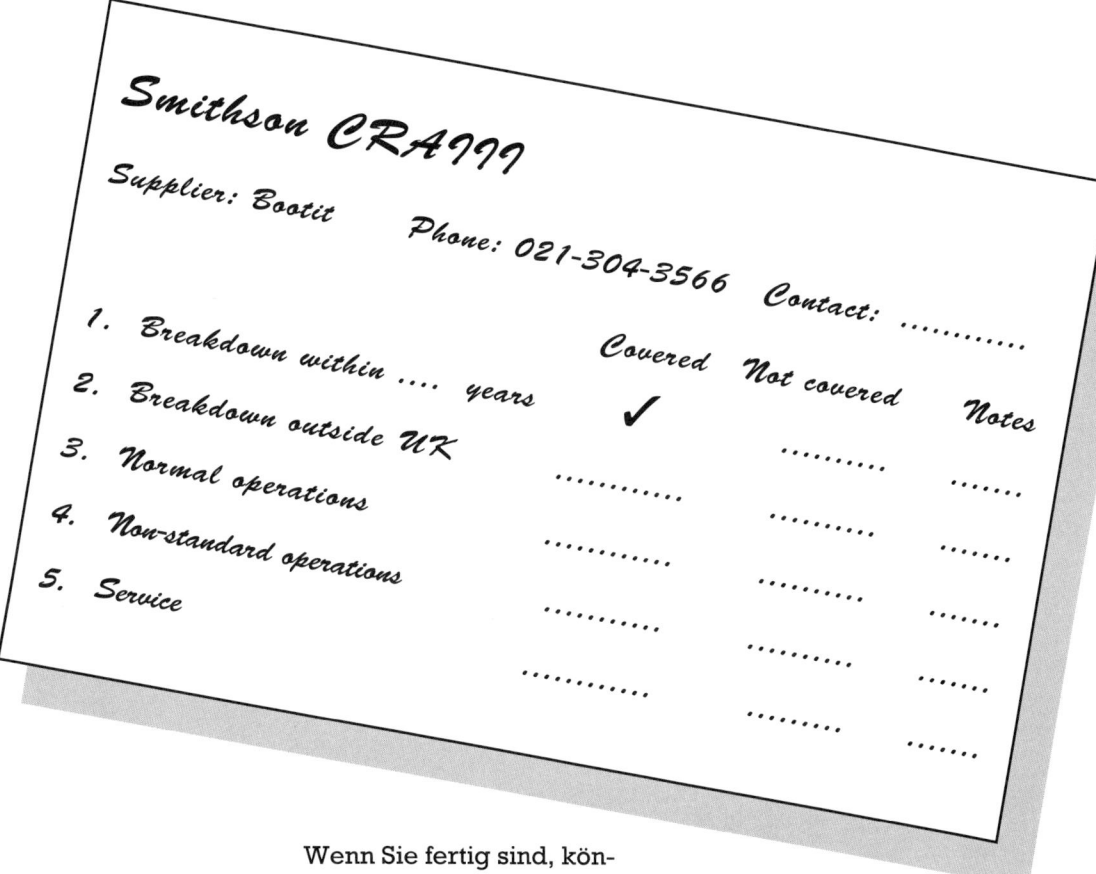

Smithson CRA999

Supplier: Bootit   *Phone: 021-304-3566*   *Contact:* ....

	Covered	Not covered	Notes
1. Breakdown within .... years			
2. Breakdown outside UK	✓	....	....
3. Normal operations	....	....	....
4. Non-standard operations	....	....	....
5. Service	....	....	....

Wenn Sie fertig sind, können Sie Ihre Notizen im Lösungsteil überprüfen.

Extract 2
An insurance claim

Im nächsten Telefongepräch geht es um einen Schadensersatzanspruch, der nicht zügig bearbeitet worden ist. Der Hintergrund: Vor einigen Monaten hatten Josephine und Harry King beschlossen, mit einem zweiwöchigen Urlaub in Brasilien, genauer in Sao Paulo, dem trüben New Yorker Winter zu entkommen. Wie alle vorsichtigen Urlauber haben sie eine Reiseversicherung abgeschlossen. In Sao Paulo angekommen mußten sie feststellen, daß ihr Gepäck nicht den gleichen Weg genommen hatte. Es sollte gar nicht mehr auftauchen. Als Josephine endlich ihr Reisebüro in New York erreichte, sagte man ihr, daß sie kaufen solle, was sie für den Urlaub unbedingt brauche, und daß man sich nach ihrer Rückkehr um eine Schadensersatzregelung kümmern werde. Josephine und Harry kauften also ein, für insgesamt 795$; und als sie wieder in New York waren, schickten sie dann auch die Schadensersatzforderung zusammen mit den Rechnungen an COVERALL, ihre Versicherung. Nach drei Monaten hatten sie immer noch keine Reaktion von der Versicherung.

Unit 6

Hören Sie sich nun auf der Aufnahme an, wie Josephine bei COVERALL anruft. Vervollständigen Sie beim Zuhören die Notizen der COVERALL-Angestellten.

COVERALL

wherever, whenever, whatever, whoever

Notizen des 1. Angestellten:
Caller's name:
Type of policy:
Type of claim:

Notizen des 2. Angestellten:
Place of loss:

Notizen des 3. Angestellten:
Insured's name: Tel:
Reason for call:
Place of loss:
Date of claim:
Action:

Vergleichen Sie Ihre Notizen mit den Angaben im Lösungsteil.

Customer service

American/British English

Now let's look at some of the differences between American and British English.

Vocabulary

Both the Coverall clerks and Mrs King used the word **vacation**; in British English the equivalent is **holiday**.

Here are some more differences you may notice:

American	British
public holiday	bank holiday
apartment building	block of flats
trailer	caravan
downtown	city centre

In British English the verbs **phone**, **ring** and **call** are all used with the same meaning; in American English the commonest verb is **call**.

Usage

In the phone call one of the clerks said: Good morning, is **this** Mrs King? In the UK, the equivalent would be: Good morning, is **that** Mrs King?

American	British
Is this Mr Brown?	Is that Mr Brown?
These details are correct.	Those details are correct.

So, in the US the phone connects the speakers physically; they regard themselves as being in the same place. In the UK, callers regard themselves as being in different places.

Language and communication skills

Conditional sentences

Let's start by looking again at some of the language from the phone call to Bootit. The speakers used a number of conditional sentences (Bedingungssätze) containing the word **if**.

Unit 6

Type 1	Yes, basically if it breaks down within the first two years, the manufacturer will repair it or replace it.
	Well, if you need any more information, I'll be happy to answer your questions.
Type 2	So, what would happen if it broke down abroad?
	As far as I can tell, sir, if it broke down outside the UK, you wouldn't be covered.

Die beiden Typen sind zum Teil ähnlich, zum Teil unterschiedlich. Beide Satzstrukturen drücken ein Verhältnis zwischen Ereignissen und ihren Folgen aus. Soweit die Ähnlichkeit. Der Unterschied besteht darin, daß der Sprecher in Typ 1 das Ereignis für tatsächlich möglich hält; der Sprecher in Typ 2 dagegen hält das Ereignis nur für eine wenig wahrscheinliche Möglichkeit. Das heißt, der Unterschied zwischen den beiden Satzmodellen liegt in der Beurteilung des Ereignisses durch den Sprecher: Typ 1 steht für eine tatsächliche Möglichkeit, Typ 2 für wenig wahrscheinliche Möglichkeiten.

Die beiden Typen unterscheiden sich durch den Tempusgebrauch.

	'If' clause	**Main clause**
Type 1	present simple	future with 'will'
Type 2	past simple	conditional with 'would'

Exercise 1

Setzen Sie die Verben im zweiten Teil der folgenden Sätze in die passende Zeitform. Üben Sie dann mit der Aufnahme die Aussprache der vollständigen Sätze. Falls nötig, sehen Sie sich die Regeln für Bedingungssätze noch einmal an.

Zuerst ein Beispiel:

If it breaks down, (we replace it).

If it breaks down, we will replace it.

1. If it broke down abroad, (we don't replace it).
2. We wouldn't repair it, (if you don't use our parts).
3. If you call before 10 o'clock, (the engineer comes in the afternoon).
4. You could buy extra cover, (if you want to).
5. If you buy this product, (we offer a special discount).

Customer service

Offering to help

Let's look again at the language used by the clerks at Coverall as they tried to sort out Josephine King's insurance problem. During the phone call, the clerks made various offers.

How can I help you?

Would you like me to connect you?

Shall I connect you?

Well, if you could give me some more details, Mrs King, I'll check out what happened to your claim.

The clerks used the following modal verb phrases (modale Hilfsverben) to make their offers:

Can I ... and **Shall I** ..., which are both question forms, **I'll** ..., which is a statement form, and the verb phrase, **Would you like me to** ..., which is also a question form.

Exercise 2

In dieser Übung sollen Sie nun Ihre Hilfe anbieten, und zwar mit den Redewendungen, die wir gerade besprochen haben. Verwenden Sie jeweils das in Klammern angegebene Verb. Zunächst ein Beispiel:

Offer to ring the caller back later. (will)
I'll ring you back later.

1. Offer to check the caller's records. (shall)
2. Offer to send the caller a fax. (would you like me to)
3. Offer to send the caller some more details. (can)
4. Offer to sort out the caller's claim tomorrow. (will)
5. Offer to put the caller in touch with a good lawyer. (would you like me to)

Structuring a phone call

Now we are going back to our first phone call between Bootit and the prospective customer for a portable bubble-jet printer. Let's look at the expressions that can be used to structure a phone call.

Getting the person you want to speak to	Could you put me through to your sales department? Could/Can I speak to ..., please? I'd like to speak to ..., please. Mr Brown, please.
Explaining your purpose	Yes, I'm ringing/phoning/calling about the Smithson bubble-jet printer. I'd like to check what after-sales service you offer.
Asking for more information	And what exactly does that cover? Excuse me, what does that mean?
Moving on	I have another question. Could I ask another question? There's something else I'd like to know.
Accepting the information	Well, that's all (I need to know) for now.
Thanking	Well, thank you very much/thanks for your help. Well, thank you/thanks for the information.
Ending the call	Goodbye/Bye.

Exercise 3

Formulieren Sie also nun Sätze, die zu den Anweisungen passen. Sie können sich die Anweisungen zuerst ansehen, wenn Sie mehr Zeit haben wollen, um die Sätze zu formulieren, aber machen Sie die Übung auf jeden Fall mit der Aufnahme. Das Beispiel zeigt Ihnen, wie es geht:

Ask to speak to Harry Malone.
Could I speak to Harry Malone, please?

1. Ask to be put through to the sales department.

2. The purpose of your call is to ask about laptop computers.

3. Ask for the exact price of that model.

4. You don't understand what an on-site warranty means.

5. Move on to your next question - about delivery.

6. Indicate that you've got all the information.

7. Thank the other party for the information.

Customer service

Communicating by phone

Although Josephine King was clearly having problems getting her claim settled, the clerks at Coverall were having problems of a different sort - communication problems.

Zunächst wollen wir uns ansehen, wie man die typischen Verständigungsschwierigkeiten meistert, die es am Telefon oder im persönlichen Gespräch gibt.

- Sie haben etwas akustisch nicht verstanden und bitten um eine Wiederholung.

(I'm) sorry, I didn't catch that.

(I'm) sorry, I didn't hear what you said.

(I'm) sorry, could I have your name again, please?

(I'm) sorry, could you repeat that, please?

(I'm) sorry, would you mind repeating that, please?

- Sie haben etwas nicht verstanden und hätten gerne eine ausführlichere Erklärung.

(I'm) sorry, Mrs King, but I don't quite understand the problem.

I'm still not entirely clear on this, Mrs King.

I'm not quite with you.

Could you go over that again, please?

Could you explain that again, please?

- Sie möchten z.B. einen Namen buchstabiert haben.

And could you spell your name for me?

Could you spell that, please?

Can you spell it, please?

Exercise 4

In dieser Übung führen Sie ein Telefongespräch. Ihr Gesprächspartner möchte eigentlich mit Ihrem Vorgesetzten sprechen, aber da dieser im Augenblick nicht zu erreichen ist, haben Sie den Anruf entgegengenommen. Der erste Abschnitt des Dialogs zeigt Ihnen, was Sie tun sollen. Sie nehmen die Rolle B.

A: *This is Ferdinand Gutierez.*
   (Ask him to repeat his name.)

B: *I'm sorry, could I have your name again, please?*

A: *Yes, my name is Ferdinand Gutierez.*

Jetzt machen Sie weiter. Sie können sich von der Aufnahme durch das Gespräch leiten lassen.

A: Listen, when are you going to sort out this bill?

B: (You don't understand the problem.)

A: I said when are you going to pay this bill? It's more than two months overdue.

B: (You didn't hear what he said.)

A: I said it's more than two months overdue.

B: (Say you'll look into it tomorrow. Ask him to spell his name.)

A: Yes, it's G-U-T-I-E-R-E-Z.

B: (Too fast. Ask him to repeat it.)

A: Yes, it's G-U-T-I-E-R-E-Z. And could you spell your name for me, please?

B: (Do as he asks!)

A: OK, I got it. Look forward to hearing from you tomorrow then. Goodbye.

Customer service

PUT IT ON PAPER

Reading

Dieser Abschnitt beschäftigt sich mit verschiedenen Schriftstücken aus dem Kundendienstbereich. Im Anschluß an die Texte des vorhergehenden Abschnitts finden Sie hier einen Brief an einen Kunden über Serviceleistungen für das verkaufte Produkt und einen Ausschnitt aus einer Versicherungspolice mit den Einzelheiten der Bedingungen bei Gepäckverlust. Wie in den anderen Lektionen werden Sie im Anschluß an die Texte Übungen zum Wortschatz und zum schriftlichen Ausdruck finden.

Model 1
A customer letter

Frank Baker hat sich schließlich dazu entschlossen, den Smithson Bubble-Jet-Drucker bei BOOTIT zu kaufen. Zwei Tage nach seiner Bestellung wurde der Drucker schon geliefert, und am nächsten Tag kam der folgende Brief.

Lesen Sie den Brief und beantworten Sie dann die Verständnisfragen.

BOOTIT COMPUTER SUPPLIES
Unit 37, Fisher Park Trading Estate
Birmingham B21 6HJ
Tel: 021-567-4986 Fax: 021-565-6783

Mr Frank Baker,
15 Hillcrest Road
YORK
YO5 7YH

12 March 1993

Dear Mr Baker,

Congratulations on your selection of a Smithson Laser Printer GH-N4490. For exceptional speed, paper handling, features and price, you cannot beat Smithson Laser Printers. Naturally, we hope that you will be very satisfied with this product and that it will provide you with hours of trouble-free printing. However, to give you even greater confidence in your printer, we are giving you

ONE YEAR ON-SITE WARRANTY*
at
NO CHARGE

In addition, we would like to draw your attention to a number of special offers that we have at Bootit at the moment. These will only be available for a limited period of time, while stocks last, so we strongly advise you to place your order very soon. In particular, as owner of a Smithson Laser Printer, I am sure you would like to take advantage of our special offers on toner cartridges. These and other unrepeatable bargains are shown on the reverse of this letter.

Your printer comes with a one-year warranty. But, for only £50 you can extend that warranty for a further twelve months - giving you a total of 2 years' cover. Just think of the peace of mind that such a warranty can give. To take advantage of this once-only offer, you must return the enclosed warranty registration card within two weeks together with your payment.

Finally, if a problem should arise, either during installation or during normal usage of your printer, call our Hotline Monday to Friday between 08.00 and 18.00 on 021-800-4567. If you would like further details about any of our products, please call our sales department on the number shown above. Alternatively you can reach us by fax or letter (see details at top of letter).

We thank you for your custom.

Herbert C. Pesterall

Herbert C. Pesterall

SALES MANAGER

*   (or 30,000 pages, whichever is the sooner)

Customer service

Comprehension

1. What mistake have Bootit made in their letter?
2. What are 'special offers'?
3. Why is Bootit's special offer unlikely to be of interest to Mr Baker?
4. How much will Mr Baker have to pay, if he wants a warranty for 24 months from the date of purchase?
5. Which number should Mr Baker call if he would like some consumables?

Vocabulary development

Wortfelder sind hilfreich, um Ihren Wortschatz zu erweitern.

Vervollständigen Sie die folgende Tabelle. Ermitteln Sie die Wortbedeutungen mit Hilfe eines Wörterbuchs. Die erste Zeile zeigt Ihnen, wie es geht.

Verb	Noun	Adjective
select	selection	selective
…………	…………	satisfied
…………	addition	…………
…………	…………	special
advise	…………	…………
extend	…………	…………
…………	registration	…………
…………	usage	…………

Model 2
An insurance policy

Auf der nächsten Seite finden Sie den Abschnitt aus der Versicherungspolice der Kings, der bei verlorengegangenem Gepäck einschlägig ist. Lesen Sie ihn durch und beantworten Sie dann die Verständnisfragen.

Comprehension

1. The carrier is
   (a) the porter who carried the luggage.
   (b) the airline which transported the luggage.
2. What must the insured get if their luggage is stolen?
3. Wear and tear is
   (a) a percentage deduction based on age.
   (b) normal damage caused by use.
4. When you make an insurance claim, what documents must you send to Coverall?
5. Give two examples of excluded items.

LOST LUGGAGE

Provided all conditions are met, Coverall will indemnify the insured against loss of luggage up to an amount of $5,000. In the case of luggage lost during transit, the insured is required to obtain an official form from the carrier; in the event of theft, the insured shall obtain police certification. These documents must accompany any claim. In addition, the insured shall provide the following:

1. A list of all items lost together with
   - store receipts, where available (these are not required for items valued at less than $50)
   - date and place of purchase
   - their replacement cost minus wear and tear

2. A list of all items bought, for which the insured is claiming. No reimbursement can be made unless store receipts are submitted.

After Coverall has received all the above documents together with a completed claim form, Coverall shall assess the level of compensation.

Coverall shall pay reasonable replacement costs, on condition that all the documentation is in order.

Exclusions
The transportation and carriage of certain articles is prohibited by Federal Law. For this reason no compensation is payable in the event of loss of or damage to such articles.

Should you require further information, please contact our office.

Customer service

Vocabulary development

Die Endung -**age** wird normalerweise /ɪdʒs ausgesprochen, wie z.B. in **luggage** und **carriage**.

Zu welchen Wörtern auf -*age* passen die folgenden Definitionen?

1. to direct or be in charge of
2. general idea which the public has of a product or company
3. goods packed and wrapped for sending by mail
4. harm done to things
5. the number which is calculated by adding several figures together and then dividing by the number of figures
6. benefit
7. amount shown as part of one hundred
8. not having enough
9. piece of news which is sent to someone
10. to make it easier for something to happen

Üben Sie jetzt auch die Aussprache dieser Wörter.

Language and communication skills

Noun + preposition/ preposition + noun

The letter in Model 1 included a number of noun + preposition phrases (Ausdrücke mit Substantiv + Präposition):

Congratulations on your selection of a Smithson Laser Printer GH-N4490.

However, to give you even greater confidence in your printer ...

I am sure you would like to take advantage of our special offers on toner cartridges.

If you would like further details about any of our products ...

It also contained a number of preposition + noun phrases (Ausdrücke mit Präposition + Substantiv):

We are giving you one year on-site warranty at no charge.

These will only be available for a limited period of time. For only £50 you can extend that warranty for a further twelve months.

Alternatively, you can reach us by fax or letter.

Let's try using some of these. Remember to check your answers with the key in your resource book.

107

Unit 6

Exercise 1

Vervollständigen Sie die folgenden Sätze mit der passenden Präposition.

1. According .... our records, the following bill has not been paid.
2. I enclose a cheque .... £50 for the additional cover.
3. I spoke to him .... the phone last week about it.
4. The price rises have had an influence .... our business.
5. There must be a reason .... the delay.
6. We expect an answer .... our question next week.
7. I'll send it to you .... fax right away.
8. There's no need .... any further discussion; we have made our decision.

Other conditional constructions

In the first section of this unit we looked at conditional sentences with the word **if**. However, there are other conditional markers (Einleitungen für ein Bedingungsgefüge). Some of them are shown in the following example sentences taken from the insurance document in Model 2.

Provided *all conditions are met, Coverall will indemnify the insured against loss of luggage up to an amount of $5,000.*

In the case of *luggage lost during transit, the insured is required to obtain an official form from the carrier.*

In the event of *theft, the insured shall obtain police certification.*

*No reimbursement can be made **unless** store receipts are submitted.*

*Coverall shall pay reasonable replacement costs, **on condition that** all the documentation is in order.*

Should you *require further information, please contact our office.*

We can group these markers as follows:

1. Ausdrücke, die eine zukünftige Bedingung einleiten, die eintreten kann, aber nicht muß:	in the event of in (the) case of	in the event that in case
2. Ausdrücke, die **if and only if** bedeuten:	provided/ providing (that) so/as long as	on condition that
3. Wort, das **if not** bedeutet:	unless	

Customer service

> 4. Inversion:
>
> With **should**:
>
> **Should you require** further information, please contact our office.
> = **If you require** further information, please contact our office. (Conditional type 1)
>
> With **were** + infinitive:
>
> **Were** the claim **to be** fraudulent, the company would not pay.
> = **If** the claim **was** fraudulent, the company would not pay. (Conditional type 2)

Exercise 2

Schreiben Sie diese Sätze um und gebrauchen Sie dabei die Ausdrücke in Klammern. Nehmen Sie alle notwendigen Änderungen vor.

1. If you deliver the goods late, we reserve the right to claim compensation. (in the event of)

2. If you can't provide proof, we won't pay. (unless)

3. If accepted, your claim will be settled within 2 weeks. (provided that)

4. If you don't agree with our decision, please contact our office. (inversion with 'should')

5. If you are injured, you must obtain a doctor's note. (in the case of)

6. Make a note of this just so that you don't forget it. (in case)

7. If and only if you can provide new information, we will review your claim. (so long as)

8. If there is a fire, leave the building immediately. (in the case of)

Using different communication channels

Eine Nachricht kann über verschiedene Medien weitergeleitet werden - mündlich, schriftlich oder visuell. Für jedes Medium gibt es wiederum verschiedene Formen, z.B. kann man schriftliche Nachrichten per Fax, Brief, Poster oder Bericht weitergeben. Die entscheidende Frage ist nun: Wie kann man eine bestimmte Nachricht am effektivsten übermitteln?

In his customer letter from Model 1, the sales manager invited Mr Baker

- to phone the Hotline in the event of problems during installation or normal usage of his printer.

- to fax or write a letter to the company for details about their products.

Unit 6

Exercise 3

Verbinden Sie jeweils die Sprechabsichten (a-g) mit dem passendsten Weg der Informationsweitergabe (1-8).

1. notice
2. phone
3. face-to-face
4. report
5. letter
6. presentation
7. memo/e-mail

(a) terms of a proposed contract
(b) technical study results and conclusions
(c) reminder to managers to submit forecasts
(d) introduction of new company product to sales team
(e) news of redundancies
(f) enquiry to supplier about prices
(g) information about staff training opportunities

Expressing obligation in writing

In speech, the verbs **must**, **have to** and **need to** are widely used to express obligations or prohibition (Verpflichtung oder Verbot). For example:

You **must** get a doctor's note. (obligation)

You **mustn't** forget a doctor's note. (prohibition)

You **needn't** get a doctor's note. (no obligation)

In writing, especially in official letters, other language forms are used. Let's look at the language used in the insurance document in Model 2:

*The insured **is required to** obtain an official form from the carrier. (obligation)*

*The insured **shall** obtain police certification. (obligation)*

*The transportation and carriage of certain articles **is prohibited** by Federal Law. (prohibition)*

*These **are not required** for items valued at less than $50. (no obligation)*

On the next page is a table of verbs which can be used in written documents.

Customer service

Obligation	Prohibition	No obligation
be obliged to		not be obliged to
be required to		not be required to
shall	shall not	
	not be allowed to	
	not be permitted to	
	be prohibited from	

Exercise 4

Formulieren Sie diese Sätze mit den angegebenen Wörtern um, so daß sie etwas formeller werden.

1. You have to get a doctor's note.
   (required/obtain)

2. You can't carry firearms.
   (prohibit/transport)

3. The insurer must indemnify the insured.
   (obliged)

4. The carrier didn't have to pay for non-essential items.
   (obliged)

5. The insured mustn't ask for an unreasonable amount.
   (permitted/claim)

Unit 6

THE BUSINESS INTERVIEW

The service element

John Lewis von der Macintosh User Group spricht über die wichtige Rolle von Kundendienstleistungen. Die untenstehenden Fragen, die sich auf die wichtigsten Punkte des Gesprächs beziehen, sollen Ihnen beim Zuhören helfen. Ihre Antworten können Sie dann anhand des Lösungsteils überprüfen.

Mac Times is one channel through which John Lewis tries to give consumers sufficient information on which to make a decision about purchasing or upgrading their Macintosh equipment.

As you listen...

1. What does John say his organization will lose if they do not provide good after-sales service?

2. He says customers' after-sales problems with computers are mostly due to which of the following:

   (a) lack of training?
   (b) equipment breaking down?
   (c) not reading the manual properly?

3. Who does he employ and what kind of service do they provide?

4. What five things do customer records enable his organization to do?

5. Who bears the cost of after-sales service, and in what way?

UNIT 7
REACHING AGREEMENT

In dieser Lektion geht es vor allem um Verhandlungen.

SAY WHAT YOU MEAN

Listening	Hören
Negotiating a purchase	Verhandlungen über einen Verkauf
Negotiating a budget	Verhandlungen über einen Werbeetat
Language and communication skills	**Sprache und Kommunikation**
Comparing and contrasting	Vergleiche
Indicating degree using 'very', 'too' and 'enough'	Steigerungsstufen mit 'very', 'too' und 'enough'
Negotiating tactics	Verhandlungstaktiken
Dealing with conflict	Schwierige Verhandlungen

PUT IT ON PAPER

Reading	Lesen
A checklist of writing rules	Goldene Regeln für die schriftliche Kommunikation
The terms of a contract	Vertragsklauseln
Language and communication skills	**Sprache und Kommunikation**
Adjectives and adverbs	Adjektive und Adverbien
Clauses with '-ing' and '-ed'	Verbformen auf '-ing' und '-ed'
Letter-writing style	Briefstil
Drafting contract clauses	Wie man Vertragsklauseln formuliert

THE BUSINESS INTERVIEW

Successful negotiating	Die Kunst des Verhandelns

SAY WHAT YOU MEAN

Listening

Zuerst eine Begriffsklärung: Verhandeln heißt, durch Diskussionen und Zugeständnisse die Zufriedenheit aller Beteiligten zu erreichen. Verhandlungen sind also nicht auf die Geschäftswelt beschränkt. In diesem Abschnitt sollen Sie sich nun aber zwei geschäftliche Verhandlungen anhören; in der ersten geht es um den Verkauf eines Produkts und in der zweiten um eine Etatbesprechung. Sie lernen, wie man auf Englisch eine Verhandlung strukturiert und wie man Konfliktsituationen meistert.

Extract 1
Negotiating a purchase

In der ersten Verhandlung auf der Aufnahme vertritt Alan McDonald die Vertriebsorganisation PROVIZ, die photographische Geräte und Video-Ausrüstungen an britische Kunden verkauft. Die meisten Kunden sind Photo-Studios, die im Auftrage größerer Agenturen, die selbst wiederum für große nationale und internationale Agenturen arbeiten, vor allem Videomaterial für Werbezwecke herstellen. PROVIZ hat ein Vertriebssystem mit Vertretern, die eine große Palette von Produkten auf Kommissionsbasis verkaufen. Der andere Verhandlungspartner ist ein potentieller Kunde, ADJUST, ein Studio, das Werbefilme auf Videobändern produziert, hier durch Brian Butler vertreten. In den Verkaufsverhandlungen geht es um den neuen ZANKI Imager - eine Maschine, mit der Computerbilder und Photographien zu einem neuen Bild zusammengeschnitten werden können.

Füllen Sie beim Zuhören das Flußdiagramm über den Verhandlungsablauf aus.

Reaching agreement

NEGOTIATION FLOWCHART

The supplier's offer   *The arguments*   *The customer's offer*

- £55,000 → → …………
- ZANKI has a much larger memory
- PAXER has a much better reputation
- …………
- Price includes delivery, ………… and ………… ………… for an early order ↔ …………, incl. disks + screen
- Disks yes; screen no
- Introduction to PROMAD; group discount of …….. → Group discount of …….. + …………

Summary

1. one ZANKI + supply of disks
2. ………………………………
3. engineer to install + an operator to train staff
4. price reduced by ……………
5. if satisfied, we encourage PROMAD to look at the machine
6. model IIa

………… → → …………

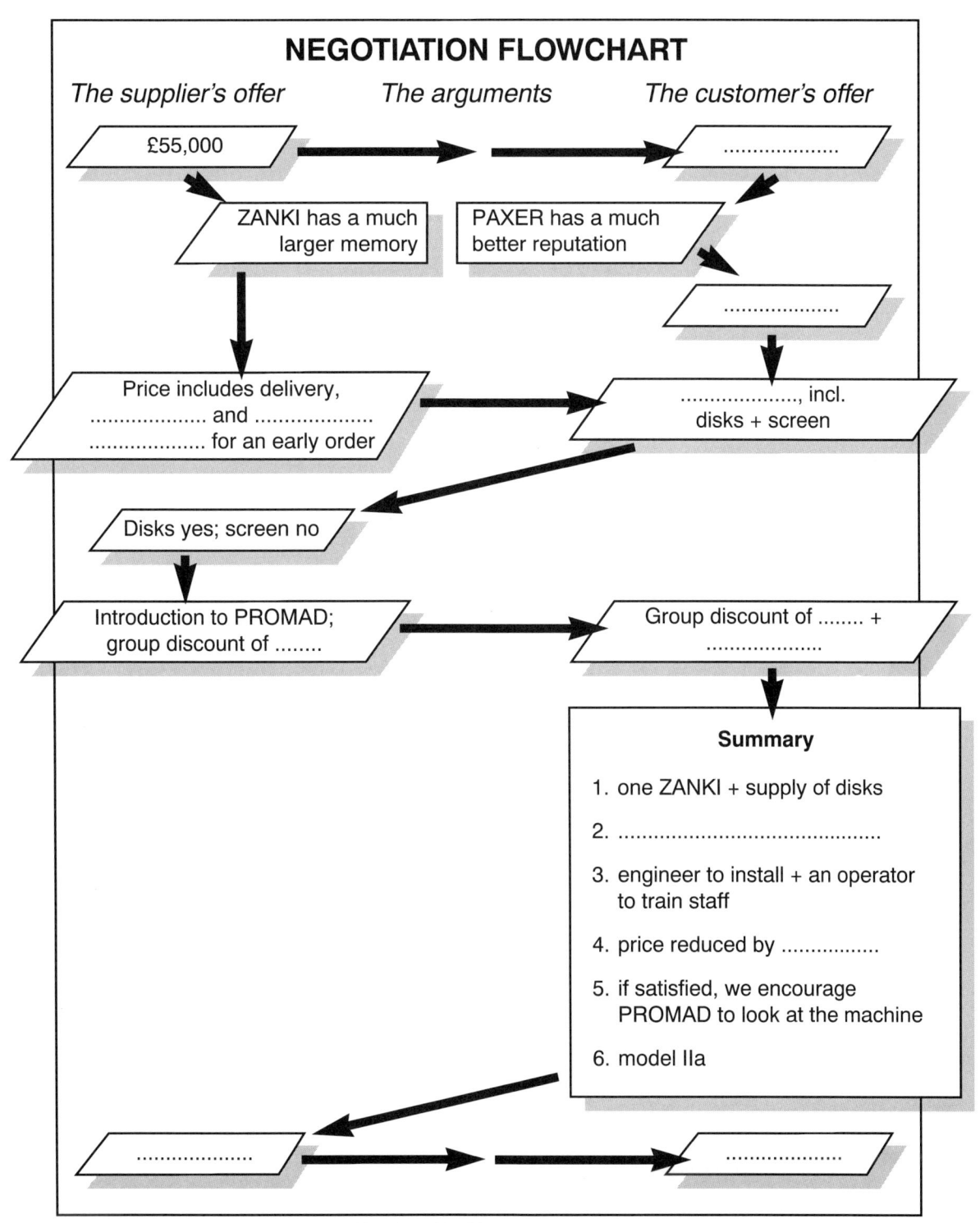

Wenn Sie sich die Verhandlungen vollständig angehört haben, dann vergleichen Sie Ihr Flußdiagramm mit den Angaben im Lösungsteil.

Unit 7

Extract 2
Negotiating a budget

Jetzt geht es zu ITC, wo der Etat für das kommende Jahr ausgehandelt wird. Bridget de Souza, Marketingleiterin, möchte ihren Werbeetat durchsetzen, doch Stephen Gaynor, der geschäftsführende Direktor, ist nicht sehr entgegenkommend. Er bezweifelt zwar nicht den Nutzen von Werbung, aber er ist ein vorsichtiger Mann, der davon überzeugt ist, daß seine strikte Kontrolle der verschiedenen Einzeletats zur jetzigen starken Position der Firma beigetragen hat. Denn während andere Firmen Verluste hinnehmen mußten, präsentiert ITC sich als ein strahlendes Beispiel für beständiges Wachstum - und dabei soll es nach Stephen bleiben.

Hören Sie nun für eine kleine Weile mit: Bridget hat Stephen gerade ihre Werbevorhaben ausführlich vorgestellt. Ergänzen Sie beim Zuhören die folgenden Notizen über den jeweiligen Stand der Verhandlungen und über die Argumente, die von Bridget und Stephen vorgebracht werden.

I·T·C

	Amount	Argument for	Argument against
Stage 1	……….	continue initiatives	……….
Stage 2	280,000	……….	can't implement all plans
Stage 3	……….	……….	keep company on target for steady growth
Stage 4	……….	can live with it	can accept it

Überprüfen Sie Ihre Ergänzungen im Lösungsteil.

Reaching agreement

American/British English

Vocabulary

Fast-moving worlds create a lot of **jargon**. One feature of American English is the creation of verbs from nouns. For example Bridget de Souza said: **Anything less will seriously impact on our efforts to deliver.** The noun **impact** (Einfluß) is converted into a verb. Here are some more examples, more common in American English than in British English.

Verb	Meaning
to broker	to act as intermediary
to bus	to transport by bus
to clerk	to work as a clerk
to bottom out	to reach the lowest point
to party	to go to a lot of parties/have fun
to major in	to graduate in a subject

Usage

Stephen said: **Bridget, no way we can agree that**. His British counterpart would have said: **… we can agree with/to that**. A number of verbs differ between American and British English in their use of prepositions.

to appeal a decision	to appeal against a decision
to protest a plan	to protest against a plan
to meet with a person	to meet a person
to visit with a friend	to visit a friend

Language and communication skills

Comparing and contrasting

Gehen wir noch einmal zu der Verhandlung über den ZANKI Imager zurück. Sie haben verschiedene Ausdrücke gehört, mit denen Produkte und Preise verglichen wurden. Auf der nächsten Seite finden Sie einige Möglichkeiten, Vergleiche auszudrücken.

Unit 7

Comparing adjectives

One-syllable (einsilbig) adjectives (**big**, **short** etc.) form the comparative and superlative forms as follows:

Comparative	**Superlative**
bigger	biggest
shorter	shortest

Two-syllable (zweisilbig) adjectives ending in -**ow**, -**y** or -**le** (**narrow**, **easy** and **simple**) form the comparative and superlative forms as follows:

Comparative	**Superlative**
narrower	narrowest
easier	easiest
simpler	simplest

Using 'more' and 'most'

Other two-syllable adjectives and longer adjectives form the comparative and superlative with **more** and **most**:

*And the price is **more reasonable** than you'd expect, too.*

*It's the **most reasonable** product on the market at the moment.*

Irregular forms

Some adjectives have irregular comparative and superlative forms:

*And if we made you an offer - and don't forget the Paxer has a **much better** reputation - we'd be talking about £37,500.*

*In fact I'd say it is **the best**.*

The same or different?

Words and expressions of similarity and difference:

*I mean it's **basically the same as** the Paxer and they're on offer for £40,000.*

*But they're **quite different** machines. The Zanki's memory is **much larger** than the Paxer's.*

*I'd say the Paxer is **similar** to the Zanki.*

Other forms of comparison

Clauses of comparison can be used as follows:

*I wish I could help you, but I'm afraid that's **as low as** the price goes.*

*I'm afraid that price is **not so/as low as** we'd like.*

Reaching agreement

Exercise 1

Sie können diese Grundregeln nun anwenden, indem Sie die folgenden Sätze so umformen, daß Sie statt eines Komparativs den Superlativ und umgekehrt benutzen. Wenn Sie wollen, können Sie diese Übung zuerst mit dem Buch machen, bevor Sie sie mit der Aufnahme versuchen. Sehen Sie sich zuerst diese beiden Beispiele an:

We can't offer a lower price.

That's the lowest price we can offer.

That's the most reliable model you can find.

You can't find a more reliable model.

1. We can't offer a better price.
2. That's the cheapest version you can find.
3. We can't sell a more expensive product.
4. That's the worst model you can buy.
5. We can't make a more generous offer.

Indicating degree using 'very', 'too' and 'enough'

Sehen Sie sich noch einmal die verschiedenen Ausdrücke an, die Stephen und Bridget verwendet haben, als sie versuchten, sich auf einen Werbeetat zu einigen. Während der Verhandlungen haben sie die Worte **too** und **very** benutzt, um ihre Argumente zu verstärken.

*My main concern as always is that if you try and stretch a budget **too** far, then you risk coming away without any tangible results.*

*Well, last year we believe that our campaigns were **very** successful.*

On the other hand, the word **enough** means that something is acceptable.

*But did you get **far enough** with last year's budget?*

*You just told me it was **enough** to achieve your objectives.*

In fact **too** and **enough** are related. **Too** means **more than enough**. For example, Stephen could say:

*That budget is **too high**; in other words it is **not low enough**.*

Then, after negotiations with Stephen, Bridget could look at the new reduced figure and say:

*That budget is now **very low**, but **not low enough** for Stephen.*

Here **very** intensifies the meaning of **low**.

Exercise 2

Ergänzen Sie die folgenden Sätze und verwenden Sie dabei einen Ausdruck mit **very**, **too** oder **enough**. Sie können Ihre Sätze mit der Aufnahme überprüfen. Zuerst zwei Beispiele:

*The product is **too expensive**; in other words it is **not cheap enough for us**.*

*That product is **very unreliable**; in fact it is **too unreliable for us**.*

1. The service is too slow; in other words it is not ....

2. Your reply was very slow; in fact it was ....

3. The campaigns were too long; in other words they were not ....

4. The offer is very late; in fact it is ....

Negotiating tactics

Geschicktes Verhandeln heißt, daß man nicht zu schnell eine feste Position erreicht. Nach einem kurzen freundlichen Gespräch zu Beginn sollte sich die Verhandlung in gut vorbereiteten und logisch aufeinanderfolgenden Schritten entwickeln. Sehen Sie sich noch einmal an, wie Brian über den ZANKI Imager verhandelt.

Wie er das Produkt mit einem Modell der Konkurrenz vergleicht, um den Preis zu drücken:

That's way over the top, as far as I can see. I mean it's basically the same as the Paxer and they're on offer for £40,000. I'd say that's a more realistic price.

Wie er die vielen Extras für nicht notwendig erklärt und so für einen niedrigeren Preis plädiert:

That may be, but to be honest, Alan, we don't need such a large memory.

Wie er für einen eventuell akzeptablen höheren Kaufpreis im Gegenzug weiteres Zubehör verlangt:

Well, we might consider £42,000, if you were prepared to supply disks and a new screen.

Reaching agreement

Gute Geschäftsbeziehungen als Verhandlungsargument:

But surely for an old and valued customer ...

Wie er Termine als Druckmittel benutzt:

I hope you're not going to throw away a deal like this just because of the summer holidays.

Wie man den entscheidenden Punkt einführt:

Oh yes, one last thing, this is the IIa we are talking about, isn't it?

Exercise 3

Jetzt sollen Sie das Verhandeln auf Englisch üben. Wählen Sie jeweils die passende Antwort.

1. Well, I'm glad to hear you're happy with your Zanki Imager. What do you think of the Zanki screen? Attractive, isn't it?

   (a) I'm sure it'll be very expensive.
   (b) What's the price tag?
   (c) That's over the top.

2. The manufacturer's price is £5,000.

   (a) We wouldn't pay that. It's not worth it.
   (b) That's a bit steep. The screen is just the same as the Scorpion.
   (c) That's a good price.

3. Oh no, they are completely different products. The graphics quality doesn't bear comparison.

   (a) Yes, but the problem is we don't need super graphics.
   (b) Yes, but the problem is the price.
   (c) Yes, but the problem is the weight.

4. Well, if, as you said, you're looking for reliability, this has got to be the machine for you.

   (a) Well, we might consider £3,500.
   (b) Well, we might consider it.
   (c) Well, we might consider £3,500, if you included the power unit.

5. I'm afraid that's the price. With a trade discount, of course.

   (a) You've got to do better than that.
   (b) Well, I can't accept that.
   (c) But we've been doing business for years.

6. We could arrange delivery in six weeks.

   (a) In six weeks! If we could agree a price, I'd expect it here in two.
   (b) In six weeks! That's out of the question!
   (c) Well, if that's the best you can do.

Dealing with conflict

Zurück zur zweiten Verhandlungsrunde, in der Bridget ihren Werbeetat genehmigt haben möchte. Bei einer solchen internen Verhandlung ist es wichtig, daß keine Seite als Verlierer dasteht, da sie ja wohl weiter zusammenarbeiten müssen. (Anders bei Allan und Brian: Auch wenn sie zu keiner Einigung über die ZANKI-Maschine kommen, werden sie trotzdem ein anderes Mal ein Geschäft abschließen können.) Es ist also wichtig für Bridget und Stephen, daß sie nicht auf bestimmten Forderungen beharren und so möglicherweise einen ernsthaften Konflikt verursachen, der dann nicht mehr zu lösen ist, ohne daß eine der beiden Parteien ihr Gesicht verliert.

Let's see how Stephen and Bridget dealt with the conflicts.

Wie man von einem strittigen Punkt ablenkt:

> *No way we can agree that.*
>
> *Well, let's talk about this company's objectives.*

Wie man die andere Seite zu einem Vorschlag auffordert:

> *And I'm saying your figure is too high.*
>
> *OK, so let me ask you what figure you envision?*

Wie man persönliche Aspekte vermeidet und das Interesse der Firma betont:

> *Stephen, I'm not here to argue percentage points. I just want what's best for this organization.*
>
> *Listen, Bridget, I don't mean to be negative, but we have to come up with a figure we both can live with.*

Wie man sich auf realistische Vorstellungen konzentriert:

> *But it is my job to keep this company on target for steady growth.*

Nachgeben:

> *I can live with $280,000, but I certainly can't implement all my plans.*

Reaching agreement

Exercise 4

Diese Übung zeigt Ihnen, wie Sie auf Englisch Konflikte in Verhandlungssituationen vermeiden können. Im folgenden verhandelt der Firmenchef mit dem Werbeleiter über die Einstellung eines zusätzlichen Mitarbeiters in der Marketingabteilung. Sie übernehmen die Rolle des Werbeleiters. Der erste Teil des Gesprächs zeigt Ihnen, wie es geht.

I can't accept that your department is so overloaded as to need another full-time clerk.
(Emphasize how the work has increased.)

Well, let's look at how the work has increased.

Jetzt machen Sie weiter. Versuchen Sie, diese Übung mit der Aufnahme zu machen.

But I'm saying a full-time clerk is out of the question.
(Invite your boss to make an offer.)

What you are proposing adds another $18,000 to the payroll.
(Emphasize the company's interests.)

How about some temporary help?
(Accept it as a short-term solution, but focus on next year.)

We'll cross that hurdle when we come to it.
(Concede that he is the boss, but emphasize the importance of solving the problem now.)

Unit 7

PUT IT ON PAPER

Reading

Model 1
A checklist of writing rules

One evening, while Alan was waiting at the Proviz office for an important phone call from a customer, he came across the following humorous article in a business magazine.

Lesen Sie den Text und beantworten Sie dann die Verständnisfrage.

Many skilled negotiators clinch the deal over the table, yet slip up when drafting the agreement. Make sure that your written documents are as well presented as your spoken arguments.

TEN GOLDEN RULES

Writing skills for every professional

1. Don't use no double negatives.
2. Verbs has to agree with their subjects.
3. Don't use commas, which aren't necessary.
4. Try to never split your infinitives.
5. Its important to use your apostrophe's correctly.
6. Correct spelling is esential.
7. Be carefully when you use adjectives; use adverbs correct.
8. Join clauses well, like a conjunction should.
9. Placing a comma between subject and predicate, is not correct.
10. Always check your text to see if you have any words out.

Comprehension Schreiben Sie die Zehn Goldenen Regeln noch einmal und verbessern Sie dabei die Fehler.

Reaching agreement

Vocabulary development

In den folgenden Wortgruppen gehört jeweils ein Wort nicht dazu. Schlagen Sie die Bedeutung der Wörter, die Sie nicht kennen, im Lexikon nach und bestimmen Sie das Wort, das nicht paßt.

1. double, single, once, treble, quadruple
2. have to, should, need to, must, to be required to
3. necessary, optional, obligatory, essential, binding
4. split, divide, separate, part, combine
5. correctly, rightly, wrongly, badly, lovely
6. careful, beautiful, spoonful, harmful, resourceful
7. like, from, to, through, after, because

Model 2
The terms of a contract

ITC, die Sie schon aus der Verhandlung über Bridgets Werbeetat kennen, haben einen Vertrag über den Vertrieb ihres Stimmensimulators Z45 ausgearbeitet. Im folgenden sehen Sie den Vertragstext.

Lesen Sie den Text und beantworten Sie dann die Verständnisfragen.

Comprehension

1. To what does Territory refer?
2. What is meant by Products?
3. Why are Territory and Products written with a capital letter?
4. How can ITC alter its prices?

Vocabulary development

Benutzen Sie Vorsilben, um Gegensatzpaare zu bilden. Zuerst ein Beispiel:

dependent   **independent**

1. agreement   4. applicable
2. related   5. effective
3. legal   6. exclusive

In offiziellen Dokumenten werden häufig die Vorsilben **here** und **there** benutzt, z.B. **hereby** für **by this agreement** und **thereto** für **to that**.

Welche Wörter mit **here** und **there** passen zu den folgenden Bedeutungen?

1. after this   3. in accordance with this agreement
2. in that document   4. as a result

DISTRIBUTION AGREEMENT

This agreement is made on 1 January 19__ between ITC Inc., having its registered office in San Diego, California, USA, hereinafter referred to as **ITC**, on the one side, and PRODUCTOS SINCOSA, having its registered office in Barcelona, Spain, hereinafter referred to as **SINCOSA**, on the other side.

Article 1

Territory and Products

1.1 **ITC** hereby appoints **SINCOSA** as its exclusive distributor in Spain and Portugal, hereinafter referred to as **Territory**, for the sale of the Z45 as well as accessories and spare parts related thereto, hereinafter referred to as **Products**.

Article 2

Legal situation of the Distributor

2.1 **SINCOSA** will buy and sell **Products** in its own name and for its own account and will act as an independent trader as regards both **ITC** and its customers.

2.2 **ITC** hereby grants permission to **SINCOSA** to apply its own name and address to the customers of **Products**.

2.3 **ITC** undertakes to sell **Products** within **Territory** only to **SINCOSA** and shall not appoint any other distributor or agent for **Products** in **Territory**.

2.4 **ITC** agrees to refer to **SINCOSA** all customers within **Territory** enquiring about **Products**.

2.5 **SINCOSA** is not entitled to sell **Products** in countries outside **Territory**.

Article 3

Prices and conditions of payment

3.1 **ITC** shall sell **Products** to **SINCOSA** according to the price list issued by **ITC** and applicable to all European distributors and being effective at the time of acceptance of **SINCOSA's** order.

3.2 **ITC** reserves the right to change its price list by giving ninety (90) days' written notice to **SINCOSA**.

3.3 Payment for **Products** purchased by **SINCOSA** shall be made by 20 per cent in cash on delivery and by 80 per cent by signed draft to be paid at sight ninety (90) days from delivery.

Article 4

Termination

ITC may terminate the agreement if the following conditions are not fulfilled:

Language and communication skills

Adjectives and adverbs

Point 7 in TEN GOLDEN RULES for writing skills shows a mistake in the use of adjective and of adverb. The sentence should be:

*Be **careful** when you use adjectives; use adverbs **correctly**.*

Let's look at the basic rules for adjectives and adverbs.

Use adjectives

1. To give more information about nouns:

   He writes good English.

2. After the verb **to be**:

   He is good at writing English.

3. After verbs of the senses (look, sound, smell, taste, feel):

   His English sounds very fluent.

Use adverbs

1. To give more information about verbs:

   He writes English well.

2. To give more information about adjectives:

   He writes extremely good English.

3. To give more information about adverbs:

   He writes English extremely well.

Exercise 1

Wählen Sie jeweils das passende Wort.

1. This machine is very *good/well* value for money.
2. You should price your products more *realistic/realistically*.
3. But this machine looks quite *different/differently*.
4. In any case it is *extreme/extremely* large.
5. I think you have been *bad/badly* informed.
6. We have looked very *hard/hardly* at your offer.

7. That price is *absolute/absolutely* fixed.

8. We are *certain/certainly* impressed by its performance.

Clauses with '-ing' and '-ed'

Look at the following sentences from the Distribution Agreement:

*ITC agrees to refer to SINCOSA all customers within Territory **enquiring** about Products.*

*ITC shall sell Products to SINCOSA according to the price list **issued** by ITC ...*

In the first sentence **enquiring** means **who enquire**; in the second sentence **issued** means **which is issued**.

Exercise 2

Schreiben Sie die folgenden Sätze um und benutzen Sie eine **-ing** oder **-ed**-Form. Ein Beispiel zeigt Ihnen, wie es geht.

An agreement which both parties have signed will be binding.

An agreement signed by both parties will be binding.

1. The goods which we supply will be delivered by 1 March.
2. We will pay compensation for any delivery which arrives late.
3. Any claim which the company makes will be thoroughly investigated.
4. We shall settle within 90 days any claim which arises from a dispute.
5. Any decision which the court arrives at shall be final.
6. The costs which arise from the case shall be paid by both parties.
7. The decision which the court has reached shall be final.
8. Any agreement which you have signed will come into force immediately.

Letter-writing style

Die Zehn Goldenen Regeln haben auf mögliche Fehler in Grammatik, Orthographie und Interpunktion hingewiesen. Aber ein guter Brief muß nicht nur korrekt, sondern auch in angemessenem Stil geschrieben sein. Der Stil hängt zum großen Teil von der Art der Beziehung zwischen den beiden Briefpartnern ab.

Reaching agreement

Daher wird ein Geschäftsbrief immer förmlicher sein als ein Privatbrief. Aber was bedeutet 'förmlich' für einen Geschäftsbrief?

Here are some characteristics:

1. The letter should look businesslike.
2. Ideas should be systematically developed and links between ideas clearly signalled.
3. Language should be appropriate in terms of vocabulary and expression, avoiding slang and colloquial expressions (umgangssprachliche Ausdrücke).
4. The style should retain an appropriate level of formality and avoid becoming too personal.

Exercise 3

Im folgenden lesen Sie einen persönlichen und informellen Brief. Formulieren Sie ihn um, so daß er formeller wird.

Paul Schroeder
Salzacherstr. 34
2356 Himmingen
Germany

Hi there, Paul!
Great to hear that you'll be passing through York during your UK tour. What do you mean by 'staying a few days'? But no problem, as we can easily put you up. If you don't fancy that, there's plenty of hotels. Oh yes, I just remembered about the travel. The trains from London normally take about 2 hours. Some of them are much slower – so find out. Of course I can pick you up at York station when you arrive. Just give me a ring before you get on the train in London.

That's all for now. See you soon.

Brian

Unit 7

Drafting contract clauses

In speech, duties (Verpflichtungen) are normally expressed with **must** and entitlements (Rechte) with **can**. However, in legal contracts a range of other forms is used.

Ausdrücke für Verpflichtungen

*ITC **undertakes** to sell Products within Territory only to SINCOSA ...*

*ITC **shall** sell Products to SINCOSA according to the price list issued by ITC.*

*ITC **shall not** appoint any other distributor or agent for Products in Territory.* (duty not to do something = interdiction)

*ITC **agrees** to refer to SINCOSA all customers within Territory enquiring about Products.*

Ausdrücke für Rechte

*ITC **may** terminate the agreement if the following conditions are not fulfilled:*

*ITC **reserves the right to** change its price list by giving ninety (90) days' written notice to SINCOSA.*

*SINCOSA **is not entitled to** sell Products in countries outside Territory.* (absence of entitlement = interdiction)

*ITC hereby **grants permission** to SINCOSA to apply its own name and address to the customers of Products.* (gives entitlement)

Exercise 4

Schreiben Sie die folgenden Sätze zu Vertragsklauseln um und benutzen Sie die in den Klammern angegebenen Wörter.

1. The Agent mustn't give information to third parties. (shall not/disclose)

2. ITC must deliver the contract items to SINCOSA. (hereby agree)

3. SINCOSA must handle all information as strictly confidential. (undertake/treat)

4. SINCOSA may end the contract in the following circumstances: (entitled/terminate)

5. ITC lets SINCOSA refuse delivery in the following circumstances: (grant permission)

6. SINCOSA can't talk to other distributors. (not entitled/approach)

Reaching agreement

THE BUSINESS INTERVIEW

Successful negotiating

Hier ist noch einmal Caroline Wiggins. Sie spricht über Verkaufsverhandlungen, wie man sie vorbereitet und möglichst erfolgreich abschließt. Die untenstehenden Fragen, die sich auf die wichtigsten Punkte des Gesprächs beziehen, sollen Ihnen beim Zuhören helfen. Ihre Antworten können Sie dann anhand des Lösungsteils überprüfen.

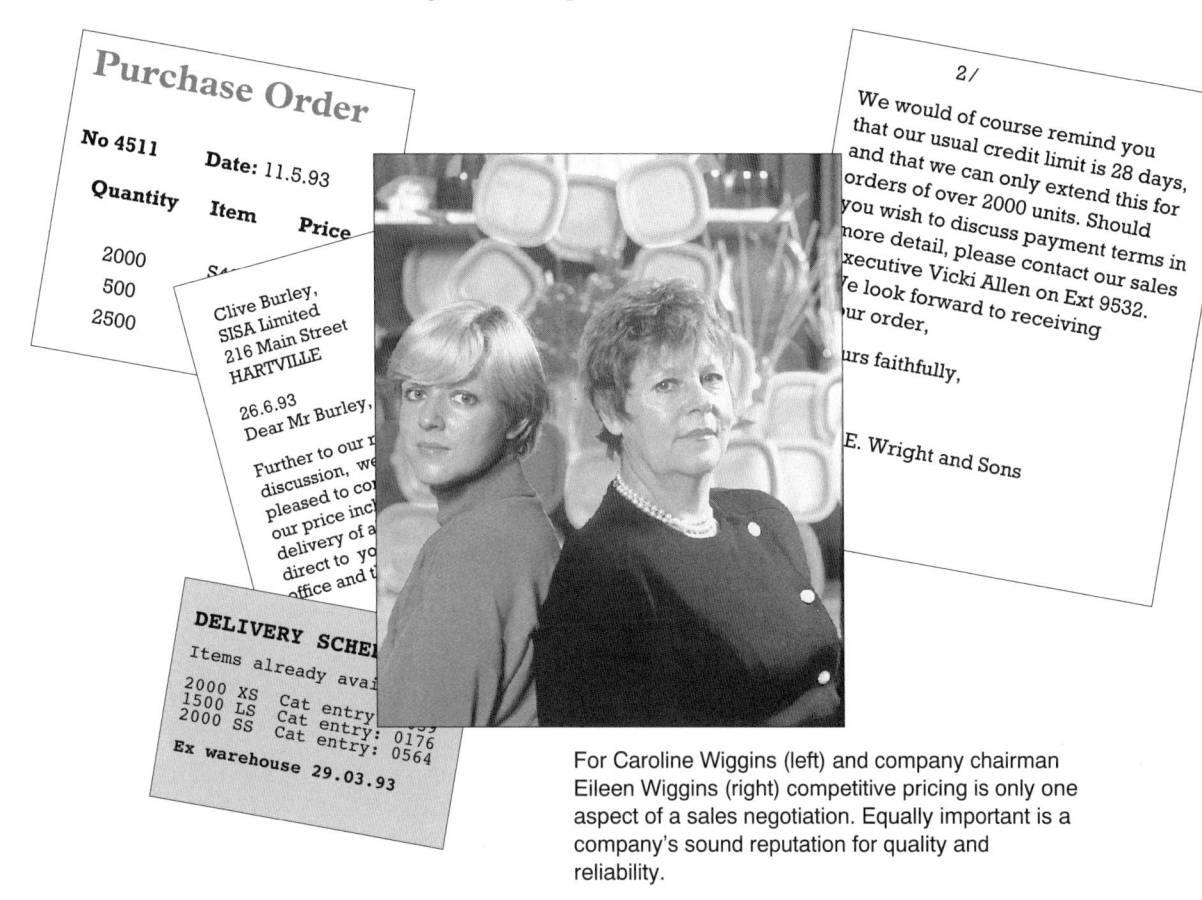

For Caroline Wiggins (left) and company chairman Eileen Wiggins (right) competitive pricing is only one aspect of a sales negotiation. Equally important is a company's sound reputation for quality and reliability.

As you listen ...

1. List briefly the three areas Caroline says are important when preparing for a negotiation.

2. What techniques does she recommend when starting actual negotiations?

3. Is price always the most important factor, in Caroline's experience? If not, what other things have to be taken into account?

4. What examples does Caroline give of bargaining factors?

5. How does she explain the term 'retrospective discount'?

UNIT 8
SOCIAL CONTACT

In dieser Lektion lernen Sie allgemeine Umgangsformen in Kontakten mit Geschäftskollegen.

SAY WHAT YOU MEAN

Listening	Hören
An end-of-year meeting	Ein Jahrestreffen
A briefing session	Einführung für Neuankömmlinge
Language and communication skills	**Sprache und Kommunikation**
Expressions of time	Zeitangaben
Reported speech	Indirekte Rede
Greetings, introductions and farewells	Wie man sich begrüßt, vorstellt und verabschiedet
Making small talk	Small Talk

PUT IT ON PAPER

Reading	Lesen
Advice on business lunches	Ratschläge für Arbeitsessen
Cross-cultural briefing notes	Wechsel von einem Land ins andere
Language and communication skills	**Sprache und Kommunikation**
Verb: '-ing' or infinitive?	Verb: '-ing' oder Infinitiv?
'As' or 'like'?	'As' oder 'like'?
Written emphasis	Betonung im geschriebenen Englisch
Sequencing information in writing	Wie man Informationen ordnet

THE BUSINESS INTERVIEW

How others see us	Wie andere uns sehen

Unit 8

SAY WHAT YOU MEAN

Listening

Warum sind gute Umgangsformen im Geschäftsleben so wichtig? Ganz einfach: Weil Sie mit Ihrem Geschäftspartner auf gutem Fuße stehen müssen, um ins Geschäft zu kommen. Man braucht nicht allein saubere Geschäftspraktiken, sondern auch angenehme Umgangsformen. Wie schätzen Sie Ihre Fähigkeiten ein, mit Menschen umzugehen?

1. Wie leicht fällt es Ihnen, mit Unbekannten ins Gespräch zu kommen?
2. Können Sie ein Gespräch durch die richtigen Entgegnungen in Gang halten?
3. Wählen Sie immer die richtigen, d.h. unverfängliche, Themen für eine Unterhaltung?
4. Wie leicht fallen Ihnen diese Dinge in anderen Ländern und Kulturen?

Wenn Sie sich noch nicht in allen Punkten sicher fühlen, dann wird Ihnen diese Lektion sicher weiterhelfen.

Extract 1
An end-of-year meeting

Das Jahrestreffen der europäischen Partner von Andrew MacIntyre, einem internationalen Finanzberatungsunternehmen, findet dieses Mal in Budapest statt. Etwa 100 Teilnehmer sind bei dem Treffen anwesend. Füllen Sie beim Zuhören die folgende Übersicht über die verschiedenen Partner aus.

Social contact

Name	Based in	Current interest/activity
Karl		
	London	
Pierre		
Eric		

Vergleichen Sie Ihre Einträge mit den Angaben im Lösungsteil.

Extract 2
A briefing session

Clive, den Sie schon auf dem Empfang kennengelernt haben, hat sich schließlich doch entschlossen, nach Pittsburgh zu gehen. Wir treffen ihn in der amerikanischen Hauptgeschäftsstelle von Andrew MacIntyre wieder. Er und seine Frau Helen werden von Ruby Turner, der die nach Amerika versetzten Angestellten der Firma betreut, mit einigen amerikanischen Gepflogenheiten bekannt gemacht.

Vervollständigen Sie beim Zuhören die Notizen.

CROSS-CULTURAL BRIEFING NOTES

Some notes to help you settle in:

1. .... Americans feel more comfortable on first name terms
2. Handshake and eye contact ....
3. Topics of conversation
   i ....
   ii ....
   iii ....
   iv ....
4. ....

Überprüfen Sie ihre Ergänzungen anhand des Lösungsteils.

135

American/British English

Vocabulary

'House and home' is a popular topic of conversation among both the British and the Americans. This is an area where Clive and Helen are likely to find some differences.

American	British
trash can	dustbin
yard	garden
bathroom	toilet/lavatory
soap powder	washing powder
thumb tack	drawing pin
appetizer	starter
dessert	sweet

Usage

A greeting which is very common in American English is **Have a nice day!** Like many Americanisms, it has gradually been crossing the Atlantic and can now be heard in the UK. Other similar wishes are shown below.

> Have a great meal!
>
> Have a good trip!
>
> Have a wonderful holiday!
>
> Have a fantastic time!
>
> Have a good game!
>
> Have a good weekend!

Language and communication skills

Expressions of time

Look at the following pair of sentences spoken at the reception:

*Yes, I've been based in London **for the last five years** and I became a partner a few months ago.*

*Oh, it's just that I had to do a lot of travelling **during the winter** and it was all getting a bit much.*

We use **for** to indicate how long an action lasted, as in **for five years**; and we use **during** to indicate a period in which an event happened, for example, **during the winter**.

Now look at the next pair of sentences:

*And I have to decide **by next month**.*

*Karl, keep that under your hat, please, **until the official announcement**.*

As these examples show, we use **by** to indicate an action which happens at or before the deadline (Stichtag) and we use **until** for an action which continues up to the deadline.

Exercise 1

Antworten Sie auf die folgenden Äußerungen mit einem vollständigen Satz und wählen Sie die passende Präposition für die vorgegebene Zeitangabe. Versuchen Sie, diese Aufgabe mit der Aufnahme zu machen, und lassen Sie sich von den Vorgaben hier im Buch leiten. Die Beispiele zeigen Ihnen, wie es geht.

How long have you been based in Frankfurt?
*I've been based in Frankfurt **for** three months.*

How long are you going to stay there?
*I'm going to stay there **until** the end of the year.*

1. When will you make your decision? (the end of next month)
2. How long will you stay there? (at least one year)
3. When did you discuss this with Martin?
   (the flight from Frankfurt)
4. How long will you be working there? (the end of next year)

Reported speech

During the cultural briefing session, Ruby and Clive used a number of reported speech forms.

Clive, you said in the questionnaire you'd already had a lot of contact with Americans, right?

And, Helen, you say that you have occasional contact.

Yes, when I worked in the city people never asked me how much I earned or what my house cost.

People will often ask if you have children and how many you have, and what they're called and where they go to school.

Reported speech (indirekte Rede) is where we quote what somebody else said or asked. For example, what Clive originally said in the questionnaire was:

I've already had a lot of contact with Americans.

When Ruby quotes him she says:

Clive, you said in the questionnaire you'd already had a lot of contact with Americans, right?

Notice the change of verb tense from **have had a lot of contact** in the direct speech to **had had a lot of contact** in the reported speech.

Now look at this direct question: Do you have children?

As an indirect question in the cultural briefing this became:

People will often ask if you have children.

Here there is no tense change.

Changing direct speech to reported speech

1. Wenn das einleitende Verb des Sagens oder Fragens im Präsens oder Futur steht, dann bleiben die Verben der indirekten Rede so, wie sie in der direkten Rede sind.

2. Wenn das Verb des Sagens oder Fragens in der Vergangenheit steht, dann verändert sich die Verbform:

   - Präsens wird Imperfekt
   - Imperfekt wird Plusquamperfekt - oder bleibt in manchen Fällen auch Imperfekt
   - Perfekt wird Plusquamperfekt
   - **will** wird **would**

Here are some examples of direct and reported speech:

Peter has just said 'I will be in the US later this year.'
(verb of speaking in present perfect tense)

Peter has just said that he will be in the US later this year.
(no tense change in reported speech)

Peter said 'I will be in the US later this year.'
(verb of speaking in past tense)

Peter said that he would be in the US later this year.
(**will** changes to **would**)

Social contact

Exercise 2

Gestern abend waren Sie bei den Browns zum Abendessen, die Ihnen sagten, daß sie in die USA gehen würden. Heute sprechen Sie mit einem gemeinsamen Freund, der mehr über die Pläne der Browns wissen will. Formen Sie Peter Browns direkte Äußerungen in indirekte Rede um. Nehmen Sie die hier im Buch vorgeschlagenen Einleitungen für die indirekte Rede und sagen Sie die Sätze dann zusammen mit den Sprechern auf der Kassette. Aber hören Sie sich zuerst zwei Beispiele an:

We are going to spend six months in the US.
Peter Brown said **they were going to spend six months in the US.**

We will be back in Europe in September.
Peter Brown said **they would be back in Europe in September.**

1. Of course, we've been to the States before.
(Peter said ....)

2. Have you ever been to the States?
(Peter asked ....)

3. I want to work abroad for a short time.
(Peter has often said ....)

4. Is it a good idea to sell our house? (Peter asked ....)

5. We will see you all in September. (Peter said ....)

Greetings, introductions and farewells

Let's look again at the greetings, introductions, replies and farewells at the Andrew MacIntyre reception.

Between people who don't know each other

How do you do? My name is Pierre Beurton.

Nice to meet you. I am Karl Schick.

By the way, let me introduce myself. My name is Eric Varkonyi.

How do you do? I'm Pierre Beurton from the Lille office.

Between people who already know each other

Hello, Karl. Nice to see you again. How are things in the Frankfurt office?

Fine thanks, Clive.

Pierre, how nice to see you again.

It's nice to see you, too.

Introducing others

Do you know Karl here?

And this is Karl Schick.

Let me introduce you to Pierre Beurton.

Unit 8

Leaving

Well, nice meeting you.	*Nice meeting you, too.*
I look forward to seeing you at the next meeting.	*Me too.*
Excuse me, I must go now. See you again.	*(Yes,) see you again.*
See you later.	*(Yes,) see you later.*
Have a good trip.	*Thanks.*

Exercise 3

Jetzt können Sie diese Ausdrücke gleich anwenden. Sie sollen je nach Vorgabe entweder antworten oder die passende Frage stellen. Machen Sie diese Übung mit der Aufnahme - wenn Sie etwas mehr Zeit für die Sätze haben möchten, können Sie auch erst mit dem Buch arbeiten. Doch zunächst ein Beispiel:

'How do you do? My name is Harvey Elliott.'
(Reply and give your name.)
'How do you do? My name is Janine Belot.'
(You must leave now. You'll see Janine in Paris.)
'Excuse me, I must leave now. See you in Paris.'

1. 'Nice to see you.' (Reply.)

2. (Ask about things in the Madrid office.)

3. (Introduce yourself.)

4. 'Do you remember me? I'm Clive Jackson. We met in Brussels.' (Reply.)

5. (Introduce your colleague Sven Johnsson.)

6. 'Well, I have to leave now. Nice meeting you.' (Reply.)

Making small talk

Now we're moving back to the cultural briefing (Einführung in die Gepflogenheiten des neuen Landes) in Pittsburgh.

During the session, Ruby, Clive and Helen mentioned a number of topics for small talk: jobs, weather, family and sport. Here are some questions you could ask for each of these topics.

Questions about jobs

What do you do?

Where are you based?

How long have you been there?

Questions about the weather

How's the weather in Pittsburgh?

What's the weather like in winter?

Social contact

Questions about family

Do you have family?

Do you have children?

How many children do you have?

What are they called?

Where do they go to school?

Questions about sport

Are you interested in sport?

Do you play golf?

How often do you play?

Exercise 4

Stellen Sie sich vor, Sie seien nach Boston versetzt worden und vor kurzem dort angekommen. Auf einer Party lernen Sie neue Leute kennen. Machen Sie diese Übung am besten mit der Aufnahme. Das Beispiel zeigt Ihnen, wie es geht:

'How do you do? My name is Samuel Smith.'
(Reply and give your name.)
'How do you do? My name is Brigitte Schultz.'

'So, Brigitte, where are you from?'
(Reply and ask Samuel where he is from.)
'I'm from Germany. And where are you from?'

Noch einmal von vorn. Und Sie sind einfach Sie selbst.

1. 'How do you do? My name is Samuel Smith.'
   (Reply and give your name.)

2. 'So, where are you from?'
   (Reply and ask Samuel where he is from.)

3. 'Originally from the UK. But now I live here.'
   (Ask Samuel what his job is.)

4. 'I work as a computer programmer.'
   (Ask how long he has been in Boston.)

5. 'Oh, I don't live here in Boston. I'm just visiting.'
   (Ask where he is based.)

6. 'In Miami.'
   (Ask about the weather there now.)

7. 'Absolutely beautiful. A wonderful outdoor life for the family.'
   (Ask if Samuel has children.)

8. 'Yes, two boys and a girl. How about you?'
   (Reply.)

Unit 8

PUT IT ON PAPER

In diesem Abschnitt sehen Sie sich einige Texte an, die die gesellschaftliche Seite des Geschäftslebens behandeln. Zu jedem Text finden Sie Verständnisfragen und Übungen zum Wortschatz.

Reading

Model 1
Advice on business lunches

In der Zeit, bevor Clive sich entschlossen hatte, in die Vereinigten Staaten zu gehen, wurde sein Arbeitstag immer hektischer: Die internen Geschäftsbesprechungen und die Treffen mit Kunden nahmen kein Ende. Hinzu kamen außerdem die Arbeitsessen. Clive griff schließlich zu "The Manager's Problem Solver", einem Buch voll praktischer Tips für die alltäglichen Probleme eines Managers, und schlug unter dem Stichwort "Social Occasions" ("Gesellschaftliche Verpflichtungen") nach.

Lesen Sie den Text auf der nächsten Seite und beantworten Sie dann die Verständnisfragen.

Comprehension

1. What disease can business lunches lead to?
2. How might a person not accustomed to wine feel after a few glasses at lunchtime?
3. What drink does the writer recommend?
4. When is the optimum time for doing business over lunch?
5. Which course does the writer recommend you should go on to after the main course?
6. Put the following courses into the correct order:

   sweet, main course, coffee, starter, cheese, aperitif

Vocabulary development

Suchen Sie im Text die Verben mit den folgenden Bedeutungen:

1. to object to
2. to make better
3. to succeed in doing

4. to make
5. to advise
6. to be accustomed to

Question

I'm obliged to lunch with clients several times a week. Work is absolutely impossible afterward. What can I do to improve my afternoon performance?

Answer

Nothing could be less businesslike than allowing lunch to render you inefficient and unproductive for half the working day. This is the path to redundancy and/or cirrhosis.

Unless you're used to drinking alcohol at lunchtime, a couple of glasses of wine could just make you lethargic.

Only by abstinence can you solve the problem. Offer your guest aperitifs and wine but don't order a full bottle and expect him or her to drink it all. Better to say, 'Would you like a glass of wine?' They'll ask if you intend to have one and you should demur in favour of mineral water. Blame a heavy night or a late work session to come, but don't weaken.

Encourage your guests to order whatever they like, but avoid anything too filling for yourself. Just after the main course is the time when most serious lunchtime work is accomplished - don't let distractions from the sweet trolley get in the way. If you, as host, go straight on to coffee, your guest will probably follow suit.

Unit 8

Model 2
Cross-cultural briefing notes

At the end of Clive and Helen's first day of cultural briefing, Ruby gave them a short article to read.

Lesen Sie den Text und beantworten Sie dann die Verständnisfragen.

THE ADJUSTMENT PROCESS

When an individual enters a strange culture, he or she is like a fish out of water. Newcomers feel at times that they do not belong and consequently may feel alienated from the native members of the culture. When this happens, visitors may want to reject everything about the new environment and may glorify and exaggerate the positive aspects of their own culture. Conversely, visitors may scorn their native country by rejecting its values and instead choosing to identify with (if only temporarily) the values of the new country. This may occur as an attempt to overidentify with the new culture in order to be accepted by the people in it.

Reactions to a new culture vary, but experience and research have shown that there are distinct stages in the adjustment process of foreign visitors.

The first stage (1) is when many people are fascinated and excited by everything new. The visitor is elated to be in a new culture.

After that (2) comes the stage when the individual is immersed in new problems such as work, home and language.

At the next stage (3) everyday activities are no longer major problems. Although the visitor feels more comfortable with the new language and culture, some aspects are still difficult to grasp.

The fourth step (4) is when individuals have been away from relatives and good friends for a long period of time and may feel lonely. Frustration and a loss of self-confidence may result. In fact, as we will see later, some individuals may remain at this stage.

At the final stage (5), a routine has been established. The visitor has accepted the habits, customs and characteristics of the people in the new culture. The visitor feels comfortable with friends, associates and the language of the country.

The following 'W' shaped diagram illustrates the periods of adjustment in a second culture and might apply to a one-year stay.

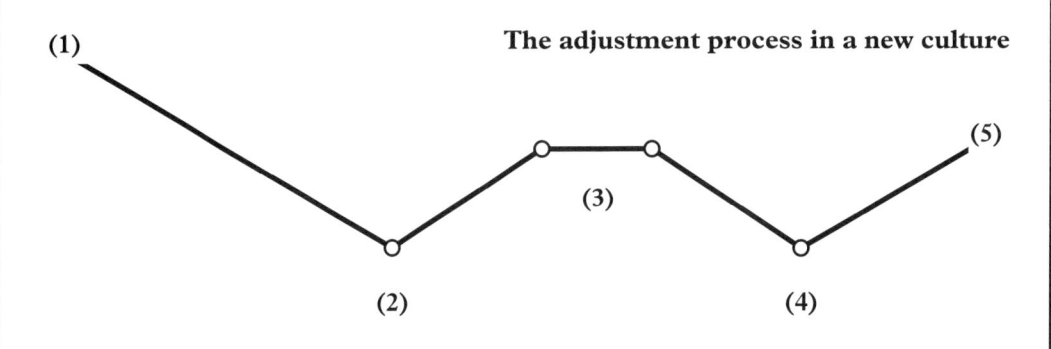

The adjustment process in a new culture

Social contact

Comprehension

Jedes der im Text erwähnten Stadien hat einen speziellen Namen. Wählen Sie jeweils den passenden Namen und setzen Sie ihn in das Diagramm ein.

initial adjustment   acceptance and integration

honeymoon period   culture shock

mental isolation

Vocabulary development

Suchen Sie im Text Wörter mit der entgegengesetzten Bedeutung:

1. negative
2. solution
3. leave
4. foreign
5. scorn
6. accept
7. permanently
8. depressed

Language and communication skills

Verb: '-ing' or infinitive?

Let's go back to Clive's problem over business lunches and look again at the advice he got.

*Don't order a full bottle and expect him or her **to drink** it all.*

*Unless you're used **to drinking** alcohol at lunchtime, a couple of glasses of wine could just make you lethargic.*

In the first sentence the **to** is a particle; in the second the **to** is a preposition.

How can we see the difference?

Try replacing the word(s) after **to** with a noun or the word **it**.

If the **to** is a preposition, the sentence will be grammatically correct.

If the **to** is a particle, the sentence won't be grammatically correct.

WRONG: Don't order a full bottle and expect him or her *to* it.

RIGHT: Unless you're used *to* it, a couple of glasses of wine could just make you lethargic.

Die **-ing**-Form wird immer nach Präpositionen benutzt.

Unit 8

Exercise 1

Vervollständigen Sie die folgenden Sätze mit der richtigen Form des Verbs in Klammern.

1. I would like to (reduce) my alcohol consumption.
2. That advice should stop you from (drink).
3. We look forward to (hear) about the results.
4. Are you really interested in (solve) this problem?
5. I'd advise you to (drink) the mineral water.
6. I certainly don't object to (drink) a little wine.
7. It is better than (accept) these terms.
8. He hopes to (contact) you next week.

'As' or 'like'?

Look at the following sentences from the article about cultural adjustment:

*When an individual enters a strange culture, he or she is **like** a fish out of water.*

*This may occur **as** an attempt to overidentify with the new culture in order to be accepted by the people in it.*

*In fact, **as we will see later**, some individuals may remain at this stage.*

As and **like** both mean **the same as** or **similar to**.

We say:

*He is **like** a fish out of water.*
(In other words, his behaviour is the same as a fish out of water, but he isn't really a fish.)

*This occurs **as** an attempt.*
(In other words, this action really is an attempt.)

Now compare the following sentences:

*He behaved **as** a son.*
(The same as a son, which is really what he was.)

*He behaved **like** a son.*
(The same as a son, but in fact he wasn't a son.)

Note also that we use **as** in a subordinate clause (Nebensatz), for example:

***As** we will see later, …*

Social contact

Exercise 2

Vervollständigen Sie die folgenden Sätze mit **as** oder **like**.

1. People who come to a new country .... immigrants are likely to suffer from adjustment problems.
2. .... we know, these problems usually resolve themselves.
3. People who don't behave .... natives are often discriminated against.
4. Visitors may criticize aspects of their native country such .... its values and culture.
5. Visitors who work .... executives are equally likely to suffer from adjustment problems.
6. When we went back it was just .... old times.
7. We knew it would be difficult, just .... you said.
8. It's not .... we imagined it was going to be.

Written emphasis

Now let's look again at the advice about how to be more effective after a business lunch. We are going to look at how to emphasize or highlight information.

Subject	Verb	Object	Adverbial phrase
I	am obliged to eat	restaurant lunches	several times a week

The normal sentence order in English is shown here, but there are various techniques we can use to be more emphatic.

1. Inversion of subject and verb after **only** and negative words/expressions such as **no** and **nowhere**:

   *Only by abstinence **can you** solve the problem.*

   *Under no circumstances **should you** order a full bottle of wine.*

2. Imperatives:

   ***Encourage** your guests to order whatever they like, but **avoid** anything too filling for yourself.*

   ***Don't let** distractions from the sweet trolley get in the way.*

3. Intensifying adverbs:

   *Work is **absolutely** impossible afterward.*

Unit 8

Exercise 3 Hier sehen Sie einen ersten Entwurf für einen Beschwerdebrief. Wie könnten Sie ihn mit mehr Nachdruck formulieren?

> Dear Mr Barnes
>
> We were disappointed with your response to our enquiry. According to our records, we placed the order more than three weeks ago and cannot understand why we have not received the goods. You should note that you in fact acknowledged our order two weeks ago. This means we can't be in any way responsible for the problem. So, we would appreciate it if you didn't try to blame us as we are sure that we are not liable.
>
> If you wish to continue supplying us, we would be grateful if you could contact us as soon as you receive this letter.
>
> Yours sincerely

Sequencing information in writing

Der Artikel über den Umzug in ein anderes Land mit anderen Gebräuchen, den Ruby an Clive und Helen weitergegeben hat, beschrieb fünf verschiedene Stufen der Anpassung, die die meisten Leute durchleben. Wenn Sie eine Reihe von Punkten haben, dann können Sie diese natürlich einfach unter den Nummern 1 - n auflisten. Das erleichtert dem Leser die Orientierung. Oder Sie können verbale Ausdrücke verwenden, um die verschiedenen Stufen der Abfolge zu kennzeichnen - so wie in Rubys Artikel. Hier sind diese verbalen Ausdrücke im Überblick:

Social contact

Beginning
- ↓ First/initially/the first step/the first stage
- ↓ Second/secondly/the second step/at the second stage
- ↓ Then/after that/at the next stage/the next step
- ↓ Finally/the final step/at the final stage

End

Exercise 4

Ruby has been asked to provide some cultural counselling for a family going back home after five years at Andrew MacIntyre's headquarters in Pittsburgh. As you can imagine, there is usually a 're-entry' adjustment process, again consisting of five stages, which are shown on the diagram below.

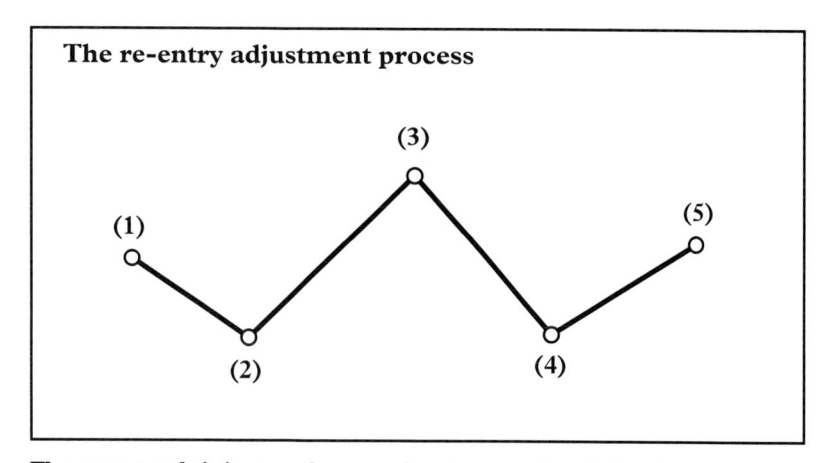

The re-entry adjustment process

(1) (2) (3) (4) (5)

The text explaining each stage is given on the following page.

Numerieren Sie die Abschnitte fortlaufend; formulieren Sie dann den Text um und verwenden Sie verbale Ausdrücke, um die Reihenfolge zu markieren, so wie in Rubys erstem Artikel.

149

- ❏ There may be confusion and emotional pain about leaving because friendships will have to be disrupted. Many people realize how much they have changed because of their experiences and may be nervous about going home.

- ❏ Family and friends may not understand or appreciate what the traveller has experienced. The native country may have changed in the eyes of the former traveller.

- ❏ A routine has been established in the new culture and the visitor feels comfortable with friends and associates in that country.

- ❏ The former traveller becomes fully involved with friends, relatives and activities, and feels once again integrated in the society.

- ❏ Immediately upon arrival in the home country, there is usually a great deal of excitement. There are parties to welcome back the visitor and renewed friendships to look forward to.

Social contact

THE BUSINESS INTERVIEW

How others see us

Catherine Perry, Managerin der PR-Agentur Good Relations in London, spricht über die Arbeitsbedingungen in der internationalen Geschäftswelt.

As an American living and working in London, Catherine Perry is used to dealing with different attitudes on each side of the Atlantic.

As you listen...

1. How does Catherine describe the relationship between the UK and the United States in their use of language?

2. How does she think companies should prepare employees for working abroad - apart from giving them information about the job?

3. What example does she give of the different ways British and American business people might set about getting new business?

4. What two phrases did Catherine use to sum up (a) the American and (b) the British attitude to actual negotiations?

5. What difference in attitudes to work does she highlight?

RESOURCE BOOK

KEY TO UNITS

1 Introducing the company   159
2 Presenting the product   168
3 Meeting customer needs   177
4 Managing projects   188
5 Results and forecasts   200
6 Customer service   211
7 Reaching agreement   223
8 Social contact   234

UNIT 1
INTRODUCING THE COMPANY

SAY WHAT YOU MEAN

Extract 1

Recording script

MK: OK, good morning, ladies and gentlemen. I'd like to welcome you all to ITCORP. My name is Mike Kowalsky and I am the Vice-President responsible for Production at ITCORP. In this short presentation this morning I'd like to give you an overview of the structure and activities of the company. In particular I've divided my talk into three main parts. First the current organization, second the key personnel and their functional responsibilities, and finally our major activities. I'll be using some charts to highlight the key information and I aim to speak for about 15 minutes. If you have any questions, I'll be happy to answer them at the end of my talk.

Right. First let's take a look at the current structure of the company. If you look at the chart here you can see that the organization is headed by John De Lucca, our current President. He is supported by four vice-presidents. As you can see, the organization is divided into four key functional departments and each VP is assisted by a team of staffers. First, we have Paul Rosenbaum, who is in charge of Research and Development here at our headquarters. Next we have Robert Leos, who is responsible for marketing. Next along is the Vice-President for Production, namely myself. And my name again is Mike Kowalsky. And finally we have Sally Brown who takes care of corporate finance. As you can see from the organigram, the four vice-presidents report directly to Mr De Lucca.

Moving on, some five years ago we introduced geographic divisions in order to bring together in one unit all the activities performed in one region. So, each division is like a separate business unit in certain aspects, but is not a truly separate enterprise because each divisional head must report to HQ. So our operations are split into three geographic areas, as you can see. First, North America, under Hank Martens. This consists of two sections - the USA and Canada; second, there's Simon Lavery, who takes care of the Middle and Far East; and finally we have Europe and Africa. Clark Mountjoy is responsible there. So, these three vice-presidents report to central headquarters. Right, so that is the current structure of the organization, the key personnel and their functional responsibilities. Now I'd like to

Key – Unit 1

move on to my second point: a review of our major activities. In order to understand the areas …

ITCORP ORGANIGRAM

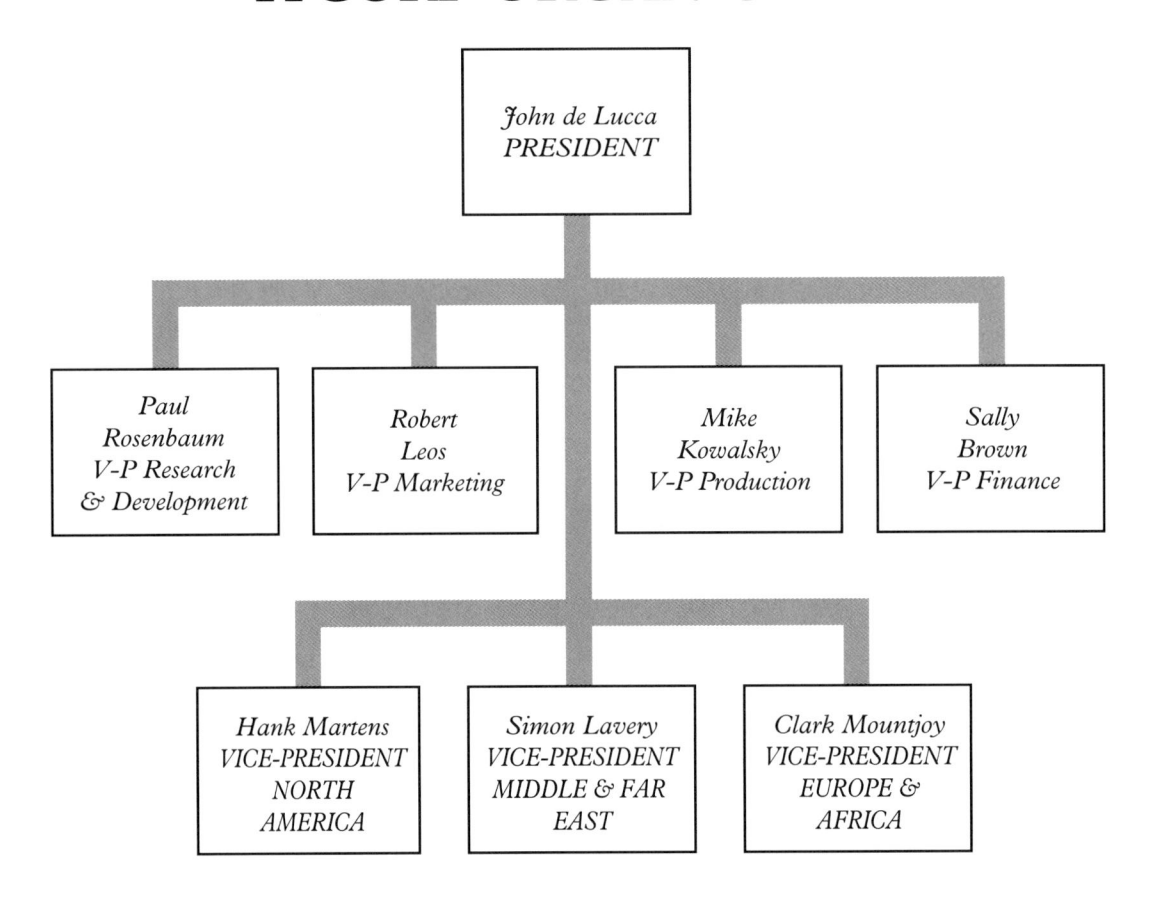

```
                    John de Lucca
                     PRESIDENT
   ┌──────────────┬──────┴───────┬──────────────┐
   Paul          Robert          Mike           Sally
 Rosenbaum       Leos          Kowalsky         Brown
 V-P Research  V-P Marketing  V-P Production  V-P Finance
 & Development

            ┌───────────────┼───────────────┐
      Hank Martens    Simon Lavery     Clark Mountjoy
     VICE-PRESIDENT  VICE-PRESIDENT    VICE-PRESIDENT
        NORTH         MIDDLE & FAR        EUROPE &
       AMERICA            EAST             AFRICA
```

Extract 2

Recording script

C: So Herr Schneider, how do you operate in the UK then?

PS: Right, this is how we operate in the UK. In the UK we have two kinds of arrangements for our customers. And, if you hang on a minute, I can show you what the full picture looks like. Yes, here we are. So, here you can see the route from manufacturer to customer. So, the goods are manufactured here.

C: Here? You mean in Germany?

PS: Yes, that's right. And then they are transported to the destination country. In this case the UK. Now, in the UK we have, as I

Key – Unit 1

said, two arrangements - firstly agents and secondly dealers. Let's look first of all at agents.

C: Right.

PS: Agents send their orders through to us at our plant in Küberg. These days they are usually sent by fax or phoned through to us. Then our local office processes them and ships the goods to them.

C: By road?

PS: Yes, normally by road, but we sometimes use rail.

C: I see.

PS: At the same time we invoice the agent for the agreed amount. After that the agent delivers the units to the customer, collects payment, and then settles our invoice. So the agent retains a commission which is a percentage of the sales price. After we have sent out our invoice we expect payment within 30 days. So, that's the agents. OK?

C: Yes, fine.

PS: OK, now moving on to the dealers. They send in their orders to us. The order is processed and then the invoice is raised. The difference between the agent and the dealer is that dealers buy goods at their own risk before they sell them on to the customer. So they are free to fix their own prices - at least according to what the market will take. So, that's the dealers. And those are the two arrangements. Is that clear?

C: Yes, quite clear thanks.

PS: At the moment we have three agents in the UK. We have been pretty successful so far and we are now interested in appointing some new agents.

C: So I understand.

PS: Now I have the agency details here. Would you like to take a copy?

C: Yes, please.

PS: And if you have any questions, please get back to me. Here's my card.

C: Thank you very much. And here's mine. There is just . . .

Key – Unit 1

KÜBEL NETWORK CHART

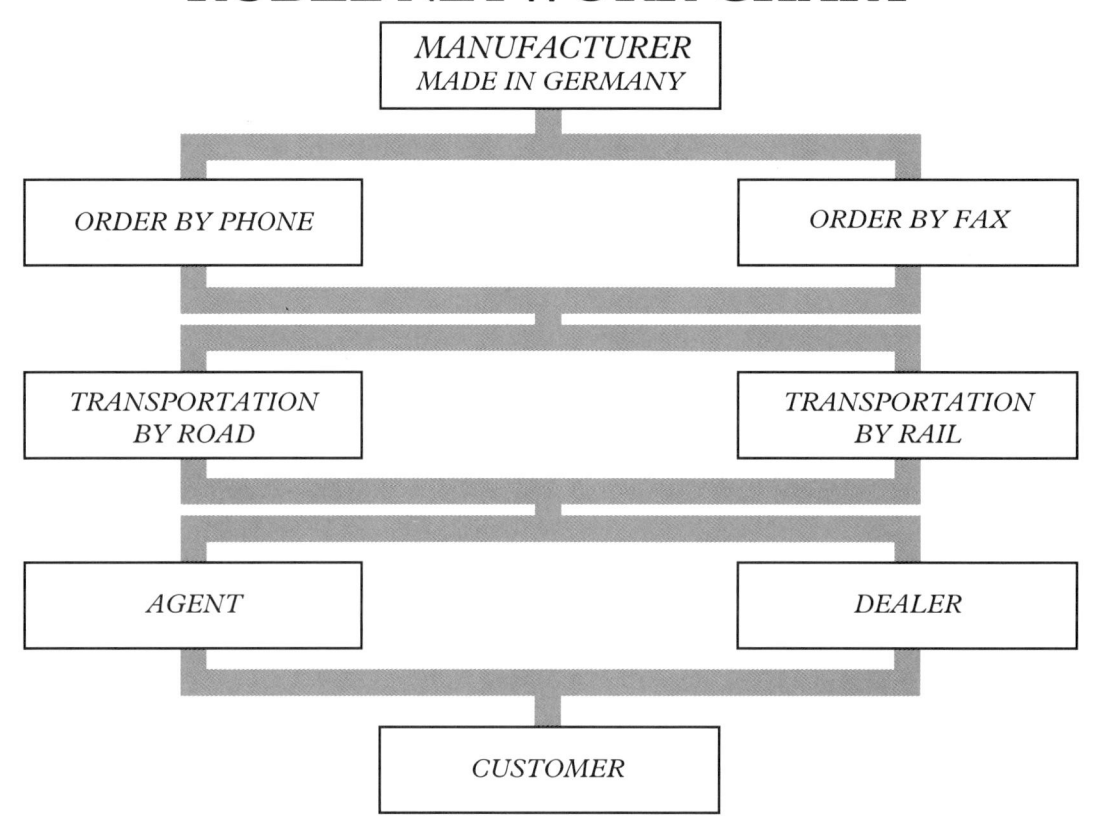

```
                    MANUFACTURER
                   MADE IN GERMANY

    ORDER BY PHONE                    ORDER BY FAX

    TRANSPORTATION                    TRANSPORTATION
       BY ROAD                            BY RAIL

        AGENT                              DEALER

                        CUSTOMER
```

Presenting the organization

Exercise 1

1. He is supported by a research team.
2. Mike takes care of the laboratories.
3. Mike reports to Paul.
4. The research team is split into scientists and engineers.
5. Susanne is in charge of finance.

6. The company has four operating divisions.
7. Marketing strategy is decided in the marketing department.
8. The marketing department is divided into three sections.
9. There are five of us who work together as a team.

Key – Unit 1

Active and passive

Exercise 2

1. First an order is received.
2. Their orders are sent by fax.
3. An order is phoned through.
4. The goods are shipped to them.
5. The goods are sometimes transported by rail.
6. The agent is invoiced as soon as possible.

Structuring your presentation (1)

Exercise 3

1. I'd like to give you an overview of the new company structure.
2. I've divided my talk into four main parts.
3. I'll be using some charts to highlight the key information.
4. I aim to speak for about 15 minutes.
5. First I'd like to consider turnover.
6. So that covers turnover.
7. Now let's move on to expenses.
8. So that covers expenses.
9. Now I'd like to move on to my final point.

Structuring your presentation (2)

Exercise 4

1. First of all let's look at the total market.
2. So, that's the total market.
3. Next there's the German market.
4. So, that's the German market.
5. So, we've looked at the two markets - the total market and the German market.
6. If you have any questions, please get back to me.

Key – Unit 1

PUT IT ON PAPER

Model 1

Comprehension

1. To help their clients perform better than their competitors.
2. No, it's team-based.
3. Leading firms around the world.
4. Board level/senior management/CEOs.
5. Physical expansion; financial performance; client relationships.
6. Most clients have kept their services from one year to the next.

Vocabulary development

1. analogous   (d) different
2. divergent   (a) similar
3. collaborative   (f) conflicting
4. challenging   (c) straightforward
5. outstanding   (e) inferior
6. vast   (b) tiny

Model 2

Comprehension

1. Over 100 years.
2. Ethical (prescription) drugs.
3. $5.7 billion.
4. It has three field sales divisions.
5. To strengthen its position in the UK pharmaceutical market.
6. Expansion of UK divisions, and internal promotion of staff.
7. GP (General Practitioner) and hospital sectors.
8. A competitive salary, pension and benefits available from a multinational.

Vocabulary development

1. excellence   excellent
2. innovation   innovative
3. success   successful
4. globe   global

Key – Unit 1

5. ambition	ambitious
6. confidence	confident
7. persuasion	persuasive
8. competition	competitive

Adjectives and adverbs

Exercise 1

Below are suggested answers. Other combinations are possible.

1. We work in a highly competitive market.
2. We need well-qualified salesmen.
3. Our task is to achieve long-term real growth.
4. We have an enviable client spread.
5. It is a technically sophisticated market.
6. We sell competitively priced products.

Introducing your company in writing

Exercise 2

Trade Stands International (TSI) is a leading provider of exhibition stands and support services.

Established in 1981, TSI has been servicing the needs of companies, ranging from small specialized firms entering new markets to well-established multinationals.

We are in a unique position to meet your exhibition needs, whether you require our simple export-pack or full, on-the-ground support.

Staffed by our 24-hour experienced teams, we can make sure your products or services are displayed to their full advantage.

Key – Unit 1

THE BUSINESS INTERVIEW

Talking about company structure

Recording script

Alan, can you tell us something about the present structure of your company and how you see that structure developing?

Yes, United Biscuits consists of five companies, four in Europe and one in the United States, which is based in Chicago but has plants all over the States. We are basically represented in snacks, confectionery and chilled and frozen foods, and each of the five companies is self-contained in its own right. It is a profit centre, it has its own Board, it has its own strategy. But overall it reports into the United Biscuits Centre which lays down the general strategy.

Internationally?

Well, one of the plans we have got in the next few years is to become a truly international company, so we are looking quite thoroughly at acquisition developments in Europe and in the Far East in particular. And our policy there, when we acquire a company or have a joint venture, is to understand fully the way that the market works and to allow that company its head because we think that the local managers understand the markets better. So for example if we acquired a snack food company in Spain, that company would report into KP which is our snack food operation but it would actually be allowed to run according to the market conditions that are there; and of course in addition to reporting into KP it would be able to take advantage of the United Biscuits Centre - with the research and development, the finance and so on that the Centre can provide.

So it's a hierarchical organization - or a flat one?

Well, we have quite a flat organizational structure. Each of the managing directors in the acquisition or joint venture companies would report in to the managing director of their appropriate company. So the Spanish snacks man would report to KP and then the KP Managing Director would report into the Chief Executive. So we are non-hierarchical - there are only three layers of hierarchical management in fact.

Where do you fit in yourself into this structure?

Well, I am part of the Group Centre, which is there to add value to what the operating companies are doing and to help them to do their job to the best of their advantage. So in the Centre we have the research and development function, we have a central

Key – Unit 1

finance department, we have a personnel director who lays down personnel policy worldwide and each of them works with their counterparts in the operating companies. I am responsible for United Biscuits communication which means I am responsible for looking at what United Biscuits needs to say about itself worldwide to all its audiences and make sure that it is said as creatively and as efficiently as possible...

As you listen ... (Answers)

1. (b) United Biscuits has four companies in Europe and one in the United States.

2. Each company is self-contained (own profit centre, own Board, own strategy), but reports into the United Biscuits Centre which lays down the general strategy.

3. (c) allow local managers to make use of their specialist knowledge and United Biscuits' central resources.

4. No, it's quite flat, non-hierarchical, with only three layers of management.

5. To help operating companies do their job to their best advantage - in other words, as well as possible.

UNIT 2
PRESENTING THE PRODUCT

SAY WHAT YOU MEAN

Extract 1

Recording script

SM: Right, let's get started. I know you're all on tight schedules, so I'm going to be brief today. We're convinced we're on to a winner and I see it as my job today to convince you too. Later we'll have time to go into the whole project in more detail. So, I'm going to take just 15 minutes to cover two major areas; firstly the market and secondly the product. I'll be using some transparencies ... you'll find copies in the pack in front of you.

So, let's take a look at the market. I'm going to confine the figures to the UK market, although, as you'll see we think the product has big potential throughout Europe. Nevertheless, initially we'll almost certainly launch it in the UK. As you can see from this first transparency, the total ice-cream market last year was worth £580 million. In product and distribution terms, this divides into two sectors: the impulse-buying, in-hand sector - in other words, the hot sunny day, let's get an ice-cream sector - and the take-home, multi-pack sector. You can see from this graph here, the in-hand sector has been pretty static over the last five years, barely keeping pace with inflation - just five per cent a year, whilst the take-home sector has risen by about 40% in value. However, as we'll see in a moment, most of this increase is accounted for by supermarkets' own label brands.

Right, so not a particularly dynamic market. Let's take a look at the competition. On this pie chart, you can see how it was carved up last year. Walls was very much the dominant brand, with 42% of the market, followed a long way behind by Lyons Maid with about 11%. But, and this is what I'd like you to bear in mind, 29% of the market was held by own label brands, sold in the major supermarket chains. What's more, and this is what I mentioned a moment ago, the own label brands account for nearly 43% of the take-home market. The remaining 18% of the market is held by niche operators and regional ice-cream producers.

Now, our feeling is that there is a major opportunity for a company like Cadtree, with its strong brands, to really develop brand loyalty for a high-quality chocolate ice-cream bar. Let me tell you how we see our product positioned.

Firstly, we take our existing Cadbar product and transform this into an ice-cream chocolate bar which retains the familiar taste of Cadbar. Technically, we have proved it can be done - you'll find production specifications in the folder you have in front of you. Commercially, the advantages are obvious. We all know the highest costs in our business are tied up in establishing a brand - this way we build on a name and a product which is already very well-established - in fact, one of the biggest selling brands in Europe - we simply add to our existing product a new application - ICE CREAM CADBAR. It's a new product but the brand already has a tremendous following - this will mean a relatively modest advertising budget. Secondly, ...

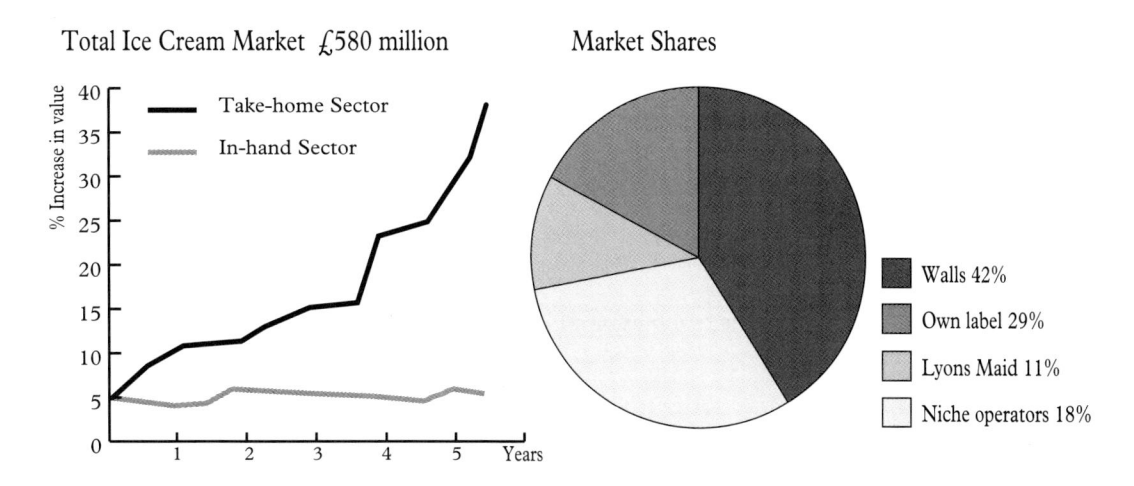

Total Ice Cream Market £580 million

Market Shares

- Walls 42%
- Own label 29%
- Lyons Maid 11%
- Niche operators 18%

Extract 2

Recording script

PS: I like the collection, Francesco. I think we can do business. What I have to check out is prices and delivery times.

FP: Of course, let's take pricing first. This table should help . . . we've listed the whole range in both men's and women's garments, . . . here you can see in the left-hand column . . . by catalogue number. Then, we've got prices in three columns - a unit price for orders under 50 pieces, a first discount for 50 to 200 pieces and then in the last column, for more than 200 pieces. All these are trade prices.

PS: Sure. We can look at retail prices in a moment.

FP: Well, you see these last two columns - the first one gives our recommended retail prices - these are the prices we will be charging in our own outlets and the last column gives the margin on the bulk order price in percentage terms.

Key – Unit 2

PS: You mean the margin if we go for orders above 200 pieces?

FP: That's right. As you can see, it's very healthy!

PS: It sure looks that way. We'd be interested particularly in your designer pants for women . . .

FP: OK, let's take a look at how prices work out on that line. They're catalogue number 9004. So, a unit price of $43, a first discount - that's on orders above 50 - bringing down the price to $38 and then a further reduction down to $35 for orders above 200 . . .

PS: Can we take that again?

FP: Of course: $43 unit price, $38 from 50 to 200 and $35 over 200.

PS: I got that. So what's the margin on the $35?

FP: As you can see here on the table, we recommend $75 as a retail price so that's a mark-up of over 100%.

PS: Fine, now what about deliveries?

Catalog no.	Unit price >50	discount price 50-200	discount price 200+	recommended retail price	margin mark-up
9001	12	9	5	15	300%
9002	58	55	50	120	140%
9003	20	19	17	30	76%
9004	43	38	35	75	114%

Describing trends

Exercise 1

1. There has been a slight fall in consumer prices.
2. Demand has dropped enormously.
3. Sales are growing slightly.
4. There has been a collapse in consumer confidence.

Key – Unit 2

5. There has been a considerable expansion in the market.
6. Sales will increase modestly.
7. There will be a substantial decrease in profits.

Describing change
Exercise 2

1. Turnover has fallen by £2 million.
2. Profits have increased to DM 250,000.
3. We have raised the dividend by 3p.
4. We forecast a rise of 40 million.
5. We are looking forward to a reduction to £20,000.

1. They raised prices last year.
2. Inflation is forecast to rise next year.
3. The tax cuts will raise inflation.
4. My taxes have risen every year of my working life.

Considering your audience
Exercise 3

1. Later we'll have time to go into more detail.
2. I'll be using some transparencies. You'll find copies in the file in front of you.
3. As you'll see in a moment ...
4. As I mentioned a moment ago ...

Balancing your argument
Exercise 4

1. Although the market was saturated, we launched a new product.
2. The marketing manager made a lot of mistakes. Nevertheless, he became Managing Director.
3. The company specialized in consumer products. However, it bought an industrial products concern.

Using visual aids
Exercise 5

1. Probably a line graph is the best in this case.
2. Probably a bar chart would do this best.
3. A pie chart would do this best.
4. A table would probably be best here.

Key – Unit 2

PUT IT ON PAPER

Model 1

Comprehension

1. Workgroup software (network group productivity software).
2. Word-processing.
3. They will already be familiar with the keys and commands.
4. It promises speed of communication and the ability to reach large groups of people.

Vocabulary development

1. Menu system — (b) Access system where user can select from list of options.
2. Hot key system — (a) Short cut using a single key to another application.
3. E-mail — (f) Allows you to prepare and send a message to an individual or a group of people.
4. Diaries — (c) A system which allows authorized users to scan other users' appointments. It also enables a user to make a common entry.
5. Scheduler — (e) A system which manages time, recording project deadlines and providing a graphic view of a group of diaries over a period of time.
6. To do lists — (d) A prioritized list of tasks with an automatic alarm to advise you of approaching deadlines.

Model 2

Comprehension

The purpose of each paragraph (1-4) in the enquiry letter is as follows:

1. Gives a reference for the letter.
2. Explains the background/situation.
3. Makes a request.
4. Ends politely.

Key – Unit 2

In the reply, each paragraph (1-4) has the following purpose:

1. Refers to the enquiry.
2. Reinforces the sales argument.
3. Responds to the request.
4. Offers more information about the enquiry.

Vocabulary development

1. edition — (d) issue
2. link up — (e) connect up
3. appreciate — (a) like
4. feasibility — (f) viability
5. implement — (h) make operational
6. delighted — (g) pleased
7. facility — (b) use (noun)
8. case history — (c) customer reference

Reinforcing your arguments

Exercise 1

1. This is not only/just a word-processing package, it is also a time management system.
2. You can scan other colleagues' diaries. In addition/On top of this, you can enter proposed dates for appointments.
3. Bringing together functions such as electronic mail and diary scheduling, the system offers the ideal networking arrangements.
4. All in all, the system represents the best value for money on the market.
5. Although it has one or two minor deficiencies, as a whole, it meets the needs of most customers.

Letter-writing expressions

Exercise 2

Dear Mr Bradshaw,

With reference to your letter dated 11 June 1993, we were delighted/pleased to read of your interest in our new accounting software.

Please find enclosed the information you requested concerning prices and installation costs. We would be grateful/appreciate

Key – Unit 2

it/be obliged if you could complete the attached form so that we can process your order as soon as possible.

We look forward to receiving your order in the next few days. In the meantime, please do not hesitate to contact us if you require further information.

American/British letter-writing styles

Exercise 3

Your ref: 052/PQ
Our ref: 22/TS
Date: 6/2/93

Gentlemen

Thank you for your letter dated May 24, 1993.

Further to your request, we enclose the documentation concerning our products.

Please do not hesitate to contact us if we can be of further assistance.

Sincerely yours

Tom Parker

Vice President - Sales

Key – Unit 2

THE BUSINESS INTERVIEW

Marketing and product strategy

Recording script

Ken, yours is a very new product. How do you see the market situation both domestic and worldwide at the moment?

There are really three markets for our product. One is consumer products to general users, the sort of people who would read books. The other is education for people learning, and the third one is professional applications, anything from train schedules to parts manuals, to insurance data - any type of professional application.

What sort of strategy have you got for marketing the product worldwide?

We have I think perhaps a survival strategy, that is to say it's a new product and a new technology, so the market worldwide is rather small and to survive and prosper we must sell a product worldwide. So we think globally and act locally. We create products that satisfy local needs but we can sell around the world.

This is through local distributors or agents?

It's developing quickly. We imagine that the main distribution channels will be the normal book distribution channels and that's the way in which they are being distributed presently.

Right. Would you say that in today's marketing world only the big can survive, that one needs to be a conglomeration in order to survive?

No, in fact quite the contrary, I think we try to be fleet of foot. We try to adapt and change very quickly. We are a small company, we have offices in Tokyo, London and San Francisco, and total staff of less than fifteen. So I think in this technology and similar companies you have to be able to move quickly - and a small company can do that whereas a large company may not be able to do that.

How do you set about in that context establishing a brand name globally? Is it an easy task?

It's not an easy task, but what we've done - we're in publishing, we publish products - is we've tried to publish products of well-known companies or co-publish products with well-known companies and we are hoping that that will give us some name recognition, and in the future we will publish our own products

Key – Unit 2

and hopefully create a specific name for ourselves - and reputation.

Do you see it taking over from traditional book publishing?

Not at all. I think it's perhaps a bit like radio or television and print media. I think that there were predictions that electronic media would take over print but they work side by side and I think that each will adapt to one another and they work together . . . it's an adjunct - not a replacement for printed publishing.

And what about competition? You are at the forefront of new technology, but are there people snapping at your heels?

There is competition but the potential for this new publishing medium is so vast that we are actually happy to see competition . . . I think that everyone benefits and we are happy to compete.

As you listen ...

(Answers)

1. (a) consumer products to general users

   (b) educational

   (c) professional applications such as train schedules or parts manuals

2. (c) survival

3. A small company can adapt quickly (try to be 'fleet of foot'). A large company may not be able to do so.

4. (b) co-producing products of/for well-known companies.

5. No. He says they will adapt to each other and work together.

UNIT 3
MEETING CUSTOMER NEEDS

SAY WHAT YOU MEAN

Extract 1

Recording script

JS: OK then, just so that we're both clear about the purpose of this first meeting. In order for me to give you good advice, it's essential I fully understand the situation the company is in.

PD: OK, yes, sure.

JS: Good. Our tour around the plant has put me in the picture as far as the testing equipment is concerned - in other words the product - I now need to know more about the company and your present market.

PD: Yes, that's quite clear. I suppose you want to ask a lot of questions?

JS: That's right. I'd like to start by checking some background information.

PD: That's fine with me.

JS: Now, if I understand it correctly, you and your family hold all the equity in the company ...

PD: Equity?

JS: I mean the shares and therefore the control of the business.

PD: Oh ... I see. Yes, that's right, we've always kept it a family business and we've no plans to change that.

JS: Right. Now, you've got three senior managers?

PD: Yes ... there's Jean Lafond, he looks after the production side ... Marc Fontaine who's in charge of Finance and Isabelle Martin, our sales manager. She already has too much work looking after our French customers - one of the things I want your advice about is how to manage the export business from this end.

JS: Of course, I understand that. I'll certainly cover that issue in my report, I promise you. Now, if I could ask you a few more questions. I'd like to check over some of the figures.

Key – Unit 3

PD: Please go ahead.

JS: First of all. Your turnover last year was just under FF24 million, wasn't it?

PD: Yes, that's correct.

JS: And these sales were solely in France, I believe?

PD: About 95%. Actually, we sold one or two test units in Italy and Spain.

JS: That's interesting. I didn't know that. Who were the customers?

PD: They were subsidiaries of our established French clients.

JS: I see. So you don't have any representation outside France? ... I mean agents or distributors.

PD: No, all our sales up until now, in France and elsewhere have been as a result of direct customer contact. Isabelle has done an excellent job these last few years. Again, what I need to know is how you operate in the UK. Do we need to set up agency agreements? Can we sell direct?

JS: Yes, that's clear. I understand your concern. In fact, that's really the key question which I am going to address in my report. If I might come back to one or two more questions?

PD: Sorry. I'm too impatient.

JS: Not at all. Consultants always ask a lot of questions but I promise you it will mean my advice will be all the better for it!

PD: Good! I like that!

JS: So, I wonder if I could ask you one or two more questions about the financial side?

PD: Yes, sure.

JS: A key element in breaking into any new market - especially a foreign one - is the level of investment. I need to know a bit more about your level of profitability and your sales and promotion budgets?

PD: Yes, I can see that. Let me just get the figures for last quarter ... Marie, nous avons besoin ...

COMPANY PROFILE

Name: Sudouest Électronique
Product: testing equipment for printed circuit boards
Ownership: Danton family
Turnover: FF 24m
Domestic sales: 95%
Export sales: 5%
Management structure:

```
                    Pierre Danton
                    Managing Director
                            |
    ┌───────────────────────┼───────────────────────┐
Jean Lafond            Marc Fontaine           Isabelle Martin
Production             Finance                 Sales
```

Customer need: advice on entry into UK market

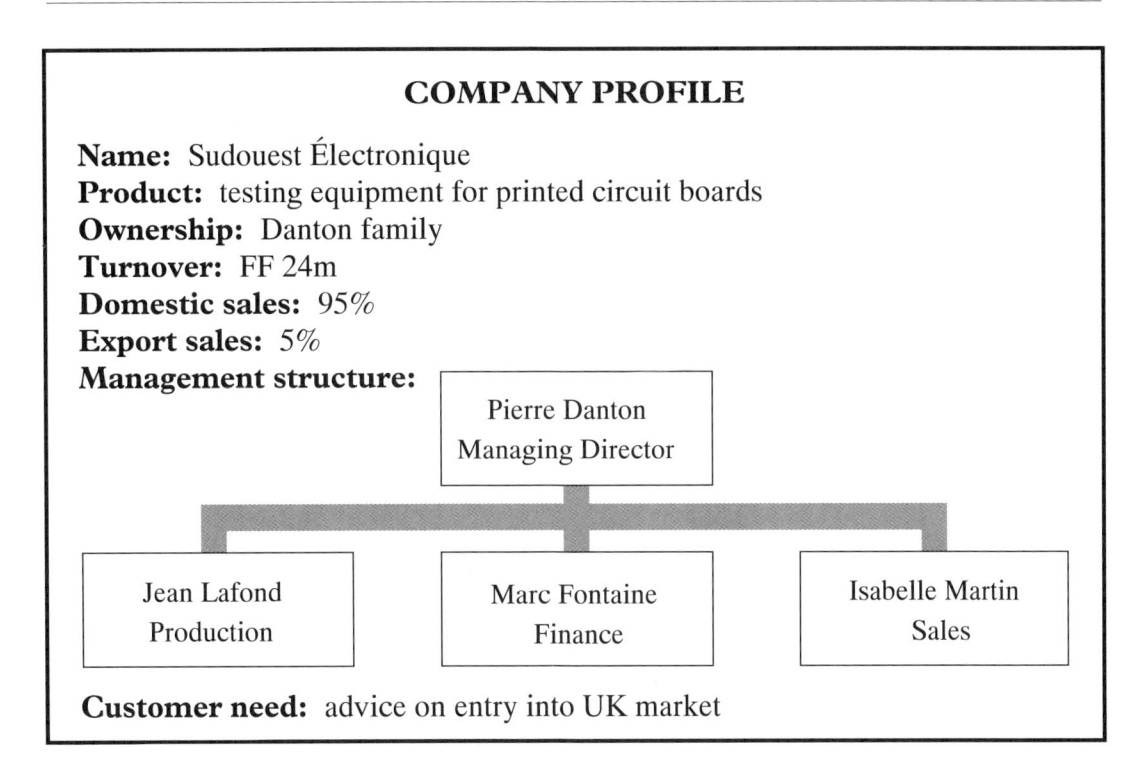

Extract 2

Recording script

JP: Well, Claire. We'd better get started. Could I ask you some questions, mainly about the company and of course the new range?

CN: Sure. Just remember I'm new to the company and they just put me in charge of this new line!

JP: A real challenge then! So Claire, just a couple of questions about the marketing team - you report to Jeff Hines, I guess?

CN: Right. Do you know him?

JP: Not really. I met him once or twice. And you don't have any market research function in the team?

CN: No, that's not true. Susan Kerly is a full-time researcher but she's too busy to work on this project.

JP: Anybody else in the department?

CN: Yes, there are two other product managers - one takes care of our hospital business, the other cosmetics.

JP: I see. So there are three product managers under Jeff Hines, plus the market researcher?

CN: That's right. We're a small team but AZTEC operates in a specialty market - we're not big.

JP: If you don't mind me asking, just how big are you?

CN: You mean in revenue terms . . . gee . . . I'd have to check . . . I guess $20 million last year.

JP: That's not so small.

CN: In our line of business it is. We're a small player.

JP: OK. Now what can you tell me about the new line?

CN: Essentially they are a range of herbal remedies which treat sickness such as headache, colds, fatigue and so on - basically the things we all suffer from!

JP: Too true . . . there's too much stress around. And you see these being sold in drug stores, over the counter?

CN: That's right. We know there's a big market out there but we're not sure the best way to pitch our promotion - that's why we've come to you.

JP: If I get your message, you're looking for the best way to tap in to the new fashion for natural cures?

CN: We don't see it as a fashion. We're serious about our products. No, we need to know more about our public - how they behave when they get sick, what do they do, what do they think.

JP: Right. Now I'm getting the picture. So we need an attitude survey to look at consumer behaviour . . .

Key – Unit 3

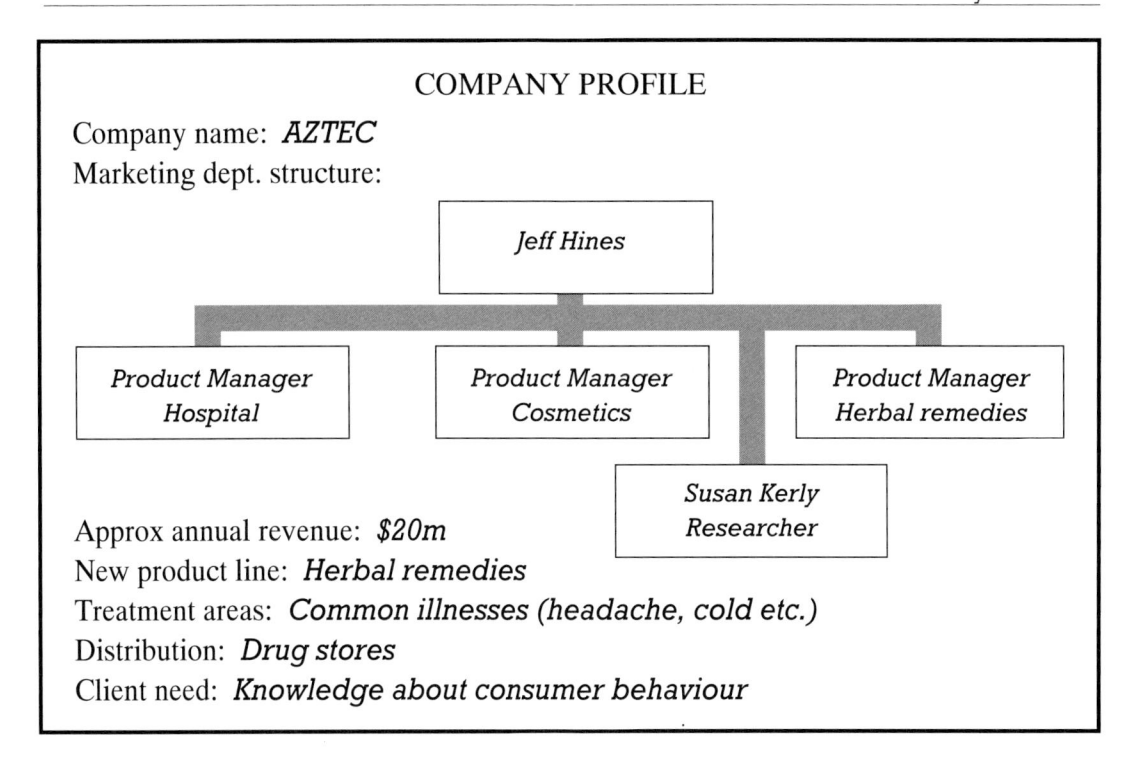

```
COMPANY PROFILE
```

Company name: *AZTEC*
Marketing dept. structure:

```
                    Jeff Hines
        ┌───────────────┼───────────────┐
  Product Manager  Product Manager  Product Manager
     Hospital        Cosmetics      Herbal remedies
                         │
                    Susan Kerly
                     Researcher
```

Approx annual revenue: *$20m*
New product line: *Herbal remedies*
Treatment areas: *Common illnesses (headache, cold etc.)*
Distribution: *Drug stores*
Client need: *Knowledge about consumer behaviour*

Question tags

Exercise 1

1. Your family hold all the equity, don't they?
2. You didn't export anything last year, did you?
3. You will appoint an agent in the UK, won't you?
4. They haven't appointed an agent yet, have they?
5. Your company is based in the south west, isn't it?
6. You weren't interested in a joint venture, were you?

Question words

Exercise 2

1. How much do they cost?
2. Where will they be sold?
3. What type of illnesses do they treat?
4. How often do they get them?
5. How long does the treatment last?
6. How old is an average consumer?

Key – Unit 3

Polite questions

Exercise 3

1. Might I ask you if you have plans to expand?
2. Could I ask you what your profits were last year?
3. Would you mind telling me what sort of problems you have with suppliers?
4. I wonder if I could ask you how much you exported last year?

Responding to questions

Exercise 4

1. Yes, that's right.
2. Please go ahead.
3. No, that's not true.
4. I'm afraid I don't have the figures on me.
5. I see.

PUT IT ON PAPER

Model 1

Comprehension

1. Question 1 is looking for (a) a definition of alternative medicine.
2. For Question 2 the survey hopes to get a negative answer.
3. In order to confirm that people take a lot/too many drugs.
4. It means that people are seeking alternative solutions.
5. This question is important because they want to sell the herbal remedies direct to the consumer.
6. They are trying to establish whether there is any price resistance to their products.

Vocabulary development

Verb	Noun	Adjective
to satisfy	satisfaction	satisfactory
to prescribe	prescription	prescriptive
to advise	advice	advisory
to consult	consultation/consultant	consultative
to imagine	imagination	imaginative/imaginable
to prepare	preparation	preparatory
to cure	cure	curative

Model 2

Comprehension

1. (a) delivery cost included.
2. (c) British Standard.
3. (c) margin of profitability.
4. The hotel she stayed in.

Vocabulary development

1. to look after   (e) Take care of the children.
2. to look forward to   (g) I can't wait to see you again.
3. to look at   (f) Don't stare at me.

Key – Unit 3

4. to look into (a) We must study this in greater depth.
5. to look for (b) I've been searching for it.
6. to look up (d) Why don't you find it in the directory?
7. to look through (c) You just need to scan the book.

Expressing frequency

Exercise 1

(Definite frequency)

1. We hold a meeting annually.
2. We organize a quarterly social event.
3. I produce the company newsletter monthly.
4. We are now planning our twice-yearly/half-yearly conference.
5. Every four months, we have a strategy meeting.

(Indefinite frequency)

6. I scarcely ever leave the office before eight.
7. I'm almost always the first to leave.
8. Usually/Normally, we have lunch in the canteen.
9. I seldom/infrequently eat out.

Adverbs of time

Exercise 2

1. It's 9.40. The bank still hasn't opened!
2. It's 9.40. The bank hasn't opened yet!
3. It's 9.40. The bank's still closed!
4. It's 15.25. The bank's already closed!
5. It's 15.25. It should still be open.
6. It's 15.25. It shouldn't have closed yet!

Question types

Exercise 3

1. Open
2. Encouraging
3. Leading
4. Closed
5. Open
6. Leading

Formal/informal language

Exercise 4

1. I'm afraid I can't come to the meeting.
2. Please could you send the package on?
3. I hope we have the chance to return/repay your kindness.
4. I'm sorry the delivery's late.

Key – Unit 3

THE BUSINESS INTERVIEW

Talking about the market

Recording script

Caroline, can you tell us something about your company, what its products are and who you sell to?

The company is a middle-sized limited company. We manufacture disposable tableware which incorporates products such as plastic cutlery, bar accessories, airline trays and the like. We mainly operate through distributor networks both at home and overseas, rather than agents because they are stockists locally and will import container loads of product. We are mainly supplying into Europe; we do supply more exotic places such as the Caribbean, the Middle East. But with a low unit cost product obviously the further we export the more expensive the freight becomes.

What about some of the differences in selling techniques in different parts of the world?

Well, obviously every region and every country has its differences, its certain flavour if you like, but I suppose if we were looking in Europe you would say that possibly in Scandinavia they were more interested in the quality of the product. They will listen to the benefits and it's quite important to build a case around the benefits you can sell them around a certain product. In southern Europe, in Spain and Italy I would say they are more price-conscious. And then possibly if you look to the Middle East, people tend I think to not like you trying to sell to them - in the sense that they will look at the range of products that you have, they will make a choice, and the harder you try and push something you are less likely to actually make that sale. So I think they are the three main areas that I would have noticed.

Finally, what sort of characteristics do you think are essential in a successful international salesperson?

They have to be able to communicate and have an ability to get on with people. I think the people concerned would have to be independent, be able to make their own decisions, negotiate at a higher level possibly in the fact you would be dealing with managing directors or chairmen of companies very often . . .

Whereas in this country, you'd be . . .

Key – Unit 3

... You'd possibly just be dealing with a normal buyer. I think obviously language is essential if you are trying to sell to a country, to have an understanding if not a very good level of language of that particular country helps, and that obviously links with the cultural background of the country as well. I think they have to be tenacious and stick at it. For example I have just recently set up a contract. I have been talking with this large manufacturing company for nearly five years. They have just signed a contract for supplying one of the largest supermarket chains in France with a range of plastic cutlery.

So, a happy ending.

Well hopefully yes, hopefully!

As you listen...

(Answers)

1. It is a middle-sized, limited company. They manufacture disposable tableware such as plastic cutlery, bar accessories, airline trays.

2. Mainly through distributors. They supply mainly into Europe, but also to the Caribbean and the Middle East.

3. In northern Europe they are more interested in quality. In southern Europe they are more price-conscious. In the Middle East they do not like you trying too hard to sell to them (pushing them) - they prefer to look at your range and make their own choice.

4. They should be able to communicate and to get on with people. They should be independent and able to make their own decisions. They should also be able to negotiate at a higher level than they may need to in the home market. They should have some understanding of the language and culture of the country they are selling to. They have to be tenacious, to 'stick at it'.

5. Talking to a large manufacturing company for five years before signing a contract for supplying one of the largest supermarket chains in France with a range of plastic cutlery.

UNIT 4

MANAGING PROJECTS

SAY WHAT YOU MEAN

Extract 1

Recording script

CH: It's good to see you again, Paolo. Do sit down. How was your trip over?

PL: Fine. The weather's better here than in Florence!

CH: That makes a change. I don't think you've met Suzanne. She's our senior engineer on this project.

PL: How do you do, Suzanne (shaking hands).

SK: Nice to meet you, Paolo.

CH: Anyway, we're very short of time this morning so I suggest we get straight down to business. I've called this meeting to finalize the timing on this project. We've basically got two items on our agenda today - firstly, the construction schedule and secondly, and very important, the schedule of payments. Are there any other items, Paolo, you want to put on the agenda?

PL: There is just one. I'd like to discuss the whole issue of the project management.

CH: I'm not sure I understand.

PL: Well I think it's vital we all agree on the decision-making process for the project.

CH: I see. Fine. Well, we'll take that at the end. Right, let's take the first item - project timing. Suzanne, you've brought along the project planner. Would you like to take us through it?

SK: Certainly. Can you both see if I put it up here?

PL & CH: Yes, that's fine.

SK: Well, as you can see, I've divided the planner into three periods - January to March, April to June and finally July and August. So, starting in the first week of January, we need to have approved your final design plans, Paolo.

Key – Unit 4

PL: That's as we agreed.

SK: So I believe. Then, the next phase - that's scheduled to take us up to the end of January, we plan to complete the excavation work.

CH: So, Paolo, we'd like you on site again at the beginning of February for the laying of foundations.

SK: That's right, we reckon this stage will take six weeks, taking us up to mid-March - that includes all the basic supplies - mains electricity, water, drainage.

PL: May I just interrupt?

SK: Of course.

PL: You don't want me here for all that time, do you?

CH: Of course not, two or three visits should be enough just to check on the work.

PL: Fine. So mid-March is the deadline for completion of the foundations?

SK: Yes, we've allowed a couple of weeks leeway before work begins on the next phase. As you know, we've decided to break the building of the complex into two stages. We aim to start by 1st April on the water sports area - that's the swimming pools, chutes, sauna etc. We've allowed a further two months for this work, before we start work on the main sports hall.

PL: So that brings us up to the beginning of June?

SK: That's right. We're still in the second period I mentioned at the start - the construction phase. That leaves us June for the sports hall.

PL: Suzanne, I'd want to be on site throughout this construction phase.

CH: Of course, we thought you would. You'll share an office with Suzanne, on site.

PL: That's fine.

SK: Good, that brings me to the final phase which we've set aside for all the internal work - decoration and finishing. We thought two weeks for all the surface decoration - that's plastering, tiling

Key – Unit 4

and painting, then a further four weeks for all the fixtures and fittings.

PL: That sounds about right. If you don't mind, I'd like to send my partner, Francesca Rizzardi, over for that part of the project. As you know, she did all the work on the design spec for it.

CH: That makes sense. Suzanne, can I just add a very important point? This schedule is very tight. We all have to remember that our client has put some very tough penalty clauses in the contract for any delays - so, for all our sakes, it's essential that we don't go over deadline.

SK: That's one reason why we've allowed an extra two weeks at the end of August for any unforeseen problems.

CH: Yes, I'm worried about that. It doesn't seem long enough to me.

SK: Oh, I don't foresee any major problems. There really shouldn't be any trouble meeting our 1st September completion date.

CH: It's good to hear you sound so optimistic! Right, so if there aren't any other questions, let's move on to the next item . . .

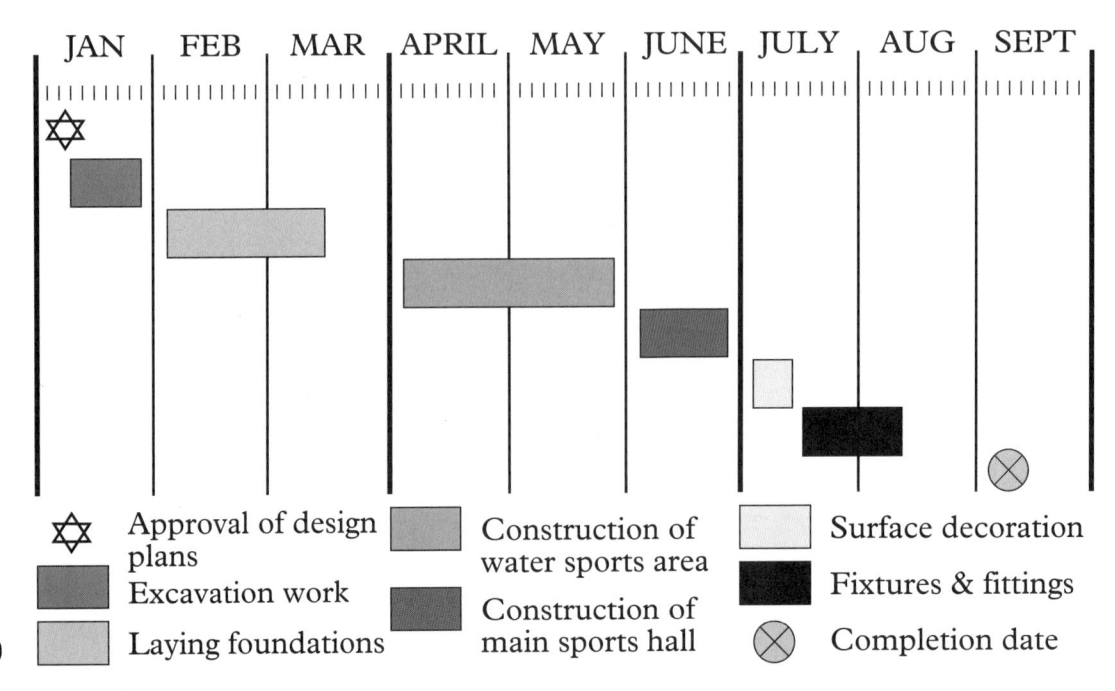

| JAN | FEB | MAR | APRIL | MAY | JUNE | JULY | AUG | SEPT |

✡ Approval of design plans
▪ Excavation work
▫ Laying foundations
▪ Construction of water sports area
▪ Construction of main sports hall
▫ Surface decoration
▪ Fixtures & fittings
⊗ Completion date

Extract 2

Recording script

HS: OK, can I just summarize where we've got to? We've agreed that we should set up our first quality circle in the finishing plant. The target for the group will be to reduce process loss rates from around 8% to under 3% over the next 12 months. What we need to decide now is who's in the group, how often they should meet and how they should work. Let's take the question of who's in the group first. Pete?

PD: Well, I reckon Stephen should be team-leader.

SC: I'm not so sure. As I understand it, the group should try to establish their own initiatives. I don't think my presence would help.

HS: Why do you say that? They're going to need some guidance. You've got experience in this area. You'll be able to point them in the right direction.

SC: I think you misunderstood me. The guys in the finishing plant are a pretty independent bunch - sure, we can give them some guidelines - but they'll work best if they're left to sort the problem out themselves.

HS: Well, you know them best.

PD: But we can't have them all sitting around talking about reducing loss rates - there won't be any production at all, if they do that.

HS: Come on Pete, nobody's suggesting that. There shouldn't be more than five or six in the circle anyway.

PD: So, who's going to decide who's in the team?

SC: I think we should leave it to them.

HS: We could certainly give them a chance to choose.

PD: You got to be joking. These guys aren't used to making decisions like that.

HS: Then it's time they started to get used to it. You are not going to improve quality without commitment from your production workers. The best way to get commitment is to involve them in the process, from the start. I agree with Stephen.

PD: Look, I know these guys. They couldn't give a damn about quality circles.

Key – Unit 4

HS: We've got to give them the chance, Pete. It's the only way that it's going to work. Stephen, can you organize a preliminary meeting to explain the objectives of the quality circle and get them to select their representatives?

SC: Certainly, I'll do that. I'll fix it for Friday.

HS: Good. Let's move on to the second question - how often they're going to meet and how they will work. Stephen, any ideas?

SC: If we plan regular weekly meetings for them, I can do some training on quality analysis and decision-making with them at the first real meeting.

HS: So ... that would be the week after next - you could report back to us the following week - say Monday, April 6?

SC: Yes, that sounds reasonable. Don't expect any miracles - it's going to take time getting this going.

PD: You bet. You guys have no idea.

HS: All right, Pete. You've made your position perfectly clear. We've agreed to give it a try, haven't we? Let me just go over what we've agreed to do. First, we're going to set up the first experimental quality circle in the finishing plant - the objective will be to reduce process loss rates from 8 to 3% over the next 12 months.

PD: That's one hell of a target!

HS: It's in line with the loss rates in our other plants.

PD: But they're not in the same business.

HS: Pete, could you drop it? I don't think your attitude is helping. So, what was I saying? Yes ... we will form a quality circle in the finishing plant with five or six group members who are self-selected. Stephen will call a preliminary meeting this Friday - that's March 27 - to explain the objectives to the finishing plant team and get them to select their representatives. The following Friday Stephen will do some training with them, then report back to us on Monday April 6 ...

Key – Unit 4

True or false?

1. No.
2. Yes.
3. No.
4. No.
5. No.
6. Yes.
7. Yes.
8. Yes.

Prepositions of time

Exercise 1

1. at
2. by
3. to
4. in/during
5. in/by
6. at/on
7. throughout
8. in/by

Future: 'will' and 'going to'

Exercise 2

A: What are you going to do at the weekend?

B: I'm going to go away to visit friends.

A: Oh, are you going to drive?

B: No, I'm going to take the train.

A: How long will/does the journey take?

B: Normally it will take/it takes 2 hours.

A: And what are you going to do with your friends?

B: I'm going to relax, take it easy.

A: Sounds great. Before you go, could you just finish those letters for me.

B: Certainly, I'll do them now.

Key – Unit 4

Chairing meetings (1)

Exercise 3

1. I'd like to introduce our new colleague from Germany.
2. Have you all seen a copy of the agenda?
3. I've called this meeting to discuss the new plant location.
4. There are three items of business on the agenda; firstly, the cost.
5. Right. Let's look at the first item on the agenda.
6. Philip, would you like to add anything?
7. I think that covers everything on that point. Let's move on to item 2.
8. We're running short of time.

Chairing meetings (2)

Exercise 4

1. What exactly do you mean by management style?
2. I'm afraid we're getting off the point.
3. Thank you Pete. Could we move on now?
4. Could you leave that now? We're running short of time.
5. So let me summarize what we've agreed.
6. That just about covers everything. Let's call it a day.

Key – Unit 4

PUT IT ON PAPER

Model 1

Comprehension
1. No.
2. It can be fed by tree bark.
3. Because they plan to install another paper machine (they say 'the first paper machine').
4. No.
5. No.

Vocabulary development
1. an update, to update, up-to-date, out-of-date, outdated
2. on schedule, as scheduled, behind schedule, ahead of schedule
3. according to plan, as planned

Model 2

Comprehension
1. The written record of a meeting.
2. Because they need to increase quality/reduce process losses.
3. They are going to select themselves.
4. In order to train the members.

Vocabulary development

1. to attend — (e) to go to a meeting
2. to be present — (i) to be at a meeting
3. apologies for absence — (h) notification you cannot attend
4. the agenda — (a) the order of business
5. the minutes — (f) the written record
6. the chairman — (c) the person in charge
7. actions — (b) steps to be taken
8. an item — (g) a point for discussion
9. to table — (d) to raise an issue/point
10. to adjourn — (j) to close a meeting with the plan to meet again

Key – Unit 4

Continuous tenses

Exercise 1

1. In June I was working in Seville.
2. At the moment I'm drinking a cup of coffee.
3. In the second half of the year, we will be selling 500 units a week.
4. For the time being, I am working in our French subsidiary.
5. I was leaving Germany when the terrorists kidnapped an industrialist.
6. I know I will be working very hard next week when the negotiations start.

Verbs of reporting

Exercise 2

1. He denied saying that in court.
2. He warned us of the danger of bankruptcy.
3. She showed us/demonstrated how to connect the machine.
4. He advised me to take a holiday.
5. She insisted that I move my office.
6. He approved the product.

Writing for different audiences

Exercise 3

(Progress report)

Despite some very bad weather in December and February, the mill construction is on schedule.

An update on how the work is progressing:

January: Installation of the central boiler began, as planned.

February: Installation of the wood-store equipment began.

March: This month administrative and technical staff will be moving into their new office block.

April: This looks like being our busiest phase so far. The paper machine will be arriving for installation over the next few months. In addition, we plan to complete site work on the water treatment plant and the paper recycling warehouse.

Writing minutes

Exercise 4

(Minutes of meeting)

Present: Chris Hughes, Suzanne King (Britbuild)
           Paolo Lombardi

Subject: Leisure Complex Project

1. Project Timing

For detailed schedule, see project planner attached.

We agreed that Paolo should visit the site two or three times during the excavation phase from February to March. Paolo confirmed that he would be present on site throughout the construction phase.

It was agreed that Francesca Rizzardi would supervise on site the final phase of the project - decoration and fittings.

Chris Hughes reminded the meeting of the importance of not going over the deadlines because of the severe penalties resulting from any delay.

2. Schedule of payments

3. Project management - decision-making process

Key – Unit 4

THE BUSINESS INTERVIEW

Talking about project management

Recording script

Dale, can you give us some examples of your company's involvement in international project management?

Certainly John. ORMS is slightly unusual in that it provides a very wide range of skills in the building industry. We don't focus solely on project management, we've also involved ourselves in design, corporate identity across a broad range of projects, so we are currently involved in an office building in Berlin, development of Marseilles airport and some hotel work in Jidda.

Oh I see, so it's a very international organization.

We try to make it so.

Right. What would you say the key to success is for a project manager?

The key for a project manager is to be the glue for the team. A team will be made up from a group of people who probably haven't worked together before and the project manager has to bring this team together and make it a whole, he must make the whole greater than the sum of the parts.

How does he go about doing that?

He has to be the person who has the overview, who has a clear vision of the client's requirements and take each of the specialists and energize them into helping the team create a better product.

What would you say some of the pitfalls are in this area, and how do you set about trying to minimize those pitfalls?

Pitfalls can generally be blamed on lack of communication. Somewhere down the line within the team, somebody hasn't talked to somebody else at the right time and the project manager has to be the person who sees that happening. He can't prevent it, it will always happen, but a manager can make these crises molehills rather than mountains.

Do you have any sort of techniques for ensuring that all mistakes are picked up before it's too late?

Key – Unit 4

The principal technique is to balance a vision for where the project is going with a very good programme. One must have clearly set out a series of stepping stones along your route completing the project and each of those stepping stones must have an end in itself.

And that you liaise with your specialists and with your clients every step along the way?

We like to achieve a finished product on each step, a report maybe or a stage during the project in which everything can come together, can be brought together, and you can produce a document or a report or a presentation which allows everybody to refocus their energies.

So these would be reports or presentations to the client, would they?

Not just the client, they would involve all members of all the design teams. It's terribly important that the people working on the project in each of the individual offices understand the whole, the whole purpose of the project.

So that everybody knows where they stand?

Yes.

As you listen... (Answers)

1. office building in Berlin

    development of Marseilles airport

    hotel work in Jidda

2. To be the glue for his team/To bring the team together and make the whole greater than the sum of its parts.

3. Lack of communication.

4. (a) having a series of stepping-stone targets.

5. By organizing finished 'products' on each step of the programme, for example a report or a presentation.

6. To the client, but also to all members of the design team.

UNIT 5
RESULTS AND FORECASTS

SAY WHAT YOU MEAN

Extract 1

Recording script

AS: Yes, so we were quite surprised to get your letter.

MC: Well, in our opinion, it's better to be cautious. That's why we've invited you in, just to review the situation.

AS: I know, but it implies that something's gone wrong.

MC: Well I'm sure you'll feel differently at the end of the meeting. Perhaps we could start.

AS: Right.

MC: Just the most important details.

PB: Right.

AS: Good.

MC: If we start at the top, the first figure is the turnover for the period - with the previous year shown next to it in brackets.

PB: So we achieved a fairly healthy increase.

MC: Yes. Now firstly we've got the gross turnover, but it's this second figure, the net turnover, which is more significant.

AS: I see.

MC: Now let's look at some of your outgoings. So, here we've got your major expenses. The third important figure is the fees you pay to your freelancers. As I see it, that's gone up quite a lot compared to last year.

AS: We realized that.

MC: The fourth big figure is salaries. That too has shown a pretty substantial rise. Can I ask, any particular reason for that?

AS: Well, I tend to think it's the additional clerical staff we took on at the beginning of last year, isn't it?

PB: Yes.

MC: I see. Well, let's skip the next few figures. Right, fifthly there is advertising and promotion. This one has really shot up.

PB: Yes, we have invested quite a lot there. Mainly in advertising. Back in the old days, we didn't need to. The clients just came to us.

MC: Well, it's certainly bumped up your expenses.

AS: I feel we'll just have to be a bit more careful in the future.

MC: Yes, quite. But if we can move on, the figure that worries me most is up here under direct costs, this sixth one: directors' fees.

PB: Well, it's very simple. At the beginning we never took anything out of the company. All that effort for little return.

MC: Well, I really think we will have to review this figure very carefully. Added together, we get this figure here - number seven: the total expenses for the period. And, if we deduct all the expenses from the net turnover, we get the net profit, number eight here.

PB: Well, we knew it would be down on last year.

MC: So, what we've got to do is get a hold . . . (fade)

Key – Unit 5

PEOPLEPOWER
PROFIT & LOSS

			This year	Last year
	Income			
1	☐	Gross turnover	445,482	425,815
2	☐	Cost of sales	46,183	38,514
	☐	Net turnover	399,299	387,301
	Direct Costs			
3	☐	Fees – freelancers	196,433	168,792
6	☐	Fees – directors	90,000	45,000
			286,433	213,792
	Expenses			
4	☐	Salaries	32,500	24,500
	☐	Rent	20,000	19,000
	☐	Telecommunications	8,423	7,180
5	☐	Advertising and promotion	15,903	8,715
7			76,826	59,395
	Depreciation			
	☐	Equipment	7,517	6,168
	☐	Fixtures	2,319	2,041
			9,836	8,209
8	☐	Net profit	26,204	105,905

Key – Unit 5

Extract 2

Recording script

JS: OK folks, I'd like to start with the regional forecasts for the coming year. I have my map here so that we can see who's proposing what for where. Although the market is pretty tight at the moment, I know that you guys have been in there, pitching pretty hard. So, let's keep up the good work. Jimmy, what have you got for us?

J: OK, the East Coast. As Hank said, competition is real stiff out there, but I've got a helluva team of salesmen working with me. So, for next year I'm going to stick my neck out and say we are definitely going to increase sales by 5%.

JS: Jim, a fine start. So, you're convinced you can make 5%?

J: That's my minimum. If one or two of my prospects come good, then I'm likely to hit 6% or I could even reach 7%.

JS: Excellent, Jim, the map's looking pretty good. Denise, what have you got?

D: Well, as I'm sure you guys all know, the Mid-West is really down right now.

JS: Denise, I totally accept that industry is down, but I can't agree with you that the situation is hopeless. We've got many fine and loyal customers out there.

D: With due respect, Joe, many of our customers are suffering just as much as we are.

JS: So?

D: Well, for next year I can't offer an increase in sales. If my calculations are correct, I might manage to repeat this year's sales. And that's based on our best scenario.

JS: Well, Denise, I'm very disappointed. The soundings I've had indicate that things are improving.

D: Up to a point I'd agree with you, but it's going to take time. In fact I think we're unlikely to see any change until the last quarter of next year.

JS: OK, Denise, we'll talk about that later. George, how are things shaping up around the West Coast?

G: We're doing fine. Our patch is fairly small, but our customers are holding up well. So, sales are bound to increase by at least 7%.

Key – Unit 5

JS: George, I really can't go along with your modest forecast. You're sitting on our best customers in a prime area and all you can offer is 7%.

G: Well, that's my worst case scenario …

JS: Listen, George, modest forecasts didn't get us where we are today! You've got to think big.

G: OK, but I definitely can't make more than 10%. That's the best scenario.

JS: So what's the best you'd be satisfied with?

G: Well, let's say 8.5%.

JS: That's better, George. Keep up the good work. Right, Paul, over to you for …

Answers

	West Coast	**Mid-West**	**East Coast**
Best:	**+10%**	**0%**	**+7%**
Medium:	**+8.5%**		**+6%**
Worst:	**+7%**		**+5%**

Present perfect and past simple

Exercise 1

1. Since last year our expenses have dropped.
2. Two months ago we recruited a new secretary.
3. Since then we have raised productivity.
4. So, you are with Smith & Partners. How long have you been there?
5. Oh, I have worked there for two years now.

Forecasting

Exercise 2

1. Our costs are likely to increase.
2. We may reduce our expenses.

Key – Unit 5

3. Overheads are unlikely to rise.
4. We are bound to increase our gross profit.
5. But we can't possibly raise our percentage profit.

Giving opinions

Exercise 3

1. As I see it the short-term future isn't healthy.
2. I feel the medium term looks better.
3. As I see it the local economy will improve.
4. I really think in the long term we are in a strong position.
5. I'm inclined to think the best policy is to maintain our prices.

Agreeing and disagreeing

Exercise 4

1. I fully agree with you.
2. I totally accept that.
3. Up to a point I'd agree with you, but I think we should continue the investments.
4. I'm afraid I can't accept that.
5. To a certain extent I'd accept that, but it will grow in the near future.
6. I'm afraid I can't go along with you on that.

Key – Unit 5

PUT IT ON PAPER

Model 1

Comprehension

1. (b) a snapshot of the company's financial position at a certain date
2. (b) owns
3. (a) a long-term basis
4. (a) can be easily converted into cash
5. (b) the cost to buy the company's assets
6. (b) the financial situation of the company

Vocabulary development

1. Tangible assets — (c) hardware owned by the company and used to operate its activities
2. Loans — (e) money your company has borrowed
3. Stock — (h) value of goods ready for sale
4. Liabilities — (f) money owed by your company
5. Debtors — (g) people who owe money to you
6. Creditors — (a) people to whom your company owes money
7. Due — (i) owed, which must be paid
8. Net — (d) after all deductions have been made
9. Provisions — (b) money set aside for liabilities that cannot be accurately forecast

Model 2

Comprehension

1. Shareholder.
2. The fact that the Berball ranges have all continued to increase market share.
3. Slowing it down.
4. Market leader.

Key – Unit 5

Vocabulary development

Verb	Noun	Adjective
impress	impression	impressive
continue	continuation	continued
prove	proof	proven
maximize/maximise	maximum	maximum
profit	profit	profitable
produce	productivity	productive
assure	assurance	assured
lead	leader	leading

Reviewing tenses

Exercise 1

1. will have to
2. am writing
3. has performed
4. turned round
5. gave
6. has today become
7. was
8. had to
9. agree
10. are beginning
11. will continue
12. started
13. have done
14. will share
15. wish

Giving good and bad news

Exercise 2

1. I regret to inform you that your job application has been unsuccessful.
2. We are pleased to advise you that we have accepted your offer.
3. Regrettably, we are unable to use your services.
4. I am delighted to welcome you to our team.
5. I am sorry I was not able to attend the meeting last week.

207

Key – Unit 5

Individual and company letters

Exercise 3

1. Dear Sirs,
    We regret to inform you that …

2. Gentlemen
    We are writing to inform you that …

3. Dear Mrs Brown,
    I am pleased to tell you that …

4. Dear Sir,
    We are sorry to advise you that …

5. Dear Madam,
    I am writing to inform you that …

Key – Unit 5

THE BUSINESS INTERVIEW

Planning for the future

Recording script

Jonathan, can you tell us a little bit about your background experience as a financial manager?

Certainly. I've been working for United Biscuits for about three years. I'm responsible for financial and management accounting at a group level, so I'm responsible for putting together information every month for the directors - and also every year in our reports to the shareholders.

Where were you before you joined UB?

Well, before UB I worked for one of the big accounting firms, in London where I trained, and then in New York.

So you've got a good experience of both sides of the Atlantic?

Yes, I've certainly seen the other side of the Atlantic.

Right . . . What would you say that the key is to successful financial reporting?

Well, one of the things that concerns me most as someone who receives information from around the world is that the information arrives on time - because if I am kept waiting then our shareholders or our directors may be kept waiting. Another thing I think is very important is accuracy. Clearly we want the information to be in compliance with our reporting policies.

And is reporting the same the world over do you think, or do you get reports in different formats from different parts of the world?

The formats are the same and they follow the group financial policy. However, there may be other reasons that companies do reporting locally, and they may have different rules to apply . . . locally.

Can you give us an example of that – what might be different?

Well, for example in France the focus tends to be much more on tax and reporting for tax purposes . . . they have a chart of accounts that they use that matches those requirements. Here in the UK the focus is much more on reporting on the stewardship of assets to shareholders.

I see . . .

Key – Unit 5

And that gives a different emphasis.

Yes . . . and what sort of things can go wrong in financial reporting? Why would they go wrong?

The rules are not always understood. We use different rules for accounting in the UK than some of our subsidiaries use overseas, and it's important that we and they understand what their methods are and also what they're required to do to satisfy our requirements.

Do you ever get into problems in terminology?

We certainly can do. You might expect that you would with the French or with the Germans; we tend to quite a bit with the Americans as well.

In what way?

Because we use different terms for the same things. We talk about stocks and they talk about inventories; we talk about provisions as being something that appears in the balance sheet and they will tend to talk about it as something that appears in the profit and loss account. We can get very mixed up over it! ... So when talking to the Americans I very often got involved in late night long distance transatlantic telephone conversations, with me trying to explain what I mean and them trying to explain what they mean.

So confusions can occur even between two English-speaking countries?

Indeed they can.

As you listen . . .

(Answers)

1. He is responsible for financial and management accounting at a group level.

2. Information should arrive on time, and it should be accurate (in other words, presented 'in compliance with our reporting policies').

3. (b) Different countries may have different emphases in their reporting.

4. | **Br. Eng.** | **Am. Eng.** |
   |---|---|
   | Stocks | Inventories |
   | Provisions appear in the balance sheet | Provisions appear in the profit and loss account |

UNIT 6
CUSTOMER SERVICE

SAY WHAT YOU MEAN

Extract 1

Recording script

(Re - Receptionist,
SA - Sales assistant)

Re: Bootit Computer Supplies. Good morning.

FB: Good morning. Could you put me through to your sales department.

Re: What's it in connection with?

FB: I'd like to speak to someone about bubble jet printers.

Re: Just one moment, sir.

SA: Sales. Can I help you?

FB: Yes, I'm ringing about the Smithson Bubble Jet printer.

SA: Yes, sir. Which model?

FB: It's the CRAIII.

SA: Yes, sir. What would you like to know?

fB: I'd like to check what after-sales service you offer.

SA: Well, during the first 24 months you are covered by the manufacturer's warranty and . . .

FB: And what exactly does that cover?

SA: Well, let me see. Yes, basically if it breaks down within the first two years, the manufacturer will repair it or replace it.

FB: So, it's covered for breakdowns for two years.

SA: That's right - within the UK, that is.

FB: Ah, but I'll be travelling with it. So, what would happen if it broke down abroad?

Key – Unit 6

SA: As far as I can tell, sir, if it broke down outside the UK, you wouldn't be covered.

FB: Well, that's not very good news for a portable printer. Are there any other exclusions?

SA: Let me see. Covered for all normal operations and . . .

FB: Excuse me, what does that mean?

SA: Well, if the breakdown happens during normal operations, Smithson will repair or replace it.

FB: I'm sorry, what are non-normal operations?

SA: Well, if you used non-standard parts or non-recommended paper, then you wouldn't be covered.

FB: You mean if I don't buy Smithson's consumables?

SA: Exactly, sir.

FB: OK, I see. I have another question.

SA: Yes, sir?

FB: Is a service included?

SA: 'Fraid not, sir. And it says that servicing must be carried out at regular intervals. If not, then the warranty may be invalid.

FB: Right, I think I've got the picture. So, I would be covered for breakdown in the UK as long as I am using the printer according to Smithson's instructions and with their consumables.

SA: That's right, sir.

FB: Well, that's all I need to know for now.

SA: OK, sir. And if you need any more information, I'll be happy to answer your questions. By the way, my name's Andrew.

FB: OK, thanks.

SA: Not at all.

FB: Bye.

SA: Bye.

Key – Unit 6

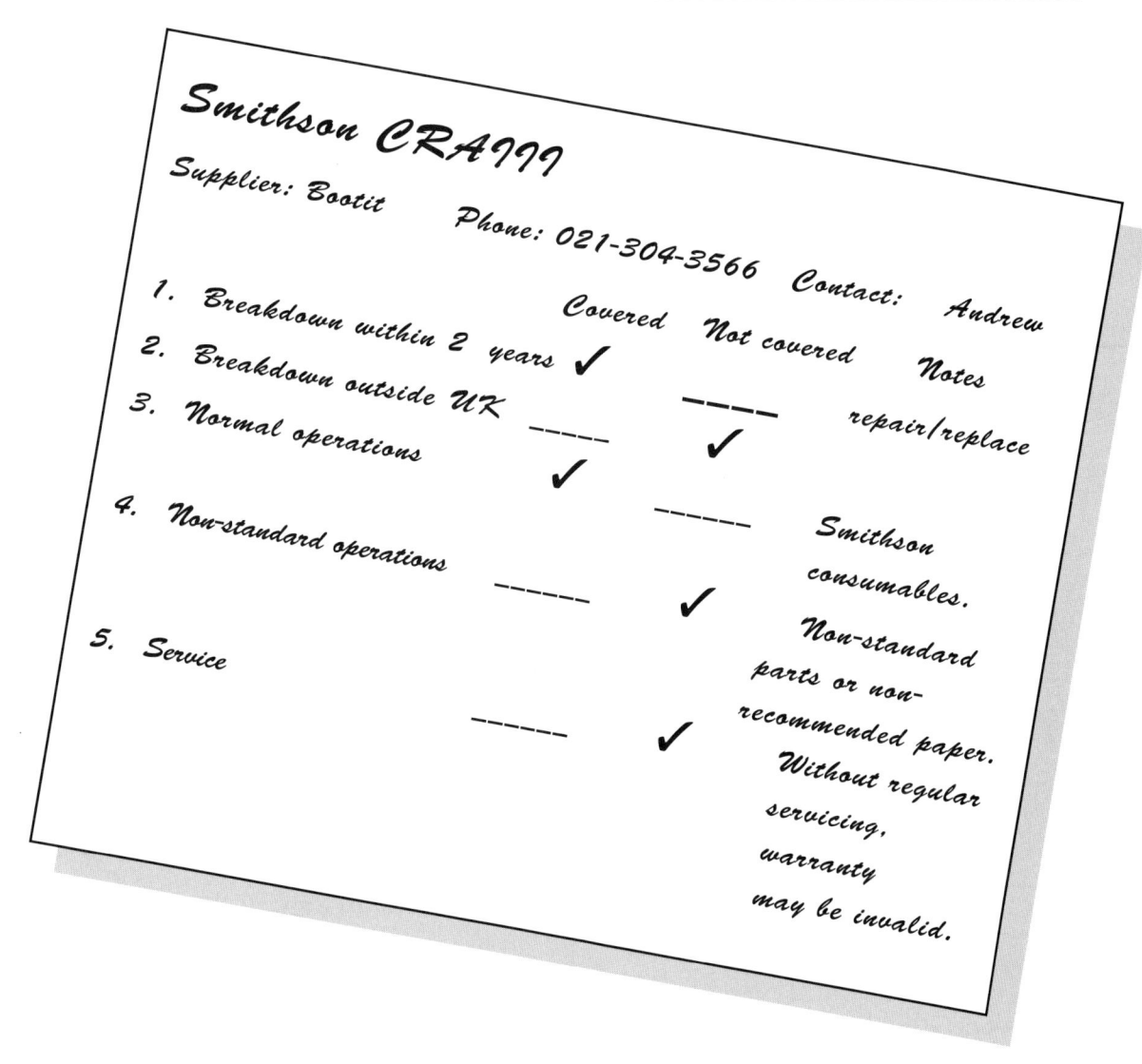

Smithson CR999

Supplier: Bootit   Phone: 021-304-3566   Contact: Andrew

	Covered	Not covered	Notes
1. Breakdown within 2 years	✓	-----	repair/replace
2. Breakdown outside UK	-----	✓	
3. Normal operations	✓	-----	
4. Non-standard operations	-----	✓	Smithson consumables. Non-standard parts or non-recommended paper.
5. Service	-----	✓	Without regular servicing, warranty may be invalid.

Extract 2

Recording script

(FC - first clerk,
SC - second clerk,
TC - third clerk)

FC: Claims department, Harry Malone. How can I help you?

JK: Good morning. My name is Josephine King. I sent in a claim form to you some three months ago.

FC: I'm sorry, could I have your name again, please?

JK: Yes, it's Mrs Josephine King.

FC: Could you spell that, please?

JK: Yes, it's K-I-N-G.

FC: OK, Mrs King, and what type of claim was it?

Key – Unit 6

JK: For lost luggage.

FC: Oh, excuse me Mrs King, was this a vacation insurance policy?

JK: Yes, exactly.

FC: Then you should be talking to our vacation claims department. Would you like me to connect you?

JK: Yes, thanks.

SC: Good morning, Mrs King, how can I help you?

JK: As I was just saying to your co-worker, we lost our luggage on vacation and put in a claim about three months ago.

SC: And where did the loss take place?

JK: At Guarulhos airport.

SC: I'm sorry, I didn't catch that.

JK: Guarulhos airport in São Paulo just after ...

SC: Excuse me, Mrs King, this is the domestic claims desk.

JK: So, who should I be speaking to?

SC: To foreign vacation claims. Shall I connect you?

JK: Yes.

TC: Good morning, is this Mrs King?

JK: Yes, it is. So when are you going to straighten this out?

TC: I'm sorry, Mrs King, but I don't quite understand the problem.

JK: It's very simple. I lost some luggage on vacation.

TC: I'm still not entirely clear on this, Mrs King. What exactly is the problem?

JK: You haven't settled the claim.

TC: Well, if you could give me some more details, Mrs King, I'll check out what happened to your claim.

Key – Unit 6

JK: But I sent them already!

TC: Yes, but I need some details to check out what's happened to your claim on the computer.

JK: OK, OK.

TC: So, Mrs King, where did the loss happen?

JK: At Guarulhos airport in São Paulo.

TC: Can you spell it, please?

JK: Yes, it's G-U-A-R-U-L-H-O-S.

TC: OK, I got that. And when exactly did you send the claim?

JK: The 12th of January.

TC: And could you spell your name for me?

JK: Yes, it's K-I-N-G.

TC: And your first name?

JK: Josephine. That's J-O-S-E-P-H-I-N-E.

TC: OK, I got that but I can't see any record of your claim on my computer. Just leave …

JK: What do you mean you can't find it?

TC: Just leave it with me, Mrs King, and I'll check it out and call you right back. Where can I reach you, Mrs King?

JK: On 234-6234. All day.

TC: OK, I'll get back to you as soon as I have some information.

JK: Thanks.

TC: You're welcome.

JK: Bye.

TC: Bye.

Key – Unit 6

COVERALL

wherever, whenever, whatever, whoever

```
First clerk's notes
Caller's name: KING
Type of policy: vacation insurance
Type of claim: lost luggage

Second clerk's notes:
Place of loss: São Paulo

Third clerk's notes:
Insured's name: JOSEPHINE KING    Tel: 234-6234
Reason for call: claim not settled
Place of loss: Guarulhos airport in São Paulo
Date of claim: 12 January
Action: check out claim and call
```

Conditional sentences

Exercise 1

1. If it broke down abroad, we wouldn't replace it.
2. We wouldn't repair it, if you didn't use our parts.
3. If you call before 10 o'clock, the engineer will come in the afternoon.
4. You could buy extra cover, if you wanted to.
5. If you buy this product, we will offer a special discount.

Offering to help

Exercise 2

1. Shall I check your records?
2. Would you like me to send you a fax?
3. Can I send you some more details?
4. I'll sort out your claim tomorrow.
5. Would you like me to put you in touch with a good lawyer?

Key – Unit 6

Structuring a phone call

Exercise 3

1. Could you put me through to the sales department, please?
2. I'm calling to ask about laptop computers.
3. And what exactly does that model cost?
4. Excuse me, what does on-site warranty mean?
5. I have another question. It's about delivery.
6. Well, that's all I need to know for now.
7. Well, thank you for the information.

Communicating by phone

Exercise 4

A: Hello, this is Ferdinand Gutierez. Listen, when are you going to sort out this bill?

B: I'm sorry, Mr Gutierez, but I don't quite understand the problem.

A: I said when are you going to pay this bill? It's shshsh months overdue.

B: I'm sorry, I didn't catch that.

A: I said it's more than two months overdue.

B: I'll look into it tomorrow. Could you spell your name for me, please?

A: Yes, it's G-U-T-I-E-R-E-Z.

B: I'm sorry, I didn't catch that. Could you repeat it, please?

A: Yes, it's G-U-T-I-E-R-E-Z. And could you spell your name for me please?

B: Yes, it's ....

A: OK, I got it. Look forward to hearing from you tomorrow then. Goodbye.

Key – Unit 6

PUT IT ON PAPER

Model 1

Comprehension

1. They thought Mr Baker had bought a laser printer; in fact he'd bought a bubble jet printer.
2. Products offered at discounted prices.
3. Because a bubble jet printer doesn't use toner.
4. £50
5. 021-567-4986

Vocabulary development

Verb	Noun	Adjective
satisfy	satisfaction	satisfied
add	addition	additional
specialize	specialist	special
advise	advice	advisable
extend	extension	extensive
register	registration	registered
use	usage	usable

Model 2

Comprehension

1. (b) the airline which transported the luggage.
2. Police certification.
3. (b) normal damage caused by use.
4. A list of all items lost, a list of all items bought and a completed claim form.
5. Firearms and illegal drugs.

Vocabulary development

1. to manage
2. image
3. package
4. damage
5. average

Key – Unit 6

6. advantage
7. percentage
8. shortage
9. message
10. to encourage

Noun + preposition/ preposition + noun

Exercise 1

1. According to our records, the following bill has not been paid.
2. I enclose a cheque for £50 for the additional cover.
3. I spoke to him on the phone last week about it.
4. The price rises have had an influence on our business.
5. There must be a reason for the delay.
6. We expect an answer to our question next week.
7. I'll send it to you by fax right away.
8. There's no need for any further discussion; we have made our decision.

Other conditional constructions

Exercise 2

1. In the event of late delivery of the goods, we reserve the right to claim compensation.
2. Unless you can provide proof, we won't pay.
3. Provided that your claim is accepted, it will be settled within 2 weeks.
4. Should you not agree with our decision, please contact our office.
5. In the case of injury, you must obtain a doctor's note.
6. Make a note of this just in case you forget it.
7. So long as you can provide new information, we will review your claim.
8. In the case of fire, leave the building immediately.

Key – Unit 6

Different communication channels

Exercise 3

1. notice — (g) information about staff training opportunities
2. phone — (f) enquiry to supplier about prices
3. face-to-face — (e) news of redundancies
4. report — (b) technical study results and conclusions
5. letter — (a) terms of a proposed contract
6. memo/e-mail — (c) reminder to managers to submit forecasts
7. presentation — (d) introduction of new company product to sales team

Expressing obligation

Exercise 4

1. You are required to obtain a doctor's note.
2. You are prohibited from transporting firearms.
3. The insurer is obliged to indemnify the insured.
4. The carrier was not obliged to pay for non-essential items.
5. The insured is not permitted to claim an unreasonable amount.

THE BUSINESS INTERVIEW

The service element

Recording script

John, how important is after-sales in your area of business, and what does it entail actually?

It's totally essential to our business. If we don't provide good after-sales service and support to our customers, then we won't get their repeat business and we won't get their word-of-mouth recommendations which will bring in more customers to our organization … It entails us answering a whole load of real or imagined problems which our customers may have with the software or the hardware that they purchased from us.

And how many of these problems are real and how many are imagined? I mean, how much of it is due to the actual machine breaking down and how much due to people just not reading their instructions carefully enough?

The majority of the problems are really imagined and are due to them not reading the manuals properly. The manuals on the whole for our particular machines - computers we deal with, which is the Mackintosh range - are exceptionally well written, but for some reason people do not read them … and they expect you to hold them by the hand and lead them through things which in most places are on the first ten pages of the manual.

So who actually does this service, and how do they do it?

Well, we employ some very good people who sit at the end of phones who are very friendly; they are courteous and they are what I would call knowledgeable generalists in that they know the computer, they know the software, and they can answer the vast majority of questions which people throw at them. And then in the background we have experts on specific topics, who can be called in if more depth is required to the problem that has been thrown at us.

And they will actually go on site presumably?

They will go on site if necessary and sort things out, and so that's not just for software, we also have hardware technicians as well.

What about customer records? What part do they play in your after-sales service?

They are very important because it enables us to know what equipment the customer has got, what problems they've had with it before, who's dealt with them before so that we can check back and find out what the sort of response was that we gave last time. And also we like to add a few little personal bits and pieces about them so we can ask them, you know, is your cat well now? and er, have you got the chimney back on after it blew off in the storm? It just lightens the conversation up a bit …

The personal touch.

The personal touch … and if we find they are aggravated, as many people can be, it helps to lighten it and we get them back on a more even course, and so it doesn't end up as a shouting match.

Who bears the cost of this service?

At the end of the day the customer, but what people don't realize is that it is expensive, and it has to be built into the cost of the equipment they buy. And this means that often what you think is a bargain may not be a bargain, because a bargain may not give you the support and service which you will require further on down the road.

Mmm. And what do you see the results of good service and support being?

As I said before, repeat business and word-of-mouth recommendation: people get a good feeling about you.

As you listen …

(Answers)

1. They won't get the repeat business (of existing customers) or word-of-mouth recommendations to bring in new customers.

2. (c) not reading the manual properly.

3. People who can answer most questions on a general level ('knowledgeable generalists'), and experts on particular topics.

4. (a) type of equipment customer has

    (b) what problems they have had before

    (c) who has dealt with them before

    (d) what their response was the last time

    (e) personal bits of information

5. The customer, through the cost of the equipment they buy.

UNIT 7
REACHING AGREEMENT

SAY WHAT YOU MEAN

Extract 1

Recording script

AM: Well, an impressive machine, isn't it, Brian?

BB: Oh, I can't deny that.

AM: And the price is more reasonable than you'd expect, too.

BB: Really? Well, what is it Alan?

AM: £55,000.

BB: That's way over the top, as far as I can see. I mean it's basically the same as the Paxer and they're on offer for £40,000. I'd say that's a more realistic price.

AM: But they're quite different machines. The Zanki's memory is much larger than the Paxer's.

BB: That may be, but to be honest, Alan, we don't need such a large memory. What we need is speed and reliability on the pre-production imaging.

AA: Well, in that case this . . .

BB: And if we made you an offer - and don't forget the Paxer has a much better reputation - we'd be talking about £37,500.

AA: I wish I could help you, but I'm afraid that's as low as the price goes. Of course, that includes delivery, installation and warranty. Don't forget that.

BB: Of course - I mean we wouldn't consider anything less.

AM: And there's a discount for an early order.

BB: Well, we might consider £42,000, if you were prepared to supply disks and a new screen.

AM: You cannot be serious, Brian. I'm sorry, anyway the screen isn't on the market yet.

BB: But surely for an old and valued customer . . .

AM: I'm sorry, Brian, that's not negotiable. The disks, on the other hand, well . . . we could offer a discount for bulk to show our goodwill. Though there is something else.

BB: Oh?

AM: I understand you're working together with Promad.

BB: Yes, that's right.

AM: We'd be interested in introducing this product to them.

BB: Well, certainly if we liked it, we'd recommend it. But if we can't agree a price for one machine, what hope is there for two?

AM: We could discuss a group discount if Promad were likely to buy a Zanki, too. Say . . . 5 per cent.

BB: Come on now - surely you wouldn't insult us with less than 10 per cent?

AM: Very well, go on.

BB: Disks included?

AM: OK, seeing as it's you.

BB: And one of your technicians to demonstrate and help for a couple of days, until we get used to it?

AM: OK. Though not until mid-September. Summer holidays.

BB: Summer holidays! I hope you're not going to throw away a deal like this just because of the summer holidays.

AM: Well, perhaps I could get one back earlier.

BB: Right. So now, let's recap. You will supply us with one Zanki, with a supply of disks, by midday on 1st September, with an engineer to install it and a competent operator to train our staff. The price will be reduced by a discount of 10 per cent on the understanding that, if we are satisfied, we will encourage Promad to look at the machine. Right? Oh yes, one last thing, this is the IIa we are talking about, isn't it?

AM: Actually no. It's the II; the IIa isn't out yet. But that shouldn't alter things.

BB: On the contrary. In fact we really couldn't go over £40,000 for Model II.

AM: OK, now we're talking Model IIa . . .

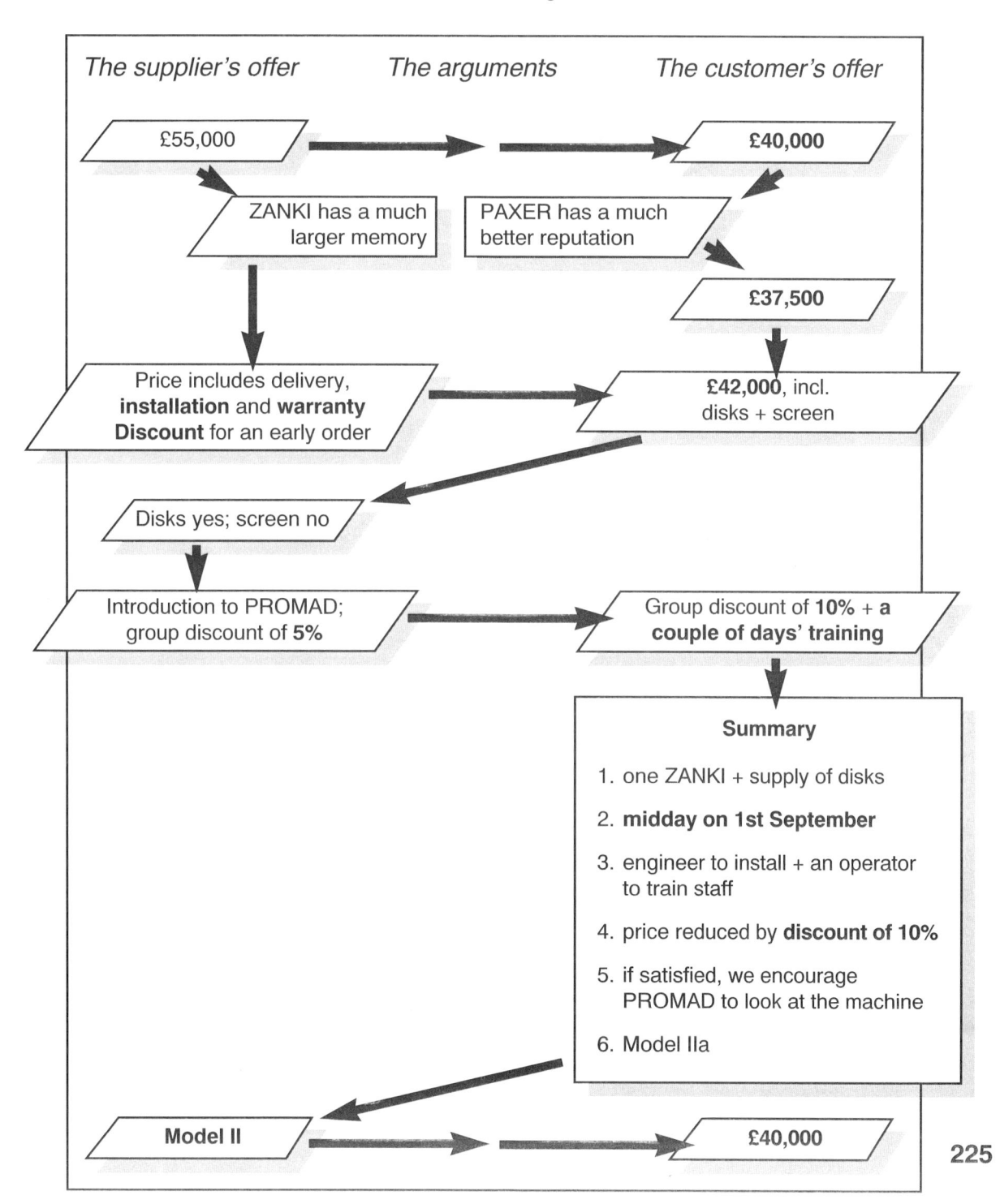

The supplier's offer	The arguments	The customer's offer
£55,000	→ →	**£40,000**
	ZANKI has a much larger memory	
	PAXER has a much better reputation	
		£37,500
Price includes delivery, **installation** and **warranty** **Discount** for an early order	→	£42,000, incl. disks + screen
Disks yes; screen no		
Introduction to PROMAD; group discount of **5%**	→	Group discount of **10%** + **a couple of days' training**

Summary

1. one ZANKI + supply of disks
2. **midday on 1st September**
3. engineer to install + an operator to train staff
4. price reduced by **discount of 10%**
5. if satisfied, we encourage PROMAD to look at the machine
6. Model IIa

| **Model II** | → | £40,000 |

Key – Unit 7

Extract 2

Recording script

SG: OK, Bridget, those plans sound fine. So where exactly do we stand on the advertising budget?

BS: Well, last year we believe that our campaigns were very successful. An excellent balance of the three classic factors: message, medium and timing.

SG: And money?

BS: Well, of course, Stephen, if we don't have the money we can't get very far.

SG: But did you get far enough with last year's budget?

BS: We certainly did, Stephen. My main concern as always is that if you try and stretch a budget too far, then you risk coming away without any tangible results. Advertising campaigns must be regular and effective to reach their target. And for that . . .

SG: . . . you need money! OK, OK. So, last year the figure was $250,000. You just told me it was enough to achieve your objectives.

BS: It was the budget we had. $250,000 is $250,000 - no more, no less.

SG: So, what are you asking for next year?

BS: Well, we estimate we need $350,000 to continue. Anything less will seriously impact on our efforts to deliver.

SG: Bridget, that's near to a 50% hike. No way we can agree that.

BS: Well, let's talk about this company's objectives. You've always said that we could make the necessary investment in advertising if we could deliver the goods. I'm saying that's what we need.

SG: And I'm saying your figure is too high.

BS: OK, so let me ask you what figure you envision?

SG: $280,000. That's a very fair percentage increase.

BS: Stephen, I'm not here to argue percentage points. I just want what's best for this organization. Without those budgets I'll have to rethink my plans.

SG: Listen, Bridget, I don't mean to be negative, but we have to come up with a figure we both can live with.

BS: I can live with $280,000, but I certainly can't implement all my plans.

SG: Well, we all have to trim a bit here and there.

BS: Stephen, at the very least I need $320,000.

SG: Bridget, please don't think that this is a personal crusade against your advertising efforts. But it is my job to keep this company on target for steady growth.

BS: I accept that. We all share the same goals.

SG: OK. Can you accept $300,000 and still implement your plans?

BS: Well, it's not going to be easy, but yes, Stephen, I suppose I can live with that figure.

SG: Good, so tell me some more about the proposed TV campaign. I was very impressed . . .

	Amount	Argument for	Argument against
Stage 1	350,000	continue initiatives	50% hike
Stage 2	280,000	fair percentage increase	can't implement all plans
Stage 3	320,000	minimum required to implement plans	keep company on target for steady growth
Stage 4	300,000	can live with it	can accept it

Key – Unit 7

Comparing and contrasting

Exercise 1

1. That's the best price we can offer.
2. You can't find a cheaper version.
3. That's the most expensive product we can sell.
4. You can't buy a worse model.
5. That's the most generous offer we can make.

Indicating degree, using 'very', 'too' and 'enough'

Exercise 2

1. ... fast enough for us.
2. ... too slow for us.
3. ... short enough for us.
4. ... too late for us.

Negotiating tactics

Exercise 3

1. (b) What's the price tag?
2. (b) That's a bit steep. The screen is just the same as the Scorpion.
3. (a) Yes, but the problem is we don't need super graphics.
4. (c) Well, we might consider £3,500, if you included the power unit.
5. (c) But we've been doing business for years.
6. (a) In six weeks! If we could agree a price, I'd expect it here in two.

Dealing with conflict

Exercise 4

Well, can you see a way out?

Well, I just want the best solution for the company.

That's OK in the short term, but what about next year?

You're the boss, but I really think we should look at it now.

Key – Unit 7

PUT IT ON PAPER

Model 1

Comprehension

1. Don't use any double negatives.
2. Verbs have to agree with their subjects.
3. Don't use commas which aren't necessary.
4. Try never to split your infinitives.
5. It's important to use your apostrophes correctly.
6. Correct spelling is essential.
7. Be careful when you use adjectives; use adverbs correctly.
8. Join clauses well, as a conjunction should.
9. Placing a comma between subject and predicate is not correct.
10. Always check your text to see if you have left any words out.

Vocabulary development

1. once - all the others involve multiplication.
2. should - all the others imply total obligation.
3. optional - all the others involve obligation.
4. combine - all the others involve separation.
5. lovely - all the others are adverbs.
6. spoonful - all the others are adjectives.
7. because - all the others can be used as prepositions.
8. twice - all the others are adverbs of frequency.

Model 2

Comprehension

1. Spain and Portugal.
2. Z45 as well as accessories and spare parts related thereto.
3. Because they have a specific definition in the contract.
4. By giving ninety days' written notice to SINCOSA.

Vocabulary development

(Opposites with prefixes)

1. agreement - disagreement

Key – Unit 7

2. related - unrelated

3. legal - illegal

4. applicable - inapplicable

5. effective - ineffective

6. exclusive - inclusive

(Legal expressions)

1. after this - hereinafter or hereafter

2. in that document - therein

3. in accordance with this agreement - hereunder

4. as a result - therefore

Adjectives and adverbs

Exercise 1

1. This machine is very good value for money.

2. You should price your products more realistically.

3. But this machine looks quite different.

4. In any case it is extremely large.

5. I think you have been badly informed.

6. We have looked very hard at your offer.

7. That price is absolutely fixed.

8. We are certainly impressed by its performance.

Clauses with '-ing' and '-ed'

Exercise 2

1. The goods supplied by us will be delivered by 1 March.

2. We will pay compensation for any delivery arriving late.

3. Any claim made by the company will be thoroughly investigated.

4. We shall settle within 90 days any claim arising from a dispute.

5. Any decision arrived at by the court shall be final.

6. The costs arising from the case shall be paid by both parties.

Key – Unit 7

7. The decision reached by the court shall be final.

8. Any agreement signed by you will come into force immediately.

Letter-writing style

Exercise 3

Paul Schroeder
Salzacherstr. 34
2356 Himmingen
Germany

Dear Paul

I was very pleased to hear that you will be passing through York during your UK tour. However, I wasn't quite sure what you meant by 'staying a few days'. Perhaps you could clarify. In any case, there is no problem, as we can easily accommodate you; alternatively we could book a hotel for you. Moving on to travel. The trains from London normally take about 2 hours. However, as some of them are much slower, I'd advise you to check. Of course I'd be happy to pick you up at York station when you arrive. Just call me before you get on the train in London.

I think that covers everything. I look forward to seeing you soon.

Yours sincerely ...

Drafting contract clauses

Exercise 4

1. The Agent shall not disclose information to third parties.

2. ITC hereby agrees to deliver the contract items to SINCOSA.

3. SINCOSA undertakes to treat all information as strictly confidential.

4. SINCOSA is entitled to terminate the contract in the following circumstances:

5. ITC grants permission to SINCOSA to refuse delivery in the following circumstances:

   OR: ITC grants SINCOSA permission to refuse delivery in the following circumstances:

6. SINCOSA is not entitled to approach other distributors.

THE BUSINESS INTERVIEW

Successful negotiating

Recording script

Caroline, we were talking earlier about different sales techniques in different parts of the world, but when it comes to actual negotiation, how would you prepare for a negotiation?

I think first off you would have to look at the geography and politics and the social/economic climate of the country you are dealing with. The company background and the personnel structures are also important, that you know the kind of company you are dealing with, its solvency, how it operates in the market - and obviously the decision, . . . whether you are dealing with the decision makers, not wasting time on visiting somebody who doesn't actually have the buying power. And thirdly, studying your own costs before you make the trip. You have got to negotiate and come to a compromise. To do that you have to know what your costs are, involved, both in terms of production and freight and any possible other add-on costs that could arrive from the whole deal.

How would you set about opening negotiations with a prospective customer?

One important aspect is to ask enough questions - don't assume anything - to find out as much as you possibly can about the way they operate, what they expect from their suppliers, what they are actually looking for, and listen very hard to what it is they say, not assume or believe you hear something different. Obviously with export you are dealing with larger volume of goods, very often important contracts; it is very unlikely that the client will agree to the first offer you make. So you are going to be involved in possibly starting off at a level you know may be slightly too high but gives you room to manoeuvre.

And is price always critical here, or are there other areas to negotiate in?

It depends on the country, it depends on the product. Obviously price is one of the main elements; whether it's always the most important depends on the particular product and situation. Once they've agreed that the product and price is suitable, then you get in to the nitty gritty about payment terms. I mean, for example it could be that their terms are 120 days payment which might not go down too well in the UK, where our terms are mainly 30 days. Then you've got the freight costs and freight terms. And if you've agreed at a price and suddenly find that you are paying for the freight, you could be looking at a ten percent on-cost.

Key – Unit 7

And finally, can you give me a couple of examples of some bargaining factors that you find useful?

Well, it might be that for example you've arrived at a point where your customer needs a price reduction, but you actually can't afford to lower your price. So what you've got to look to do really is to look for something where you are offering added value - that could mean that you are prepared to pay towards publicity costs, advertising, exhibitions whatever - or you could be looking possibly to make a proposal on the basis of a retrospective discount. That would mean at the end of - for example - the first year's trading you would pay retrospectively your customer say a two percent discount on the complete volume of your business. So you are not actually giving a price reduction per unit, it's something that's tied to the overall global aspect of this that you're developing.

As you listen ...

(Answers)

1. (a) geography, politics and social economic climate of the country you are dealing with.

   (b) background and personnel structure of the company you are dealing with (e.g. solvency, how it operates in the market, who the decision makers are)

   (c) studying your own costs (e.g. production, freight, any other possible 'add-on' costs)

2. Ask questions about how the customer operates, and what they expect from you. Start discussions of price at a level where you have room to manoeuvre.

3. No. Payment terms (number of days' credit) and freight costs and terms can also be important.

4. Offering 'added value' by helping to pay publicity, advertising or exhibition costs, or by offering a retrospective discount.

5. At the end of the first year's trading you would pay your customer a discount on the complete volume of business.

UNIT 8
SOCIAL CONTACT

SAY WHAT YOU MEAN

Extract 1

Recording script

C: Hello, Karl. Nice to see you again. How are things in the Frankfurt office?

K: Fine, thanks, Clive. Though I've had my hands full with the Brill acquisition. And how are things in the London office?

C: Oh, not too bad, not too bad.

K: You don't sound too enthusiastic.

C: Oh, it's just that I had to do a lot of travelling during the winter and it was getting a bit much.

K: Executive stress, eh?

C: In fact the reason I'm under pressure is that I've been asked to join the fiscal team in Pittsburgh. And I have to decide by next month.

K: That sounds really exciting.

C: I know, but it's a difficult decision.

K: Yes, it's a tough one.

C: Oh, here comes Pierre. Karl, keep that under your hat, please, until the official announcement.

K: Yes, of course.

C: Pierre, how nice to see you again.

P: It's nice to see you, too.

C: Do you know Karl here?

P: No, I don't think so. How do you do? My name is Pierre Beurton.

Key – Unit 8

K: Nice to meet you. I am Karl Schick. Please call me Karl.

P: OK. And please call me Pierre.

C: So what do you think of the Paris of Eastern Europe?

P: Well, it has a certain . . . how do you say . . . ambience. The river, the bridges, the cafes.

K: An excellent choice for a conference. By the way, who's going to be in charge of the new office here?

C: Eric over there is going to be the partner in charge. Eric, can you spare us a minute?

E: Yes, of course.

P: You are very fortunate coming out here.

E: Yes, I know. You see my family comes from Hungary and so I speak the language. By the way, let me introduce myself. My name is Eric Varkonyi.

P: How do you do? I'm Pierre Beurton from the Lille office. And this is Karl Schick.

K: From Frankfurt.

E: Nice to meet you.

C: Gentlemen, will you excuse me, please? Business calls. See you later.

K: See you later.

P & E: Bye.

K: So, have you been working with Clive?

E: Yes, I've been based in London for the last five years and I became a partner a few months ago.

P: And a foreign posting already. I'm quite jealous, when I think that after ten years with the firm, I spend most of my time helping local companies to avoid bankruptcy!

Key – Unit 8

Name	Based in	Current interest/activity
Karl	Frankfurt	Brill acquisition
Clive	London	Asked to join fiscal team in Pittsburgh
Pierre	Lille	Advises local companies how to avoid bankruptcy
Eric	London	Open office in Budapest

Extract 2

Recording script

R: Clive, you said in the questionnaire you'd already had quite a lot of contact with Americans, right?

C: Yes, I normally feel quite at home with my American colleagues.

R: And, Helen, you say that you have occasional contact.

H: Yes, that's right - at receptions and dinner parties, things like that.

R: OK, the first thing you'll notice is that Americans feel much more comfortable on a first name basis. It's quite normal to call someone by their first name right from the start and we tend to repeat people's names a lot when we first meet them because it helps to fix them in our memory.

C: Yes, it's a little strange for us, because we Brits like to keep our distance till we've established at least an acquaintance.

R: Yes, aha, I've noticed that, Clive! OK, the next point is the handshake and the eye contact. Let's see how yours measure up. Clive . . .

Good, that's a nice firm handshake . . . Helen . . . No, that's what we call . . . a dead fish.

H: Thank you very much!

Key – Unit 8

R: We say that a weak handshake means a weak character. So, Helen, let's try again . . . Much better. And it's quick - usually just a couple of pumps.

C: Oh, I didn't know that.

R: And you look the other person straight in the eye.

H: OK, so you've introduced yourself and you're on first name terms. What do you talk about?

H: The weather.

R: Yes.

C: Jobs. What do you do? Where are you based? How long have you been there?

R: What you do and who you're with is a major topic of conversation; but not money. I guess that's the same in the UK.

C: Yes, when I worked in the City people never asked me how much I earned or what my house cost.

R: Right. Family is important, too. People will often ask if you have family, if you have children and how many you have, and what they're called and where they go to school. But that's often after you met someone a couple of times.

C: What about sports?

R: Yes. Sport is always good, but remember - it can be controversial - like politics! . . . Now another important thing about talk in general is feedback. You know what I mean? You got that?

H: Er, yes, I think so.

R: That was just a demonstration. We are very verbal; we need a lot of feedback to feel comfortable. So, we spend a lot of time checking that the other person understands and agrees with what we say. So, you'll hear a lot of 'right?' 'am I making myself clear?' 'okay?' . . . Okay, any questions? There we go.

H: Well, actually there was something I wanted to ask . . .

Key – Unit 8

Cross-cultural briefing notes

Some notes to help you settle in:

1. Names
   Americans feel more comfortable on first name terms
2. Handshake and eye contact
   Firm handshake and direct eye contact
3. Topics of conversation
   i weather
   ii jobs
   iii family
   iv sports
4. Importance of feedback

Expressions of time

Exercise 1

1. I'll make my decision by the end of next month.
2. I'll stay there for at least one year.
3. I discussed this with Martin during the flight from Frankfurt.
4. I'll be working there until the end of next year.

Reported speech

Exercise 2

1. Peter said that they had, of course, been to the States before.
2. Peter asked if I had ever been to the States.
3. Peter has often said that he wants to work abroad for a short time.
4. Peter asked if it was a good idea to sell their house.
5. Peter said he would see us all in September.

Greetings, introductions and farewells

Exercise 3

1. Nice to see you, too.
2. How are things in the Madrid office?
3. By the way, let me introduce myself. My name is ....
4. Hello, Clive. Nice to see you again. How are you?
5. Let me introduce my colleague Sven Johnsson.
6. Nice meeting you, too.

Making small talk

Exercise 4

1. How do you do? My name is ....
2. I'm from .... And where are you from?
3. What do you do, Samuel?
4. How long have you been in Boston?
5. So where are you based?
6. What's the weather like there now?
7. Do you have children?

Key – Unit 8

PUT IT ON PAPER

Model 1

Comprehension

1. Cirrhosis.
2. Lethargic.
3. Mineral water.
4. Just after the main course.
5. Coffee.
6. Aperitif, starter, main course, cheese, sweet, coffee.

(Note: in the UK and the US, the cheese is often eaten after the sweet or dessert.)

Vocabulary development

1. to object to - to demur
2. to make better - to improve
3. to succeed in doing - to accomplish
4. to make - to render
5. to advise - to encourage
6. to be accustomed to - to be used to

Key – Unit 8

Model 2
Comprehension

The adjustment process in a new culture

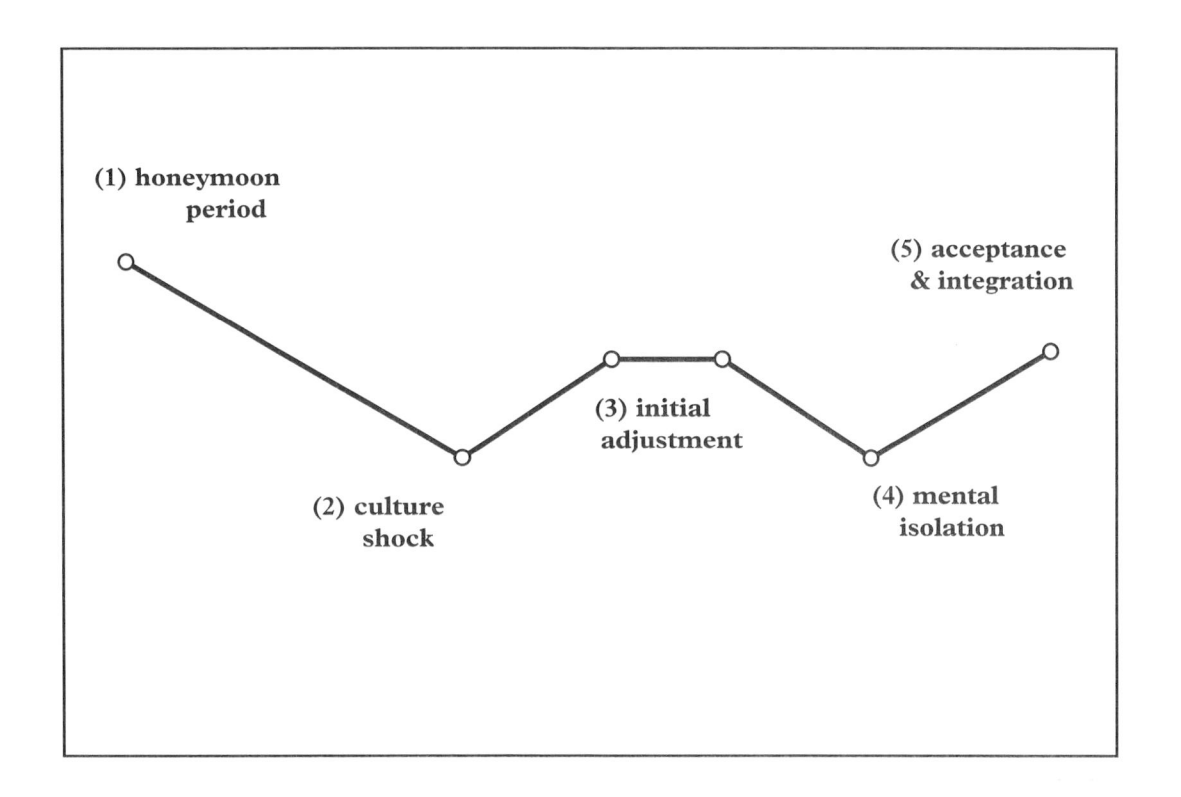

(1) honeymoon period

(2) culture shock

(3) initial adjustment

(4) mental isolation

(5) acceptance & integration

Key – Unit 8

Vocabulary development

1. negative - positive
2. solution - problem
3. leave - enter
4. foreign - native
5. scorn - glorify
6. accept - reject
7. permanently - temporarily
8. depressed - elated/excited

Verb: '-ing' or infinitive?

Exercise 1

1. reduce
2. drinking
3. hearing
4. solving
5. drink
6. drinking
7. accepting
8. contact

'As' or 'like'?

Exercise 2

1. as
2. as
3. like
4. as
5. as
6. like
7. like/as
8. as

Key – Unit 8

Emphasizing information

Exercice 3

Dear Mr Barnes

We were **most** disappointed with your response to our enquiry.

According to our records, we placed the order more than three weeks ago and cannot understand why we have not received the goods. **Note** that you in fact acknowledged our order two weeks ago. This means **in no way can we be** responsible for the problem. So, **don't try** to blame us as we are **absolutely** sure that we are not liable.

If you wish to continue supplying us, **please contact** us as soon as you receive this letter.

Yours sincerely

Sequencing information in writing

Exercice 4

Suggested answer:

1. The first stage is when a routine has been established in the new culture and the visitor feels comfortable with friends and associates in that country.

2. After that there may be confusion and emotional pain about leaving because friendships will have to be disrupted. Many people realize how much they have changed because of their experiences and may be nervous about going home.

3. The third stage is immediately upon arrival in the home country, when there is usually a great deal of excitement. There are parties to welcome back the visitor and renewed friendships to look forward to.

4. At the next stage family and friends may not understand or appreciate what the traveller has experienced. The native country may have changed in the eyes of the former traveller.

5. Finally the former traveller becomes fully involved with friends, relatives and activities, and feels once again integrated in the society.

THE BUSINESS INTERVIEW

How others see us

Recording script

Catherine, as someone who has worked both in the States and in the UK, can you tell us what some of the differences are between how Americans and the British behave in a business context?

Well I think as most people would expect, British people are much more subtle in their approach to things and in the way they communicate. We've all heard that America and England are two countries divided by a common language; a lot of the way the British people use the language is very different than Americans. We may think we understood what you said - we use the same words - but the meanings are often very different; and Americans tend to be seen as quite brash, upfront, direct, where the British are more subtle in their approach.

And what sort of briefing or background do you think a company should give an employee before expatriation?

I think companies should of course tell the person all about their job, how the company operates in the country they are going to, but just as importantly they should tell them about the everyday stresses and how your life will change, that the living conditions are different - things that you take for granted today, such as going to the grocery store, could be very different … Another thing I think companies should tell expats about is that they will be different: they will be foreign and they should learn to laugh at themselves and the perceptions that others have of their nationality. We all have stereotypes about nationalities and if we're alone in another country we shouldn't take it personally - people may share those with you. I was a bit unprepared in England, there is some, perhaps, anti-American feelings, or just simply misunderstandings about what Americans are like. People want to talk to you about those, to validate or invalidate them.

So it's important that you don't take yourself too seriously.

Absolutely. Yes.

What about the different ways that the two nations approach doing business?

I think in America people are more apt to pick up the telephone. If you see something in a newspaper that tips you off to a possible new client, you generally pick up the phone, and get directly to the decision maker. In England there is a tendency to write a letter, and then do a telephone call as a follow-up.

Key – Unit 8

Right. And in terms of when they actually get into the office to do negotiations - again different attitudes there?

Very different attitudes, I think in England we tend to go in and want to speak about their 'possible needs' and put together a possible ... you know maybe get a brief - and in America you want to know, can we do business? Is there some potential here? Let's get down to it. ... And when you are pitching and actually selling to someone, Americans are not embarrassed at all to say 'I want your business.' You know, when are you going to make a decision, let's get going ... where I think British people will say 'Well, you get back to me when you're ready.'

What about difference in attitude to work between different countries?

Well I think where I'm from, on the West Coast of America, we believe that work should be fun; and I think we work very hard, we also play very hard, and we feel strongly that you should enjoy your work, where I think in England and elsewhere in Europe, people work very hard, but work is work and that's the difference.

As you listen ...

(Answers)

1. Two countries divided by a common language.

2. Tell them about everyday stresses and how life will change - even buying things in a grocery store will be different. Prepare them for dealing with possible stereotype views, and not to take themselves too seriously.

3. In the United States, people are more likely to pick up the phone, get direct to the decision maker. In England, there is a tendency to write a letter first.

4. (a) US: I want your business.

   (b) British: Well, get back to me when you're ready.

5. On the US West Coast in particular, they believe that work should be fun. In Europe, 'work is work'.

STRUCTURAL GLOSSARY

Adjectives and adverbs	Adjektive und Adverbien	UNITS 1 and 7
Adjectives, comparison of	Adjektive, Steigerung	UNIT 7
'Already, 'still' and 'yet'	'Already, 'still' und 'yet'	UNIT 3
'As' or 'like'	'As' oder 'like'	UNIT 8
Comparing and contrasting	Vergleiche	UNIT 7
Conditional sentences	Bedingungssätze	UNIT 6
Continuous tenses	Verlaufsformen	UNIT 4
Contract clauses	Vertragsklauseln	UNIT 7
Degree, with 'very', 'too' and 'enough'	Maßangaben mit 'very', 'too' und 'enough'	UNIT 7
Emphasizing information	Hervorhebung	UNIT 8
Forecasting	Prognosen	UNIT 5
Frequency	Häufigkeit	UNIT 3
Future: 'going to' and 'will'	Futur: 'going to' und 'will'	UNIT 4
Obligation	Verpflichtung	UNIT 6
Offering to help	Hilfe anbieten	UNIT 6
Prepositions	Präpositionen	UNITS 4 and 6
Present passive verb forms	Präsens Passiv	UNIT 1
Present perfect and past simple	Perfekt und Präteritum	UNIT 5
Question tags	Bestätigungsfragen	UNIT 3
Question words	Fragewörter	UNIT 3
Reported speech	Indirekte Rede	UNIT 8
Reporting, verbs of	Verben des Berichtens	UNIT 4
Sequencing information	Reihenfolgen	UNIT 8
Tenses, review of	Wiederholung der Zeitformen	UNIT 5
Time, expressions of	Zeitangaben	UNIT 8
Trends, describing	Beschreiben von Trends	UNIT 2
Verb: '-ing' or infinitive?	Verb... '-ing'-Form oder Infinitiv?	UNIT 8

Structural glossary

Adjectives and adverbs

(UNITS 1 and 7)

We use adjectives

1. to give more information about nouns:
   competitive advantage

2. after the verb **to be**:
   He is **confident**.

3. after verbs of the senses (**look, sound, smell, taste, feel**):
   His English sounds very **fluent**.

We use adverbs

1. to give more information about verbs:
   The environment is changing **rapidly**.

2. to give more information about adjectives:
   highly interactive groupings

3. to give more information about adverbs:
   He writes English **extremely** well.

Adjectives, comparison of

(UNIT 7)

If the adjective has one syllable, the forms are:

cheap	cheaper	cheapest
high	higher	highest

If the adjective has two syllables and ends in **-y**, **-ow** or **-le**, the forms are:

easy	easier	easiest
narrow	narrower	narrowest
simple	simpler	simplest

For other two-syllable adjectives and longer adjectives, the forms are:

reasonable	more reasonable	most reasonable
expensive	more expensive	most expensive

Irregular adjectives

good	better	best
bad	worse	worst

Structural glossary

'Already', 'still' and 'yet'
(UNIT 3)

We use **already** in positive sentences to mean **by now**:

He's already visited the UK three times.

We use **yet** in negative sentences to mean **by now**:

He hasn't visited the UK yet.

We use **still** in positive and negative sentences to mean **up to now**:

He still hasn't started work on the report.

Notice the position of these words.

already: before the verb (see above) or at the end of the sentence

We've received your report already.

yet: usually at the end of the sentence (see above)

still: usually with the verb

'As' or 'like'
(UNIT 8)

As and **like** both mean **the same as** or **similar to**, but there is a difference in usage. We use **as** in the following situations:

He works as an adviser. (that is his real job)

We use different methods, such as cross-cultural training to help with cultural adjustment. (for example)

The best solution is as follows. (as now to be told)

As we will see later, some individuals may remain at this stage. (here **as** is a conjunction (Konjunktion) and so is followed by a full verb)

We use **like** in the following situations:

It works like magic. (it isn't magic, but it works wonderfully well)

New ideas like these have kept us ahead in the market. (similar to)

Skills like interviewing need thorough development. (**like** is a preposition (Präposition) and so is followed by the **-ing** form of the verb)

Structural glossary

Comparing and contrasting
(UNIT 7)

1. For comparison of adjectives see **Adjectives, comparison of** above.

2. A clause of comparison consists of one or two clauses:

The Zanki's memory is much larger than the Paxer's.
(one clause)

The Zanki's memory is much larger than the Paxer's is.
(two clauses)

We can make a clause of comparison with:

- a comparative form **+ than** (see the example above)
- **as ... as**:

That's as low as the price goes.

- **not so ... as**:

The Zanki is not so powerful as the Paxer.

Conditional sentences
(UNIT 6)

Beide Formen des Konditionalsatzes drücken ein Verhältnis zwischen Ereignissen und ihren Folgen aus. In Typ I hält der Sprecher das Ereignis für tatsächlich möglich, in Typ II für nur wenig wahrscheinlich. D.h., der Unterschied zwischen Typ I und II spiegelt die unterschiedlichen Ansichten des Sprechers über das Ereignis wider.

If the equipment breaks down, we will replace it. (breakdown is a real possibility)

If the equipment broke down, we would replace it. (breakdown is a remote possibility)

Die beiden Typen unterscheiden sich im Gebrauch der Zeitformen.

	'If' clause	**Main clause**
Type I	present simple	future with **will**
Type II	past simple	conditional with **would**

Es gibt noch andere Möglichkeiten, einen Bedingungssatz einzuleiten:

1. Ausdrücke, die sich auf eine Möglichkeit in der Zukunft beziehen

in the event of

in the event that

in (the) case of

in case

In the event of a breakdown, please contact our office.

2. Ausdrücke für 'wenn und nur wenn'

provided/providing (that)

on condition that

so/as long as

We will replace the equipment, provided that it has been properly maintained.

3. 'wenn nicht'

unless

No refunds will be made unless there is proof of purchase.

4. Inversion

(a) with **should** for Type 1 conditionals:

Should you require further information, please contact our office.
(If you require further information, please contact our office.)

(b) inverted construction with **to be** for Type 2 conditionals:

Were the claim to be fraudulent, the company would not pay.
(If the claim was fraudulent, the company would not pay.)

Continuous tenses
(UNIT 4)

We use continuous tenses (**to be** + verb + **-ing**) when we refer to an event which:

1. is happening now:

I'm reading this exercise. (present continuous)

2. will be happening at a definite moment in the future:

I'll be leaving home at 07.30 tomorrow. (future continuous)

3. was happening at a certain moment in the past:

I was reading the newspaper when the phone rang. (past continuous)

Structural glossary

Expressing degree with 'very', 'too' and 'enough'
(UNIT 7)

Too means **more than enough**:

That budget is too high.

(Nicht akzeptabel, weil es nicht niedrig genug ist.)

Very means **at a high level**:

The budget is very high.

(Es kann noch akzeptabel sein, auch wenn es sehr hoch ist.)

Enough means that it is at an acceptable level:

The budget is low enough.

(Beachten Sie, daß 'enough' nach dem Adjektiv steht.)

Drafting contract clauses
(UNIT 7)

In speech, duties (Verpflichtungen) are normally expressed with **must** and entitlements (Rechte) with **can**. In formal documents, the following forms can be used:

1. Duties

undertakes to   shall   agrees to

The company undertakes to/agrees to/shall sell these products. (The company must sell these products.)

2. Entitlements

reserve the right to   is entitled to   grant permission (allow)

The company reserves the right/is entitled to market the products outside Europe. (The company may market the products outside Europe.)

Emphasizing information
(UNIT 8)

1. Inversion von Subjekt und Verb nach **only** und nach negativen Ausdrücken wie **no** und **nowhere**.

Under no circumstances can we accept your excuse.

2. Imperativ

Eat whatever you like.

Don't do business with them.

3. Verstärkende Adverbien

This is absolutely ridiculous.

That is totally absurd.

Structural glossary

Forecasting

(UNIT 5)

Wie man Prognosen formuliert, hängt davon ab, mit welcher Wahrscheinlichkeit sie eintreffen werden. Der Grad der Wahrscheinlichkeit reicht von wahrscheinlich bis völlig unmöglich. Die folgende Übersicht zeigt Ihnen die jeweils passenden Ausdrücke.

Certain	*We are definitely/certainly going to increase sales.* *Sales are bound/certain/sure to increase.*
Probable	*I'm likely to increase sales.* *Sales are likely to increase.* *Sales should increase.*
Possible	*I may/might/could manage to increase sales.*
Improbable	*We're unlikely to increase sales.* *Sales are unlikely to increase.*
Impossible	*I definitely can't increase sales.* *Sales certainly won't increase.* *Sales can't possibly increase.*

Expressing frequency

(UNIT 3)

Die Ausdrücke für Häufigkeit lassen sich einteilen in solche für eine bestimmte Anzahl von Wiederholungen und solche für eine unbestimmte Anzahl von Wiederholungen.

1. **Definite frequency**

Once a year	annual (adj.) annually (adv.)
Twice a year	half-yearly/six-monthly (adj.)
Three times a year	every 4 months (adv.)
Four times a year	quarterly (adj.)
Six times a year	bi-monthly (adj.)
Twelve times a year	monthly (adj.)

2. **Indefinite frequency**

Adverbs of frequency	Approximate % frequency
Never	0%
Hardly ever/scarcely ever	5%
Rarely/infrequently/seldom	10%
Occasionally	35%
Sometimes	50%
Often/frequently	75%

Structural glossary

Usually/normally/generally/regularly	95%
Always	100%

Future: 'going to' and 'will'
(UNIT 4)

Will is used in the following situations:

1. wenn Sie etwas eben erst beschlossen haben:

   'Could you give me those figures?'

   '**I'll** phone them through.'

2. wenn Sie hoffen, glauben oder erwarten, daß etwas geschieht:

   I hope they **will** sell the house.

3. im Hauptsatz eines einfachen Bedingungsgefüges:

   Profits **won't** fall if we reduce our costs.

Use **going to**:

1. wenn Sie etwas schon vor längerem beschlossen haben:

   We're **going to** spend our holidays in Barbados.

2. wenn Sie aus der gegenwärtigen Situation vorhersehen können, daß etwas eintreten wird:

   The clouds are dark. It's **going to** rain.

Expressing obligation
(UNIT 6)

In speech, the verbs **must, have to** and **need to** are widely used to express obligation (Verpflichtung). In written documents we can often find the following forms:

Obligation	Prohibition	No obligation
be obliged to		not be obliged to
be required to		not be required to
shall	shall not	
	not be allowed to	
	not be permitted to	
	be prohibited from	

Structural glossary

Offering to help
(UNIT 6)

'Can I help you?' is an offer of help in the form of a question;

'I'll help you.' is an offer in the form of a statement.

We can use the following verb phrases to make offers:

1. Modal verbs:

Can I ... and **Shall I ...** which are both question forms.

I'll ... which is a statement form.

2. Full verb phrase:

Would you like me to ...? which is also a question form.

Prepositions
(UNITS 4 and 6)

1. **Point of time prepositions**

at	six o'clock midnight
on	Saturday April 10 Christmas Day
by	the end of July (indicates a deadline = at the latest) (see also **Expressions of time**)
till/until/up to	15 March (indicates an end point)
since	April 10 (indicates a beginning point)

2. **Period of time prepositions**

in	July the autumn (Am. Eng. fall) the morning the middle of ...
at	night the weekend (Am. Eng. on the weekend)
during	the meeting (see also **Expressions of time**) the lesson
for	two days twelve months
throughout	August the project

3. **Preposition + noun phrases**

at	a price/cost/charge of ...
for	£50 (amount of money)
by	fax/letter/phone (but **on** the phone)

Present passive verb forms

(UNIT 1)

1. The verb phrase consists of two parts:
- the relevant part of **to be**, i.e. **am, is** or **are**
- the past participle (usually verb + **-ed**)

The order is processed and then the invoice is raised.

2. We use the passive:
- to avoid mentioning the doer

Orders are usually sent by fax.

(Wer bestellt, spielt in diesem Fall keine Rolle.)

- in process descriptions

Next the goods are transported to the customer.

(Da es sich hier um eine Reihe von Vorgängen handelt, spielt es keine Rolle, wer jeweils im einzelnen Fall das Subjekt ist.)

- in impersonal language

The proper forms must be used for all documents.

(Die passiven Verbformen werden häufig in formellen Schriftstücken verwendet, wenn der Ton ganz neutral sein soll.)

Present perfect and past simple

(UNIT 5)

Das Perfekt wird verwendet, wenn die Handlung in einer Beziehung zur Gegenwart steht:

1. für eine Handlung in der nicht näher bestimmten Vergangenheit, die bis in die Gegenwart oder die Zukunft hinein eine Wirkung zeigt:

We have read the accounts.

(Wir sind jetzt mit dem Lesen fertig und deshalb in der Lage, darüber zu sprechen.)

2. für eine Handlung innerhalb eines noch nicht abgeschlossenen Zeitraums:

Our expenses have increased this year.

(Das Jahr ist noch nicht zu Ende.)

3. für eine Handlung, die in der Vergangenheit begann und noch andauert:

We have supplied you with programmers for the last five years.

(Wir haben mit den Lieferungen vor fünf Jahren begonnen und liefern immer noch.)

Das Präteritum wird verwendet, wenn die Handlung einfach in die Vergangenheit gehört:

We read the accounts last week.

Our expenses increased last year.

We supplied you with programmers five years ago.

The following markers are used with the past simple:

> yesterday
>
> last ...
>
> ... ago
>
> at that time

Question tags

(UNIT 3)

Eine Bestätigungsfrage ist ein Ausdruck, der eine Aussage in eine Frage verwandelt, ohne die Wortstellung zu verändern; es wird oft gebraucht, um sicherzustellen, daß man richtig verstanden hat:

Your turnover last year was just under 24 million francs, wasn't it?

Bildung von Bestätigungsfragen:

1. die gleiche Zeitform wie das Verb der Aussage:

*You worked for Sudouest Électronique, **did**n't you?*

2. Eine negative Bestätigungsfrage folgt auf eine positive Aussage und umgekehrt:

*Last year **was** a success, was**n't** it?*

3. Entsprechend der Form des Verbs im Aussagesatz werden Hilfsverben (**be**, **have** oder **do**) verwendet:

*We have**n't** exported this year, **have** we?*

*We work**ed** hard last month, did**n't** we?*

Structural glossary

Question words
(UNIT 3)

Here is a brief summary of question words:

Questions about	Question word
Place, location	Where?
People	Who?
Things	What?
Specific things/people	Which ...?
Reasons	Why?
Time	When?
Manner/method	How?
Duration	How long?
Distance	How far?
Age	How old?

Reported speech
(UNIT 8)

Die indirekte Rede gibt wieder, was ein anderer sagt oder fragt.

Paul said, 'I have just arrived.'
(Direct speech: 'I have just arrived.')

Paul said that he had just arrived.
(Reported speech: that he had just arrived.)

Die Regeln für die Umwandlung von direkter in indirekte Rede:

1. Wenn das einleitende Verb des Sprechens oder Fragens im Präsens oder Futur steht, dann ändert sich die Verbform der direkten Aussage oder Frage nicht.

They often ask, 'Do you have any children?' (direct speech)

They often ask if you have any children. (reported speech)

2. Wenn das einleitende Verb des Sprechens oder Fragens in einer Vergangenheitsform steht, dann ändert sich die Verbform der direkten Aussage oder Frage wie folgt:

present	past
past	past or past perfect
present perfect	past perfect
will	would

Paul asked, 'When are you leaving the US?' (direct speech)
Paul asked when we were leaving the US. (reported speech)

Structural glossary

Verbs of reporting
(UNIT 4)

We can group verbs of reporting as follows:

Describing	Saying	Proposing
to describe	to say	to suggest
to present	to tell	to advise
to demonstrate	to announce	to recommend
to show	to declare	to propose
	to disclose	
Thinking	to notify	**Expecting**
to think	to inform	to expect
to believe	to report	to anticipate
to consider	to state	to forecast
to wonder		to warn
	Ordering	to threaten
Asking	to order	
to ask	to command	**Agreeing**
to request	to insist	to agree
to question	to authorize	to decide
to demand	to instruct	to confirm
		to approve
Disagreeing		to admit
to disagree		
to deny		
to refuse		
to decline		

Sequencing information
(UNIT 8)

Mit Hilfe der folgenden Ausdrücke können Sie eine Aufzählung oder eine Reihe von Punkten strukturieren, so daß es Ihren Lesern leichter fallen wird, dem Text zu folgen:

Beginning

First/initially/the first step/the first stage
Second/secondly/the second step/at the second stage
Then/after that/at the next stage/the next step
Finally/the final step/at the final stage

End

Structural glossary

Review of tenses
(UNIT 5)

1. **The present simple.** Diese Zeitform bezeichnet ein Ereignis oder eine Handlung, die nicht nur auf den gerade gegenwärtigen Augenblick beschränkt ist:

   We produce components for the motor industry.

2. **The present continuous** (see also **Continuous tenses** earlier). Diese Zeitform bezeichnet ein Ereignis oder eine Handlung, die (nur) gegenwärtig stattfindet oder vorübergehend ist:

   At present we are working on a project to improve quality.

3. **The past simple** (see also **Present perfect and past simple** earlier). Diese Zeitform bezeichnet ein Ereignis oder eine Handlung, die beendet ist und ganz in der Vergangenheit stattgefunden hat:

   Last year we opened a new office in Amsterdam.

4. **The present perfect** (see also **Present perfect and past simple** earlier). Diese Zeitform bezeichnet ein Ereignis oder eine Handlung in einem Zeitraum, der noch nicht beendet ist oder der nicht angegeben ist:

   Over the past five years, we have launched more than 20 new brands in the US market.

5. **The future with will** (see also **Future** earlier). Diese Zeitform bezeichnet ein Ereignis oder eine Handlung, die in der Zukunft stattfinden wird:

   We will continue to invest in new product development.

Expressions of time
(UNIT 8)

1. **For** shows how long an action lasted:

   for five years

2. **During** shows the period during which an event happened:

   during the winter

3. **By** is used to indicate that an action happened at or before the deadline:

   I must decide by the end of next month.

4. **Until** shows an action which continues up to the deadline:

   I must work in London until the end of next month.

Structural glossary

Describing trends
(UNIT 2)

1. Bewegung nach oben

We use verbs like **increase, rise, go up, grow** or **expand**:

Sales have increased rapidly.

We also use nouns like **increase, rise** or **growth**:

There has been a rapid increase in sales.

2. Bewegung nach unten

We use verbs like **decrease, fall, drop, go down, decline** or even **collapse**:

Prices have fallen dramatically.

We also use nouns like **decrease, fall, drop, decline** or **collapse**:

There has been a dramatic fall in prices.

3. Stagnation

We use words like **static, stable, constant** or **stagnant** with the verb **to be** or sometimes **to remain**:

Share prices have remained constant.

The market was stagnant last year.

Verb: '-ing' or infinitive?
(UNIT 8)

We use the **verb + '-ing'** form

1. in the continuous verb forms (see **Continuous tenses** earlier)

2. after prepositions:

I look forward to seeing you.

3. after certain verbs including:

consider   enjoy   finish   suggest

I enjoyed meeting you.

We use the **infinitive** form

1. to combine verbs together:

They agreed to come to the meeting.

2. after most adjectives:

We are glad to accept your proposals.

VOCABULARY

A **accessory** (n) Zubehör(teil). *The photocopier comes with some accessories.*

account for (v) begründen, rechtfertigen. *We need to account for price increases.*

acquisition (n) Aufkauf. *The company has made a number of acquisitions.*

administration (n) Verwaltung. *The office administration is inefficient.*

advertising (n) Anzeigen, Werbung. *What is our advertising budget?*

after-sales service Br. Eng. (n) Kundendienst. *Our after-sales service promises call-out within 24 hours.*

agency (n) Agentur, Vertretung. *We are interested in an agency agreement.*

agenda (n) Tagesordnung. *There are four items for discussion on the agenda.*

agent (n) Vertreter. *Our agent in Italy wants more commission.*

applicable (adj) anwendbar, anzuwenden. *The regulations are not applicable.*

application (n) Anwendung(smöglichkeit). *We need to find a new application for the product.*

appoint (v) ernennen, berufen. *He was appointed to the board.*

assets (n) Vermögenswerte, Aktiva. *This company's main assets are in equipment and materials.*

attitude survey (n) Meinungsumfrage. *We are carrying out an attitude survey on health.*

B **background** (n) Hintergrund, Ausbildung. *He has an engineering background.*

bargain (n) günstiges Angebot. *There are good bargains in the shops at the moment.*

brand (n) Marke. *Coca Cola is the world's best-known brand.*

brand loyalty (n) Markentreue. *Customers feel brand loyalty to well-established products.*

Vocabulary

break into (v) erobern, sich etablieren. *It's difficult to break into export markets.*

budget (n) Haushalt(splan), Etat. *We agreed a new budget for the year.*

bulk order price (n) Mengenrabatt. *If we order 20,000 we would expect a bulk order price.*

business unit (n) Bereich, Sparte. *The company's activities are divided into business units.*

C **campaign** (n) Kampagne. *We are launching the product with a big advertising campaign.*

capacity (n) Kapazität, Auslastung. *The factory is operating at 50% capacity.*

carriage (n) Transport(kosten). *The price includes the cost of carriage.*

carve up (v) aufteilen. *The market has been carved up by two major producers.*

cash at bank (n) flüssige Mittel. *The latest balance sheet shows an increase in the cash at bank figure.*

cash in hand (n) Bargeld. *It's dangerous for a business to hold too much cash in hand.*

catalog Am. Eng., **catalogue** Br. Eng.(n) Katalog. *You'll find our prices in the catalog.*

challenge (n) Herausforderung. *We face a real challenge.*

Chief Executive Officer (n) Abbr. **CEO** Vorstandsvorsitzender, Hauptgeschäftsführer. *She's been made CEO of our new subsidiary in Washington.*

claim (n) Anspruch, Forderung. *We put in a claim on our insurance policy.*

claim form (n) Antrag(sformular). *Please fill in the claim form.*

clerical (adj) Büro-. *We employ three staff at clerical grade.*

collection (n) Kollektion. *Our Autumn collection includes many new dress designs.*

column (n) Spalte. *You'll find the figure in the third column.*

commission (n) Provision. *The salespeople are paid 10% commission.*

compensation (n) Entschädigung. *You will receive compensation for the damage caused.*

Vocabulary

compete (v) konkurrieren. *We compete with two other major suppliers.*

competent (adj) kompetent, zuständig. *You are not competent to judge this.*

competition (n) Wettbewerb, Konkurrenz(kampf). *There is a lot of competition in the market.*

competitive (adj) konkurrenzfähig, wettbewerbsfähig. *Our prices are not competitive.*

competitor (n) Konkurrent. *We have three major competitors.*

conform (v) entsprechen. *Our products must conform to EC regulations.*

consultant (n) Berater. *We have called in a consultant to advise on strategy.*

consulting (adj) Beratungs-. *We employ a team of consulting staff.*

consumables (n, pl) Spesen. *The cost of consumables is not included in the contract.*

corporate finance (n) Finanzausstattung, Unternehmensfinanzen. *Our corporate finance department deals with raising large sums of money for investment.*

creditor (n) Gläubiger. *Our creditors are putting pressure on us to pay.*

current (adj) aktuell, gegenwärtig. *Our current problems have their roots in earlier mistakes.*

current assets (n) Umlaufvermögen. *Current assets exceed current liabilities.*

current liabilities (n) kurzfristige Verbindlichkeiten. *Our long-term loans are not included in current liabilities.*

custom (n) Kundschaft. *We need to keep their custom if we are to maintain sales.*

customer (n) Kunde. *Our customers have become more demanding.*

D **damage** (n) Schaden. *Our insurance policy covers us for any damage caused by fire.*

deadline (n) Stichtag, Frist, Termin. *We must keep to the deadline.*

dealer (n) Händler. *We distribute the product through dealers.*

debtor (n) Schuldner. *Our debtors include Phisons, one of our major customers.*

Vocabulary

decision-making (n) Entscheidungsfindung. *Decision-making processes can be very long.*-**deliver** (v) liefern. *We can deliver within two weeks.*

delivery (n) Lieferung. *We can't promise delivery before next week.*

department (n) Abteilung. *The marketing department is based at headquarters.*

development (n) Entwicklung, Erschließung. *We need to invest more in research and development.*

diary (n) Terminkalender. *My diary is absolutely full for the next two weeks.*

direct costs (n) direkte Kosten. *Our gross profit can be calculated by deducting direct costs from our sales.*

discount (n) Preisnachlaß, Rabatt. *We are offering a promotional discount.*

discount for bulk orders (n) Mengenrabatt. *Our discount for bulk orders is based on 1% per 100 units.*

distribution (n) Vertrieb. *Our distribution network covers the whole country.*

distributor (n) Wiederverkäufer. *One of our distributors has been selling our competitor's products.*

dominant (adj) führend, beherrschend. *Cadtree has a dominant position in the market.*

dynamic (adj) dynamisch. *This is a young and dynamic company.*

E

economic climate (n) Konjunkturklima. *The present economic climate is rather depressed.*

electronic diary (n) Terminkalender auf dem Computer. *All other users of the network have access to my electronic diary.*

electronic mail (n) Abbr. **e-mail** E-mail.
E-mail enables us to transmit messages throughout the world.

enterprise (n) Unternehmen. *The government has tried to encourage an enterprise culture.*

equity (n) Eigenkapital. *The directors hold most of the equity in the company.*

establish (v) gründen, etablieren. *We have established a new subsidiary in Argentina.*

expenses (n) Spesen, Kosten. *Travel expenses have risen too much.*

Vocabulary

F **faithfully** (adv) (letters) **yours faithfully** hochachtungsvoll, mit freundlichen Grüßen. *I await your reply. Yours faithfully G. Mancini.*

feasibility (n) Wirtschaftlichkeit, Durchführbarkeit. *We are carrying out a feasibility study on the new plant.*

fee (n) Honorar, Gebühr. *He charges a daily fee of $900.*

finance (v) finanzieren. *We need to finance this investment internally.*

finance (n) Finanzierung, (Finanz-) Mittel. *The bank is providing the finance for product development.*

fiscal (adj) steuerlich, Finanz-. *Fiscal measures usually mean putting up taxes.*

fix (v) festsetzen. *The exchange rate has been fixed at DM2.8.*

fixed assets (n) (Sach-) Anlagevermögen. *Our fixed assets are mainly in the form of property.*

framework (n) Rahmen, Bestimmungen. *The market is controlled by a legal framework.*

freelancer (n) Freiberufler. *We use freelancers rather than employed staff.*

functional (adj) Sach-. *The organization has three functional departments: finance, personnel and marketing.*

funds (n) Geld(er), Mittel. *Do we have sufficient funds to cover this investment?*

G **goal** (n) Ziel. *We have set general goals for each division.*

goods (n) Waren. *The goods are transported by ship.*

goodwill (n) Firmenwert, geschäftliches Ansehen. *It is very difficult to value the goodwill in the company.*

gross (adj) brutto. *Our gross income exceeded $20 billion.*

guideline (n) Richtlinie. *We have set out guidelines for order-handling.*

H **head** (v) leiten. *The company is headed by a woman.*

headquarters (n) Hauptverwaltung, Firmensitz. *We have moved our headquarters outside London.*

healthy (adj) gesund. *The balance sheet looks very healthy.*

hold up (v) stabil sein. *Our sales are holding up despite the recession.*

Vocabulary

hot key access (n) Hot-Key-Access, direkter Zugriff. *The new software gives you hot key access to new applications.*

hotline (n) Telefondienst. *We have set up a hotline to handle customer enquiries.*

I **impact** (n) Auswirkung. *The launch of our new product has had a great impact on our sales.*

implement (v) einführen, realisieren. *It's easier to decide new strategy than to implement it.*

implementation (n) Einführung, Realisierung. *We expect full implementation of the plan by the end of the year.*

impulse-buying (n) Spontankauf. *Impulse-buying accounts for the sales of most ice creams.*

install (v) installieren. *The new machines will be installed next week.*

installation (n) Installation. *Installation costs have gone up.*

insurance policy (n) Versicherungspolice. *My insurance policy says nothing about invalid claims.*

intangible assets (n) immaterielle Vermögenswerte. *Some companies include goodwill as an intangible asset.*

invalid (adj) ungültig. *This insurance policy is invalid because you haven't paid the premium.*

investment (n) Investition. *Our biggest investment was in new machinery.*

invoice (v) eine Rechnung schicken, abrechnen. *You should invoice us at the end of the month.*

invoice (n) Rechnung. *We received your invoice yesterday.*

item (n) Punkt. *There are three items on this meeting's agenda.*

J **joint venture** (n) Joint-venture. *This is a joint venture between a local company and a multinational.*

K **keep pace** (v) schritthalten. *Our prices have kept pace with inflation.*

key (adj) zentral, entscheidend. *The key factor is price, in my opinion.*

L **launch** (v) auf den Markt bringen. *The new product will be launched next month.*

Vocabulary

launch (n) (Markt-) Einführung. *The product launch is scheduled for 5th May.*

leader (n) Führer. *They have been market leaders for many years.*

leeway (n) Spielraum. *We need some leeway to negotiate.*

line (n) Linie, Sortiment. *This new product line is selling well.*

line of business (n) Geschäftszweig. *We have opened up a new division to look after our chemical line of business.*

live with (v) akzeptieren. *I suppose I can live with a price of £20,000.*

look forward to (v) sich freuen auf. *We are looking forward to meeting you next Sunday.*

M

management buyout (n) Management-buyout. *They couldn't find an outside buyer so they decided to go for a management buyout.*

managing director (n) Geschäftsführer, Vorstandsvorsitzender. *He has been appointed managing director.*

manufacturer (n) Hersteller. *Kitsons are major glass manufacturers.*

margin (n) Spanne. *Our profit margin varies between 10 and 15%.*

market leader (n) Marktführer. *Mars is the market leader in the confectionery business.*

market research (n) Marktforschung. *Before we develop the product, we must do some market research.*

market share (n) Marktanteil. *Cadtree hold a 35% market share.*

maximize (v) maximieren, das Beste machen aus. *We must maximize our market position.*

media (n) Medien. *I can't understand why the media are so interested in the royal family.*

medium (n) Werbeträger. *We need to decide which medium to use: TV, radio or the press.*

memo (n) Mitteilung, Notiz. *Could you send a memo to all staff about the new smoking regulations?*

menu system (n) Menüsystem. *The software uses a menu system so that users can easily select which option they want.*

message (n) Nachricht, Aussage. *Our advertising message must be clear and simple.*

Vocabulary

modest (adj) bescheiden, geringfügig. *There has been just a modest increase in sales.*

multi-pack (n) Großpackung. *The multi-pack product enables customers to make considerable savings.*

N   **net** (adj) netto. *Net sales were lower than expected.*

net current assets (n) Nettoumlaufvermögen. *Our net current assets are too low.*

network (n) Netz. *We have set up a distribution network to cover the region.*

niche (n) Nische, Marktlücke. *Specialized producers can achieve high profits in certain niche markets.*

O   **offer** (n) Angebot. *We are going to invite offers from any supplier.*

on site (adv) vor Ort, an Ort und Stelle. *This work will be carried out on site.*

open-plan (adj) Großraum-. *We work in open-plan offices.*

operate (v) betreiben. *We operate our factories independently.*

organigram (n) Organisationsschema, Organigramm. *The organigram shows how the company is structured.*

organization (n) Organisation. *It is a very hierarchical organization.*

outgoings (n) Ausgaben. *The outgoings exceed revenue.*

outlet (n) Verkaufsstelle, Laden. *We have retail outlets in all major cities.*

outperform (v) übertreffen, erfolgreicher sein. *Our subsidiaries are outperforming the parent company.*

overseas (adj/adv) Übersee-, im Ausland. *Most of our sales are made overseas.*

overview (n) Überblick. *I'm not interested in the detail, just give me an overview.*

own label brand (n) Hausmarke. *Many supermarket chains sell their own label brands.*

P   **pants** Am. Eng., **trousers** Br. Eng. (n) Hosen. *I'm going to buy a smart pair of pants.*

partitioned (adj) abgeteilt, separat. *I prefer to work in a partitioned office.*

patch (n) Bezirk. *There are two salespeople working on this patch.*

penalty (n) Strafe. *There is a penalty clause in the contract in case of late delivery.*

percentage point (n) Prozentpunkt. *Our share price has increased by two or three percentage points.*

personal computer (n) Abbr. **PC** PC, Personalcomputer. *There are eight PCs connected to the network.*

personnel (n) Personal. *The personnel department takes care of salaries.*

pie chart (n) Torten-, Kreisdiagramm. *The pie chart illustrates market shares.*

pitch (n) Verkaufsstrategie, -argument. *Our sales pitch is to emphasize price and reliability.*

plant (n) Werk. *Our plant in Ohio is operating at 50% capacity.*

portable (adj) tragbar. *A portable PC enables you to work while travelling.*

presentation (n) Präsentation. *He talked about the new product range in his presentation.*

presently Am. Eng. (adv) gegenwärtig. *We are presently increasing our sales force.*

presently Br. Eng. (adv) in Kürze. *We will break for lunch presently.*

president (n) Präsident, Vorstandsvorsitzender. *She has been appointed as President and Chief Executive Officer.*

pricing (n) Preisgestaltung. *Our pricing strategy has been too cautious.*

prime (adj) erstklassig, vorzüglich. *We acquired a prime site for redevelopment.*

printer (n) Drucker. *The quality of our documents has improved a lot since we bought a laser printer.*

process loss rates (n) Ausschußquote. *The high process loss rates are mainly due to machine breakdown.*

product manager (n) Produktleiter. *She is the product manager in charge of launching the new AZ1000.*

production (n) Produktion. *Our production figures have been poor due to machine failure.*

productivity (n) Produktivität. *We have increased productivity by automating the assembly line.*

Vocabulary

profitability (n) Rentabilität. *Higher productivity has increased our profitability.*

profit centre (n) Profitcenter. *Each division of the company is a profit centre with its own management.*

project planner (n) Projekttagebuch. *This project planner shows the progression of the project.*

project timing (n) Zeitplan für ein Projekt. *The project timing is very tight, so we can't afford to slow down.*

promotion (n) Werbung, Absatzförderung. *We intend to follow a classic sales promotion campaign in the shops.*

property held for disposal (n) zum Verkauf stehende Grundstücke. *We hope to either sell or let all property held for disposal.*

provisions (n) Rückstellungen. *We have had to make provisions for bad debts in the balance sheet.*

Q **quality circle** (n) Qualitätszirkel. *We use quality circles to engage the employees more in the future of the company.*

questionnaire (n) Fragebogen. *We ask consumers to answer all the questions on the questionnaire.*

R **raise** (v) erhöhen, anheben. *My boss raised my salary when I said I wanted to leave.*

range (n) Sortiment. *We stock a range of goods from cheap to expensive.*

reach (v) erreichen. *It will be difficult to reach our sales targets.*

reasonable (adj) vernünftig, angemessen. *I am prepared to offer a reasonable price.*

recap (v) zusammenfassen. *Could you just recap that last point?*

receipt (n) Quittung. *My company wants to see all receipts for expenses such as taxis, meals etc.*

reception (n) Empfang. *We are holding a reception for our foreign agents before the main sales conference.*

recommended retail price (n) empfohlener Einzelhandelspreis. *The manufacturer suggests a recommended retail price to the retailer.*

redundancy (n) Entlassung. *The company has just announced 2,000 redundancies.*

registered office (n) eingetragener Firmensitz. *Our registered office is still in the centre of town, even though all our operations have been moved out to the suburbs.*

reimbursement (n) Rückerstattung. *I expect reimbursement for my expenses on this project.*

reliability (n) Zuverlässigkeit. *We can measure reliability by the number of breakdowns per year.*

repeat business (n) Folgeaufträge. *If you look after the customers you will get their repeat business.*

replacement (n) Wiederbeschaffung. *You should make sure your policy covers the cost of replacement.*

report (v) berichten, untergestellt sein. *I report to the Finance Director.*

representation (n) Vertretung. *We haven't got any representation in the north of the country.*

representative (n) Repräsentant, (Handels-) Vertreter. *Our sales representatives are responsible for a sales territory.*

research (n) Forschung. *Research and development (R and D) costs are covered by the production divisions.*

responsibility (n) Verantwortung, Pflichten. *We have clear levels of responsibility.*

retail price (n) Einzelhandelspreis. *The retail price is 20% higher than the manufacturer's price.*

retain (v) einbehalten. *We need to retain some profits for taxation.*

revenue (n) Einnahmen. *Our sales revenue is 10% up this year.*

review (n) Überprüfung, Revision. *We are carrying out a review of social benefits.*

review (v) revidieren, kritisch analysieren. *We reviewed our advertising policy.*

rival (n) Konkurrent. *We have two major rivals in this market.*

S **salary** (n) Gehalt. *He is paid an annual salary of $55,000.*

sales (n) Verkauf, Absatz. *We forecast sales of 450 units in the first quarter.*

scan (v) lesen. *The reader scans the bar code on each product.*

schedule (n) Zeitplan. *The project is on schedule so far.*

Vocabulary

scheduling system (n) Terminplaner. *The software includes a scheduling system which enables users to plan their time more effectively.*

scorn (v) verspotten, verächtlich bezeichnen. *The newspapers scorned the new invention as a cheap imitation.*

section (n) Sektion, Bereich. *The department is divided into four sections.*

sector (n) Sektor. *The most profitable sector at the moment is health care.*

sell on (v) weiterverkaufen. *The department stores sell our products on to the final users.*

settle (v) begleichen, beilegen. *This dispute still hasn't been settled.*

shape up (v) sich erholen. *The business is shaping up after a bad period.*

share (n) Anteil. *We hold a 45% share of the market.*

share Br. Eng. (n) Aktie. *Many people bought shares when the company was privatized.*

ship (v) verschiffen, versenden. *The goods are shipped to Australia twice a month.*

shoot up (v) in die Höhe gehen. *Our share price has shot up.*

software (n) Software. *You can buy this software package anywhere.*

sort out (v) lösen. *I'm sure we can sort out this problem.*

sounding (n) Erkundigung. *We have been taking soundings on the employees' reactions.*

spare parts (n) Ersatzteile. *The cost of spare parts is covered by the warranty.*

staff (n) Personal, Mitarbeiter(stab). *There are only 25 staff left in head office.*

staffers Am. Eng. (n) Mitarbeiter. *We've got two or three staffers working for the Senior Vice President.*

stand (v) stehen. *Where do you stand on this issue?*

static (adj) konstant, stagnierend. *Sales have been static for the last two months.*

steady (adj) kontinuierlich, stetig. *We have experienced steady growth this last year.*

stiff (adj) hart, stark. *There will be stiff competition in this market.*

stock (n) Vorrat, Lagerbestand. *I'm afraid that our stock is too low to meet your order. Could you wait two weeks?*

stocks Am. Eng., **shares** Br. Eng. (n) Aktien. *Company stocks have fallen recently.*

strategic (adj) strategisch. *He is responsible for strategic planning.*

strategy (n) Strategie. *We need to look at our long-term product strategy.*

stretch (v) dehnen. *There's no more money so you'll have to stretch your existing budget.*

subsidiary (n) Tochtergesellschaft. *Our French subsidiary is managed by a Frenchman.*

supplier (n) Lieferant, Zulieferer. *Kitsons have been our major supplier for many years.*

supply (v) liefern. *Kitsons have supplied our raw materials for a long time.*

sustainable (n) langfristig, dauerhaft. *We are only interested in sustainable growth.*

T **talent** (n) Begabung. *We are looking for someone with a talent for figures.*

tangible assets (n) Sachanlagevermögen. *Our tangible assets are made up of property and machinery.*

target (n) Ziel. *Our sales were precisely on target.*

team-leader (n) Gruppenleiter. *We chose a new team-leader from the existing members.*

tight (adj) eng, knapp. *The project timing is very tight - there's no room for any delay.*

to do list (n) Liste von unerledigten Aufträgen. *The system will sort your to do lists into order of priority.*

tough (adj) schwierig, hart. *There are some tough competitors in this market.*

trade price (n) Wiederverkaufs-, Großhandelspreis. *The trade price is 15% lower than the retail price.*

trader (n) Händler. *He ran his firm as a sole trader.*

train (v) ausbilden. *We need to train all the new staff.*

transparency (n) Folie. *I used a transparency to present the results.*

Vocabulary

transportation Am. Eng., **transport** Br. Eng. (n) Transport. *Transportation costs have risen a lot.*

trim (v) beschneiden. *We need to trim costs in all areas.*

turnover (n) Umsatz. *Our annual turnover is around $45 million.*

U **unit price** (n) Stückpreis. *The unit price is £25 but we offer generous discounts for bulk orders.*

V **vacation** Am. Eng., **holiday** Br. Eng. (n) Ferien. *We're taking our vacation in the summer.*

value (n) Wert. *The dollar has dropped in value.*

vice-president (n) Vorstandsmitglied, Direktor. *She's vice-president in charge of sales.*

W **warranty** (n) Garantie. *The product comes with a 12 month warranty.*

well-established (adj) alteingesessen, etabliert. *We've been in business for 50 years, so we're pretty well-established.*

word processing (n) Textverarbeitung. *We use a standard word processing package.*

workgroup facilities (n) Ausstattung für Arbeitsgruppen. *The workgroup facilities include electronic mail and diaries.*

workgroup software (n) Software für Arbeitsgruppen. *The workgroup software enables all our staff to intercommunicate.*

worth (adv) **to be worth** sich lohnen. *It's not worth investing so much money.*